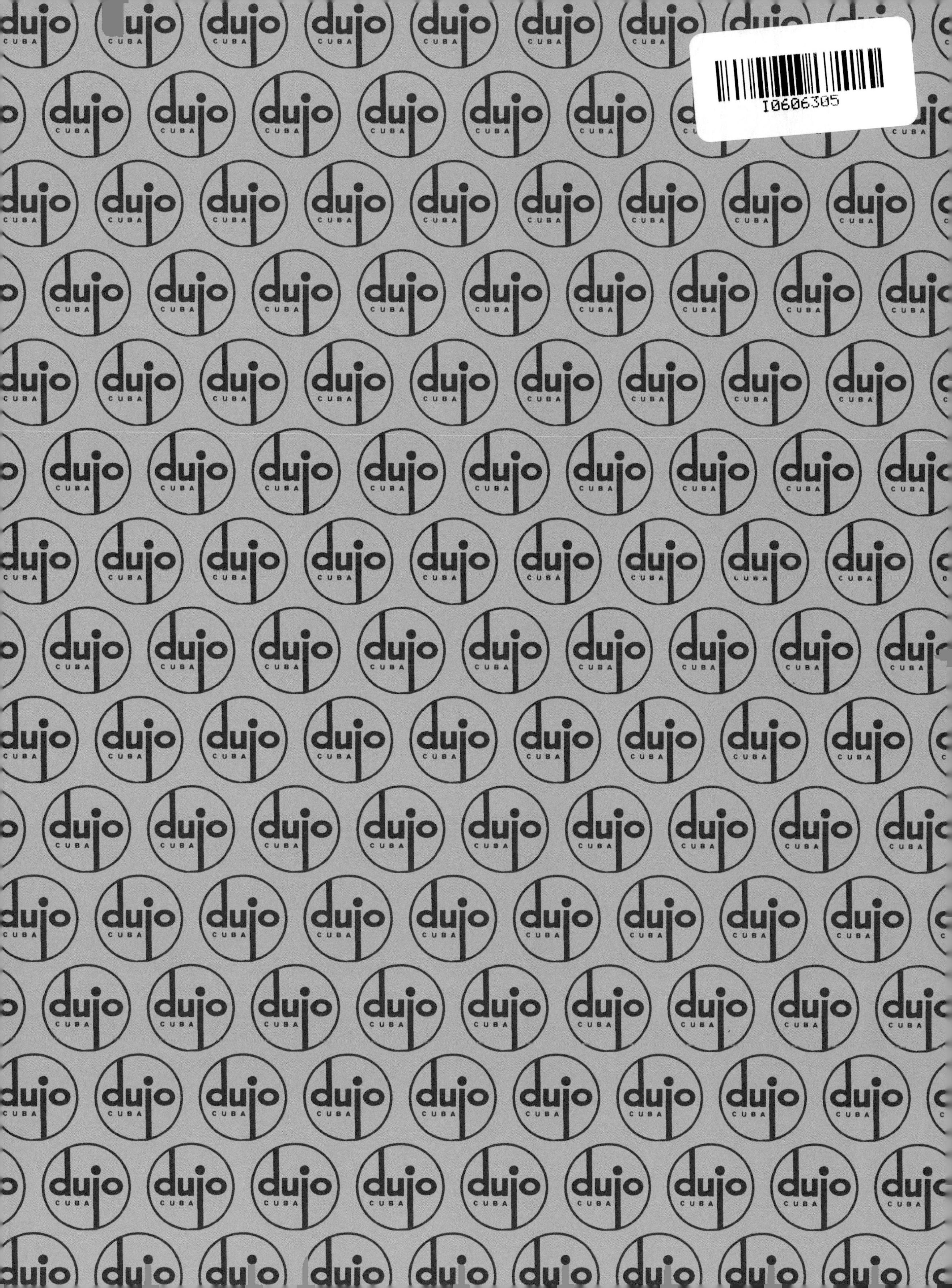

dujo
CUBA
I0606305

A MODERNIST REGIME

★

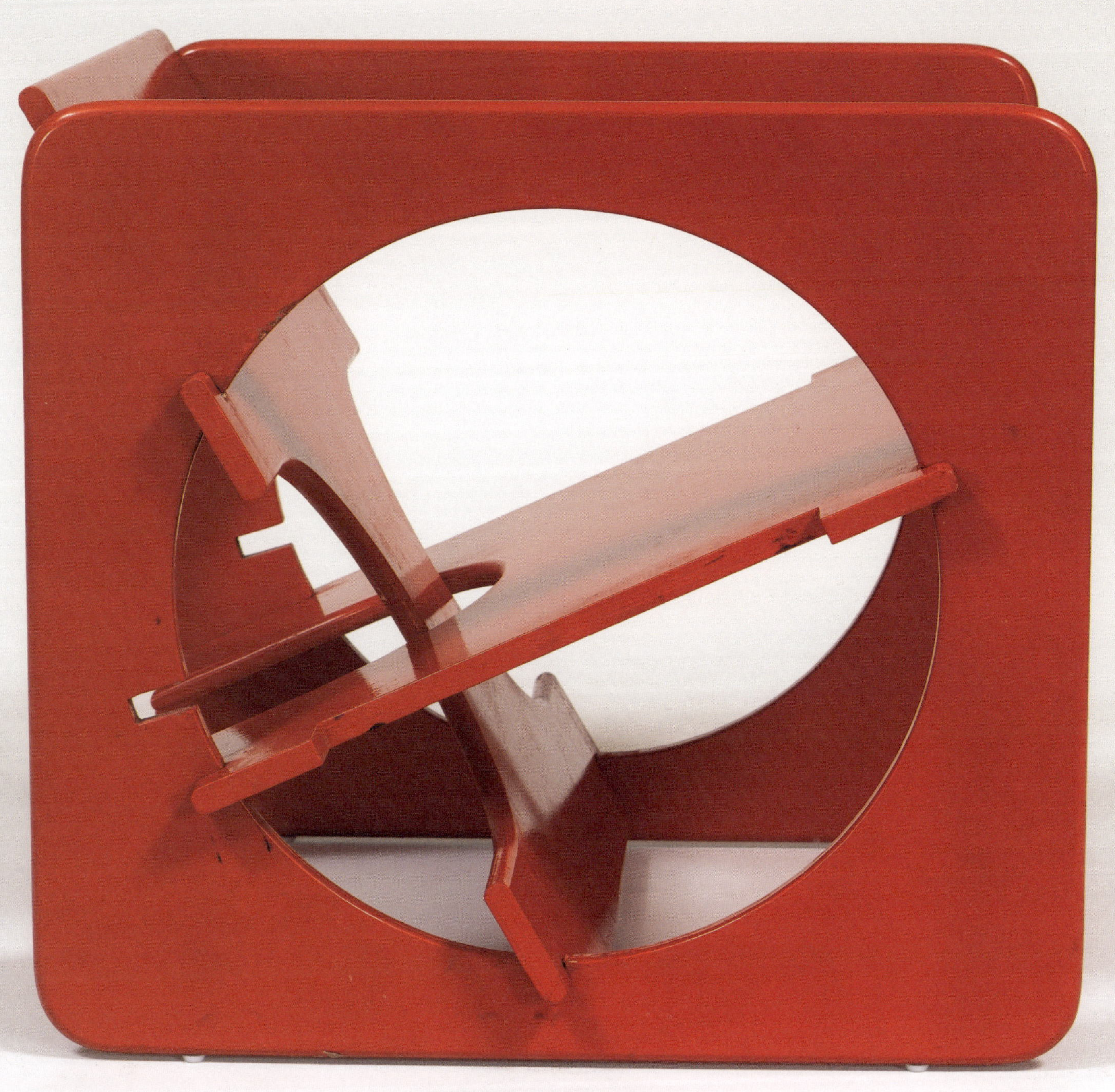

Heriberto Duverger, *Yab-Yum Lounge Chair*, 1968–1972, for the Ministry of Light Industry, lacquered plywood. Collection Cuban Modern. Photo: David Avilés

A MODERNIST REGIME

ABEL GONZÁLEZ FERNÁNDEZ AND LAURA J. MOTT WITH
ANDREW SATAKE BLAUVELT AND ANDREW RUYS DE PEREZ

CUBAN MID-CENTURY DESIGN

Rizzoli Electa, New York, New York
Cranbrook Art Museum, Bloomfield Hills, Michigan

TABLE OF CONTENTS

Foreword: A Modernist Regime

A Modernist Regime: Cuban Mid-Century Modernism might seem, at first glance, an unusual subject for a museum exhibition and publication for Cranbrook Art Museum, situated as it is in the suburbs of metropolitan Detroit—thousands of miles from Cuba. However, when the opportunity arose to work on such a project, we did not hesitate.

Our sister institution, Cranbrook Academy of Art, is often called the "cradle of mid-century design" in America, and for good reason. In the late 1930s, the academy was a hothouse of immense design talent, including Florence Knoll Bassett, Charles and Ray Eames, Harry Bertoia, Eero Saarinen, Ralph Rapson, Don Albinson, Marianne Strengell, Harry Weese, Benjamin Baldwin, and many others who came later, especially after World War II. Both major companies synonymous with modern design in America (and around the world), Knoll and Herman Miller, have deep connections to Cranbrook. But it was, in fact, this pantheon of iconic figures of mid-century design that called on us to re-examine the notion of "mid-century design" beyond the confines of the US. While more has been published in recent years about Cuban mid-century architecture, little to nothing has been written and exhibited on the country's furniture design program in the immediate years following the Cuban Revolution in 1959. What has captured the attention of some scholars and curators, early on and over the years, has been Cuban graphic design of the 1960s and 1970s, in particular the country's acclaimed propaganda and film posters.

I am grateful for the long-held interest in the period's furniture by artist Marco Castillo and the initial research of Abel González Fernández into this subject, which started this journey. I am also indebted to the work and passion brought to the project by Chief Curator Laura Mott and Andrew Ruys de Perez, our curatorial fellow. What has been unearthed are parallel stories of the development of furniture design in Cuba in the early years following the Revolution—a moment that many artists, architects, and designers believed might deliver on the egalitarian socialist promises of a modernism that seemed to have gone astray when it fled European fascism during the Second World War and landed in places like the United States. In this story of modernism, we are faced with dual narratives: on the one hand, the survivance of a more conventional-looking mid-century modern furniture crafted out of solid wood and other natural materials and produced in the artisanal workshops of Cuba, represented by figures such as Gonzalo Córdoba; and on the other, the more unconventional designs of collectives such as the Light Industry Group, which embraced new materials, technologies, and forms that reflected the contemporary cultural landscape of the late 1960s and early 1970s. As González Fernández argues in his essay (see pages 16–27), this bifurcated approach to the

Fidel Castro on the *Turiguano Couch*, designed by Gonzalo Córdoba for Dujo Muebles. Courtesy Laura Córdoba

problem of furniture design replicated the same class dichotomies of capitalism that the Revolution claimed to banish—one design for the powerful and another for the proletariat. Perhaps worse, as González Fernández and Mott (see pages 228–238) describe in their respective essays, both enterprises and creative approaches ultimately succumbed, as did so much else in Cuba, to dismal fates meted out through bureaucratic efficiencies and authoritarian expediency.

My initial impression upon seeing images of Dujo and EMPROVA furniture and the prototypical furnishings of the Light Industry Group was to think of furniture design in Cuba as a kind of condensed microcosm of modern design from the 1950s to the 1970s. Trying to place the work into my known universe of design, I drew associations between Córdoba's work for Dujo and EMPROVA and the wooden furniture we associate with Scandinavian design from people like Børge Mogenson and Hans Wegner, including their use of woods such as teak and mahogany, or the use of woven seating such as cane with the work of Marcel Breuer or Pierre Jeanneret or companies such as Thonet. Of course, all of these European designers drew upon a material palette and set of techniques that harkens back to the Global South—even the rejection of heat-trapping upholstery in favor of more breathable seating surfaces provided by woven plant fibers is a consideration in tropical climates—things that Clara Porset (see pages 34–41) saw and understood.

The work of the Light Industry Group had direct precedents and parallels with both early and contemporaneous experiments in modern art, architecture, and design. For instance, the use of strung cord, like rope, for seating can be found in innumerable chair designs of the 1950s in the US, but it also finds a precedent in the ubiquitous Acapulco chair originating in Mexico in the same period, which, in turn, drew upon the centuries-old hand-strung hammocks of indigenous Maya for inspiration. Reinaldo Togores's red and green chairs (see pages 201 and 204) update these experiments by utilizing colored plastic cord while experimenting with both wood and tubular metal chair frames—the combination of color, material, and stringing arrangement of the cord, whose patterns interact with each other depending on one's position, evoke the kinetic light installations of Op Art artists, such as Julio Le Parc (*Lumière alternées*, 1966). The slotted, do-it-yourself furniture (see page 197) by Eva Björklund, a Swedish designer who found herself in Cuba, and María Teresa Muñiz Riva's *Jigsaw* series find a parallel in Danish designer Kristian Solmer Vedel's children's furniture of the 1950s, but one driven by a no-waste approach to materials, a necessary condition in a situation of resource scarcity. The Ministry of Light Industry's plan to create whole new lines of furniture made from manufactured wood derived from processed sugarcane fiber (see pages 178–183) drew more directly on the introduction of particleboard, flat pack shipping, and do-it-yourself user assembly that had just started to percolate in the industry. Their *MueblePared*, or *Furniture Wall* concept (see page 185), finds precedent in George Nelson and Henry Wright's proposal for their *Storage Wall* concept in the 1940s. However, some thirty years later, the introduction of color, the use of particleboard panels instead of traditional pieced wood cabinetry, and the emphasis on the wall's ability to subdivide spaces and thus to zone different activities, more than the focus on storage capacity alone, can be considered important differences and advances. Additionally, the Light Industry Group's early use of then-new hardware such as concealed and self-closing door hinges and cam locks and screw bolts to join panels together—instead of adhesives and nails—would revolutionize the furniture industry with technologies that companies such as IKEA would exploit on a global scale.

All this said, the point is not a genealogy of innovation, but rather the circulation of commonly held ideas and goals and the integration of new technologies: many designers were trying to make furniture more cheaply and efficiently, and thus more accessible to more people. These were also the goals of Cuba's Ministry of Light Industry (see pages 186–199). When one reads the words of designers from this period (see pages 212–221), they strike a very similar chord to designers working outside of Cuba at the same moment, but within capitalist economies undergoing their own internalized critique, who were also facing similar constraints of time, material, user needs, safety and environmental concerns, social demands, and funding shortfalls. In many ways, the consistent throughline of this story is modernism itself. Modernism predated the Revolution, of course, yet remained malleable and fresh enough after it to be the go-to language for a much-desired transformation of society—initiating a modernist regime. However, modernism could not always shake off its bourgeois connotations, especially after its transformation under American postwar capitalism. In the end, this kind of modernism could not compete with the even more expedient, if not dour, solutions imported from the Soviet Union.

If modernism is something that has been inherited in so many places around the world, it is because it is often tied to another global project, colonialism. Given the Western orientation of modernism in general and its evolution at mid-century in the US in particular, the opportunity to better understand how this movement became internationalized could help us to begin to decolonize this grand narrative. Cuba at mid-century offers an especially useful case study as the island nation transitioned from a capitalist society and economy under the dictatorship of Fulgencio Batista to a socialist-communist one under Fidel Castro. The majority of the history of modern design has been analyzed under the rubric of industrialization via capitalism—in fact, design and capitalism are so synonymous and intertwined that economics almost always go unspoken. In the Cuban context, the economy is inevitably foregrounded.

Cuba also presents an interesting subject for design history given the country's colonial history and multicultural legacy. As historians and curators shift the focus of attention away from the Global North, it is Cuba in the Global South that provides an interesting entry point. "Discovered" by Christopher Columbus on his infamous journey in 1492, Cuba would never be the same again. The indigenous peoples of the Caribbean islands, in Cuba and elsewhere, now referred to as the Taíno, suffered a genocidal fate. The introduction of sugarcane plantations and with it slavery by the Spanish enslaved generations of Africans and their ancestors in order to satisfy the sweet tooth of consumers in Europe and North America. The later introduction of Asian peoples, particularly Chinese men, as contract laborers in Cuban sugarcane fields helped create one of the oldest and largest Chinatowns in Latin America. This multiracial mix, as it combined with Spanish colonial administrators and settlers and their descendants, adds yet another layer of social and cultural complexity.

The story that unfolds in the following pages lets us explore how the project of modernism was transformed and transfigured through the evolution of Cuba's economy from a capitalist, albeit authoritarian, framework to the problem of how and what to design in an economy that would be centrally planned and controlled after the Revolution, which also promised to liberate Cuba's multiracial society. Could the early modernism of the Bauhaus in Weimar Germany or a newly minted Russian avant-garde in the Soviet Union in the 1920s and their egalitarian missions to help transform the everyday lives of ordinary citizens be salvaged under the auspices of a country that had just freed itself four decades later from the neocolonialism of "Yankee imperialism"?

European modernism was transformed as it was introduced to pre-revolutionary Cuba—navigating the long history and tradition of a developed Colonial-era architecture and design that themselves were adapted to the climatic conditions of the tropics, the artisanal knowledge of the island, and the local material resources at hand. In what ways would climate, materials, and productive capacity limit or liberate the design of objects in a new Cuba? In what ways would modernism be transformed in the post-revolutionary period or in what ways would it simply be reframed and thus remain relatively untransformed? In what ways would design itself be changed in a society that sought to bypass the pitfalls of capitalism—designing for needs versus designing for wants; creating designs that do not signify social status or reinforce class hierarchies; making products that resist planned obsolescence; producing objects that fulfill functions but also remain artful; designing from the perspective of collective action instead of following an individual creative pursuit?

In the early days, the Revolution was meant to shape the "new man," liberating people from the tyranny of the past—certainly capitalism and imperialism but also colonialism, racism, and sexism by trying to level the inequities of society, at least in rhetoric if not always in practice. If so, how would design respond to such issues of social justice, and what if anything could be learned by their attempts? These are just some of the many questions that arose and that I hope the exhibition and publication begin to answer. This project does not and cannot answer all these questions. However, the surfacing of such questions is of initial importance because it provides a trajectory of inquiry for today's and tomorrow's scholars. We welcome and look forward to more chapters being added by others to this fascinating yet incomplete story of Cuban mid-century design, as well as other stories that center the Global South, while allowing us to critically re-examine our own cherished histories and legacies.

Andrew Satake Blauvelt, Director
Cranbrook Art Museum

Gonzalo Córdoba, *Guamá Lounge Chair*, 1959, for Dujo Muebles, mahogany and yarey. Collection Cuban Modern. Photo: Daniel Martín Corona

Introduction and Acknowledgments

The origins of *A Modernist Regime: Cuban Mid-Century Design* begin in 2017 with two unrelated but serendipitous encounters. In May 2017, the exhibition *The Museum of the Machines*, curated by our co-curator Abel González Fernández, was presented at the mid-century home of artist Marco Castillo in Havana, Cuba. Castillo had been part of Los Carpinteros (The Carpenters) from 1992–2008, a collective whose contemporary artwork was influenced by architecture, design, and the guild tradition of artisans and skilled laborers in Cuba. Due to his interest in mid-century design, particularly in Latin America, Castillo had begun to explore the design history of the island and had created a collection of original Cuban modern furniture, the first of its kind in Cuba. He brought in curator González Fernández to undertake the research and make an exhibition. In late December 2017, I was in Havana as a Warhol Curatorial Research Fellow doing studio visits for my exhibition and publication *Landlord Colors: On Art, Economy, and Materiality* (2019). I came to visit Castillo in his studio, and while he sat in a chair by Reinaldo Torgores, he began to tell me about this little-known design story and its connection to the political history of Cuba. The next week, I first encountered González Fernández at a workshop of talks and performances at the house of artist Tania Bruguera, where Castillo was also in attendance, and sitting in that living room together, a seed was planted that would grow into years of research, conversation, and collaboration and eventually culminate in *A Modernist Regime: Cuban Mid-Century Design* and its companion contemporary art exhibitions and *Marco Castillo: Hands of the Collector* and *A Modernist Regime: A Contemporary Lens*, which all debuted together at the Cranbrook in the summer of 2024.

As a curator at Cranbrook Art Museum, I had been enveloped in the legendary mid-century design history of Cranbrook Academy of Art, where icons such as Eero Saarinen, Charles Eames, Ray Eames, Florence Knoll, George Nelson, and Harry Bertoia amongst others all studied and made historic contributions to the mid-century aesthetic and built environment. One of the essential missions shared by myself and director Andrew Satake Blauvelt is to diversify the scholarship and knowledge base in our field of contemporary art and design, so the story of an unknown Cuban design history was a fascinating prospect. Andrew Satake Blauvelt, an established authority in design history, was able to see the larger implications of this Cuban collection of furniture in other cultural contexts and also drew parallels to the country's graphic design history. The combination of our mission and the transcontinental connections created the framework of the exhibition and publication.

Elena Serrano, *Day of the Heroic Guerrilla (October 8)*, 1968, poster for OSPAAAL, offset lithography and screenprint on paper. Collection Lincoln Cushing/Docs Populi

The furniture featured in the exhibition is the result of extensive research by González Fernández and Castillo, and this history has been difficult to discover and unearth. This is primarily due to the Castro regime, which had essentially eliminated creative authorship because it was considered part of bourgeois culture, so it had not funded, preserved, or documented Cuba's modernist heritage since the Revolution. Rather like a rumor, this history has been transmitted by word of mouth, from witness to witness. There is almost no published literature, and the archives have been kept within private families, or held within the government domain, or, perhaps, discarded. The reason González Fernández was familiar with this history was from lived experience; his grandfather, Rodolfo Fernández (1930–2003), is one of the protagonists of this story. He had worked as an architect on a team led by Mario Romañach (1917–1984), one of the most prominent architects of Cuban modernism, who was also a professor at Harvard, Cornell, and the University of Pennsylvania. Rodolfo Fernández collaborated with Romañach on the interior design of what would become the Fernández family home in Havana in 1958, a year before the Revolution.

After the historic shift in power to Castro's regime, Rodolfo was integrated into a select group of architects whose professional experience was utilized by the new government. The interior design of the Fernández family house is a perfect metaphor for the hybrid style that generated the paradoxical continuity of the Cuban Republic (1902–1959) into the Revolution. In the family home are the wooden trusses that were conceived by Romañach in 1958; framed examples of works by Cuban abstract painters such as Mario Carreño; and a significant work by Pop artist Raúl Martínez, *The Big Eater* (1967), which satirically addresses the struggles of his society. Pre-Columbian handicrafts are showcased on shelves designed by Rodolfo Fernández in 1968. A Saarinen *Womb Chair* (1946) is placed next to an *Isla Table* (1964) by Gonzalo Córdoba, the most prolific designer of modern Cuban furniture. Since architecture is a costly endeavor, few projects of architectural importance would be built after 1959, and high design would ultimately remain in the realm of exclusivity.

Likewise, Marco Castillo's studio, which hosted *The Museum of the Machines* exhibition, is a part of mid-century design history and is located in the Havana neighborhood of Nuevo Vedado, an area of modern upper-middle-class urbanization that was built during the 1950s. The house was completed in 1958; however, the residence was taken from its owners by the new government and assigned to Commander René Vallejo, who was Fidel Castro's doctor. Through a group of architects trained by the new regime, Vallejo added another floor and balconies to the original house, as well as commissioned additional furniture that closely replicated the original design. Living within this history ultimately led Castillo to create Cuban Modern, the first important collection of these design objects and the vast majority of loaned furniture objects in this exhibition.

A Modernist Regime: Cuban Mid-Century Design is built on the hard work and dedication of González Fernández and Castillo. The exhibition and publication scholarship are immensely indebted to Andrew Satake Blauvelt, Director, and Andrew Ruys de Perez, the Jeanne and Ralph Graham

Curatorial Fellow, who contributed as researchers and writers to every aspect of the publication, with additional assistance by Bridget Bartal, the MillerKnoll Curatorial Fellow, and Kat Goffnett, Assistant Curator of Collections. We would like to extend our gratitude to Susana Mohammad, who oversees Marco Castillo's collection, for all her important work in bringing the exhibition to fruition. The research conducted has truly benefited from firsthand accounts by the architects and designers, including Eva Björklund, Joaquín Galván, María Teresa Muñiz Riva, and Reinaldo Togores, and some who, unfortunately, passed before this exhibition opened, such as Gonzalo Córdoba and Heriberto Duverger. We would like to thank for their assistance in research, expertise, and organization Luis Rámirez, Laura Córdoba, Omara Ruiz Urquiola, Kevin Ávila, Claribel Calderius, Gladys Bidot, Sabrina Fanego, Sean Kelly, José Manuel Mesías, Ana María Fernández Gómez, Lourdes A. Hernández, the Korda family, Andrés Garrudo, Leandro Feal, Reynier Quer, Hamlet Lavastida, Rigoberto Díaz, Julio Llopíz Casal, Mirta Gómez Macle, and Rodolfo Fernández Suárez. We would also like to thank all of our very dedicated staff at Cranbrook Art Museum for their individual and collective efforts in successfully organizing, installing, interpreting, marketing, funding, and activating the exhibition and publication. A complete list of contributors appears on page 239 of this book.

A special thanks to Lorraine Wild (CAA, BFA Design, 1975) and Xiaoqing Wang at Green Dragon Office in Los Angeles for their beautiful and thoughtful design of this book and to Margaret Chace, Sarah Scheffel, and Isabel Venero at Rizzoli for their support and assistance in realizing the publication.

We would like to thank the lenders to this exhibition, including Marco Castillo, Eva Björklund, María Teresa Muñiz Riva, Reinaldo Togores, Lincoln Cushing, and Youmi Efurd at Wofford College and most especially the artists, architects, and designers whose work we are delighted to include in our presentation. For the Cranbrook Art Museum presentation, we extend our gratitude to the Gilbert Family Foundation, the Andy Warhol Foundation for the Visual Arts, the National Endowment for the Arts, and the George Francoeur Art Museum Exhibition Fund for their generous support of this project.

Collectively, the curators would like to dedicate this book to Ana María Fernández Gómez, whose loving memory and family legacy permeate this project.

Laura J. Mott, Chief Curator
Cranbrook Art Museum

CUBAN MID-CENTURY DESIGN

A MOD
REG

ABEL GONZÁLEZ FERNÁNDEZ

ERNIST
IME

The story of Cuban modernism parallels the country's existential conflicts: the tensions between the local and the global; between the leisure economy of the tourist and the work ethic of industrialization; between European and North American culture and Afro-Cuban and Taíno roots; between colonial desire and national agency. A mural by the iconic Cuban caricaturist Conrado Massaguer represents these contradictions (fig. 1). Made for a private restaurant on the second floor of the Cuban pavilion at the 1939 New York World's Fair in New York City, the mural showed an array of male historical figures such as the New York City mayor Fiorello La Guardia playing Cuban maracas, accompanied by President Roosevelt playing the bull fiddle while amused by a Cuban girl dancing on stage. The drawing scandalized Cuban authorities, who were afraid that the image "could offend some of those portrayed." Still, Mayor La Guardia approved the mural's content, according to the *New York Times*.[1]

The scene of a handful of powerful men enjoying themselves with a Cuban dancer persisted in the imagination of the pre-revolutionary independent Cuban Republic (1902–1959); however, for a significant part of the Cuban intellectual tradition this image carried with it the embarrassing, stereotypical features of a neocolonial banana republic. It embodies the humiliation of playing a role crafted for tourism—hospitality, sex, dancing bodies in rhythm—catering to the burgeoning global capitalist economy championed by the 1939 New York World's Fair. Reports on the fair's Cuban pavilion depict the construction and display of a vernacular Cuban village with restaurants and bars, including a reproduction of Havana's well-known bar Sloppy Joe's, one of the favorite destinations of American tourists of that time. The poster at the pavilion, also illustrated by Massaguer, reads "Visit Cuba," pointing to the foundation of a visitor economy facilitated by the emerging mobility of commercial aviation and the automobile, economic sectors well represented in the vast and groundbreaking pavilions of American industrial companies such as Ford, Lockheed Aircraft Company, and General Motors, among others. These pavilions, which placed Cuba in the category of pleasure and amusement, reinforced the colonialist mindset in which the agency of progress is produced in the North and spreads to the South, building upon an imagined notion of the "underdeveloped" country.

Clara Porset

Among its staff writers, *Social* had the privilege of counting on the Cuban designer Clara Porset from 1930 to 1933, whom Massaguer, a founder of the magazine, had invited to cover a section on interior decoration. Porset is a foundational figure of Latin American modernism because of her essential work in Mexico,[2] Cuba, and the United States, with a fascinating history yet to be fully uncovered. Born in 1895 in the central province of Matanzas, to an upper-middle-class family, Porset conducted several educational trips to Europe and the US at different moments and levels of her education. In 1914,[3] Porset attended high school at the Academy of the Sacred Heart in New York. From 1925 to 1928, she studied art, architecture, and design at Columbia University's School of Fine Arts. She traveled to Paris the same year to take courses in aesthetics and philosophy at the Sorbonne and art history and architecture at the École des Beaux-Arts. Before returning to Cuba in 1930, Porset enrolled at the furniture design school developed by the studio of architect, designer, and French illustrator Henri Rapin. While traveling around Europe, she encountered the ideas and work of the Bauhaus, which profoundly impacted her social, theoretical, and formal design vision.

Bringing together her education, her writings at *Social*, and her professional experiences, in 1931, Porset gave a foundational lecture for Cuban and Latin American modern design at the Havana Auditorium entitled *Contemporary Interior Decoration in Cuba: Its Adaptation to the Tropics* (see pages 34–41). Porset spoke about some of the most radical ideas of architecture and design of the time, advancing the principles of functionalism, the perfection of forms, purity of materials, and "the relation of masses, not of superimposed elements."[4] Inspired by readings of Adolf Loos and early modernist designers such as Francis Jourdain and Djo-Bourgeois, Porset attempted to address one of the fundamental problems of Cuban modernism: the tension between a globalizing and expansive international style, in line with the industrial development of capitalism, and the local contexts encountered in its expansive path. In this case and beyond, she analyzed modernism and its relationship with the tropics in a strictly Cuban context. The implicit question behind this essay is the most critical question of a whole generation of Porset's contemporary Cuban intellectual figures, such as curator José Gómez Sicre, writer José Lezama Lima, artists Amelia Peláez, and Massaguer, among many others: how to develop and educate a country in Western standards without

Fig. 1 Conrado Massaguer, sketch of the mural in the Cuban pavilion at the 1939 New York World's Fair.

Fig. 2 Clara Porset, *Cuban Butaque*, 1960, linden tree wood and leather. Collection Cuban Modern. Photo: David Avilés

colonial mimicking of the US and Europe and produce an independent postcolonial economy?

The answer Clara Porset found to this question is a triad of verbs—learn, adapt, and produce—reflecting the national values given by nature (tropical climate) and culture (the Cuban colonial architectural tradition understood as transmission of potential meanings). The lecture, as brilliant as it was austere, shows enthusiasm for a vision of architecture as a totalizing art, called to merge form, color, and light and to eliminate the barriers between craftsmanship and art. Here, architecture is seen as a machine, with furniture, painting, and design acting as its gears. Instead of using the term "decoration," Porset suggested using a more avant-garde concept, "the art of organizing enclosed spaces," which reflected the modern philosophy of the Bauhaus. Under the precepts of dialogue, harmony, and functionality between structures, the text expands on the analysis of the coexistence between the tropical wisdom accumulated by Cuban colonial architecture and the new architecture of modernism. The designer proposes an organic transition that maintains the advantages of shutters, the patio, and the arcades of the tropical colonial house to avoid the excessive heat and to moderate the intensity of the tro-pical light. For some cases, Porset recommends excess. For instance, she proposes designing lattices and louvers for windows and terraces instead of closed and uniform glass panels, maximizing the entry of light and the refreshing sea breeze of the tropics. For other furniture, she recommends austerity, as when she criticizes cushions on wicker, wood, and rattan furniture, which would bring unnecessary heat to the intrinsic freshness of organic tropical materials.

From 1930 to 1934, Porset managed her interior design studio in Havana, located at the America building in the Vedado neighborhood, the center of the city's modern life. In the same spirit as her groundbreaking lecture, she developed her design ideas in the magazine *Social*. Here, Porset provided updated information to Cuban readers about the vanguard tendencies in architecture and design, writing articles about the new buildings and tenets of The New School for Social Research in New York; about the "machine for living" of the Van der Leeuw House in Rotterdam by the architects Leendert van der Vlugt and Johannes Brinkman; about artistic commercial offices designed in Paris by Charlotte Perriand, Le Corbusier, and Pierre Jeanneret, and about interior design in New York. In these texts, Porset strongly advocates for what she calls the "new architecture," pulling concepts like the "machine for living" by Le Corbusier and advancing rationalism and functionalism in architecture. In her article "Interiores norteamericanos: Los de ahora" ("North American Interiors, Now"), the author harshly criticizes interior design tendencies in New York, dismissing the American style as "tacky": "There is no sobriety in them and no sincere simplicity. They are a conglomerate of unrelated furniture, objects without relation to each other. The furniture is treated individually according to the old concept and for purely decorative purposes."[5] Porset contrasted this decorative practice with the production of modern architecture by champions such as Le Corbusier or Walter Gropius. Like Adolf Loos in his classic manifesto,[6] she uses the metaphor of maturity, comparing the childhood of the American people to an aged and wiser Europe.

In 1932, Porset attended Black Mountain College in North Carolina, an experimental pedagogical institution where Josef Albers, formerly of the Bauhaus and a close friend of hers, directed the arts. After several projects in Havana, the designer relocated to Mexico City in 1940, where she developed an extensive body of work and became a pioneer and promoter of Mexican and Latin American modern design. From Mexico, Porset and her husband, the Mexican muralist, painter, and communist militant Xavier Guerrero, were the Latin American winners of the competition *Organic Design in Home Furnishings*, launched by the Museum of Modern Art (MoMA) in New York in 1940 and exhibited in 1941 at the museum. The MoMA exhibition catalog entry about the winners reads: "The group by Guerrero [and Porset[7]] was conceived as peasant furniture, to be made of pine with webbing of *ixtle* (vernacular for Mexican vegetable fiber) in the cot and chair. The wall case has a screening of jute in the sliding doors and at the end."[8] Among the winners of the American section of the competition were Eero Saarinen and Charles Eames, who presented their groundbreaking molded plywood chairs developed at Cranbrook Academy of Art. MoMA's catalog of the show rated Cranbrook's designers' work as "the most advanced of all these systems . . . In an ordinary chair, there are a seat and a back that supports the body at two or three points. In the case of a usual, large, upholstered chair, the body sinks into a general softness until it reaches support."[9]

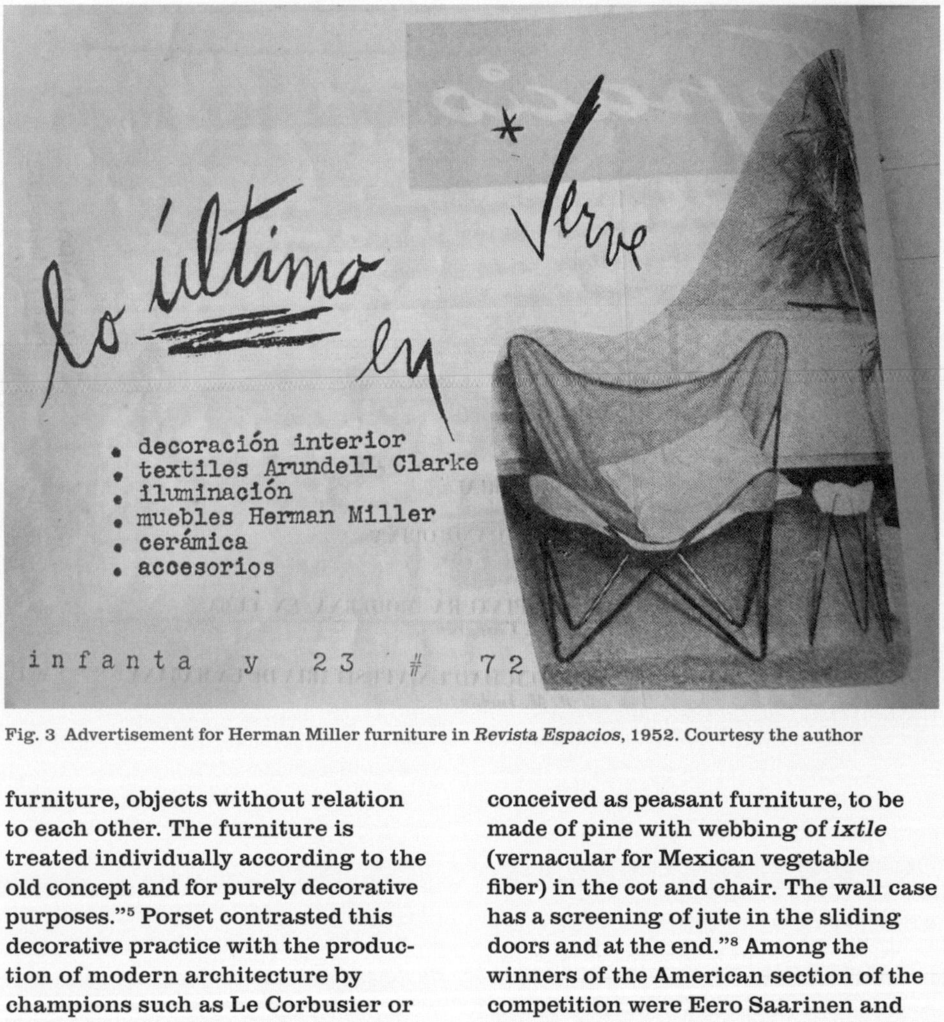

In the following years, Porset developed her iconic lounge chair, the *butaque* (fig. 2), and used it for different projects, including houses designed by the modern Mexican architects Luis Barragán and Enrique Yáñez. For this chair, Porset took inspiration from the *butaque yucateco* (a lounge chair of the Yucatán Peninsula), a piece of colonial furniture developed in the Caribbean area of Mexico with vernacular materials and a highly organic design. Experimenting with an array of materials, such as textiles, leather, and ixtle, a natural fiber, Porset followed each one of the tenets that she conceived for her lecture in Havana in 1931. In the *butaque*, Porset blended modernism and colonial tradition; incorporated craft into the production (she never industrialized her process); and used local materials and indigenous Mexican ancestral craft knowledge of weaving techniques and materiality to produce a unique piece of unupholstered furniture that would become an iconic example of modern Latin American design, renowned for its idiosyncratic simplicity, elegance, and functionality. In addition, the perfect arc of the seat of the *butaque* resembles the *dujo* chair, a precious object from the Taíno, an indigenous culture in pre-Columbian Cuba, used for ritual ceremonies in which early cigars, music, and dance were present. In Mexico City, Porset established a commercial furniture office and healthy design practice; she taught architecture and curated the groundbreaking and foundational exhibition at the Palacio de Bellas Artes, *El arte en la vida diaria: Exposición de objetos de buen diseño hechos en México* (*Art in Everyday Life: Exhibition of Good Design Objects Made in Mexico*), the first design exhibition held in Mexico. However, despite her life in Mexico, Porset did not lose her connection to Havana, where she often traveled to organize conferences, lectures, and public

Fig. 3 Advertisement for Herman Miller furniture in *Revista Espacios*, 1952. Courtesy the author

programs on design,[10] in addition to creating designs for the interiors of private houses, such as the rocking chairs created for the family residence of Orlando Álvarez in Havana in 1958.

Havana of the 1950s

As scholars Victor Deupi and Jean-François Lejeune have argued, Cuban modernism is rooted in finding the *Cubanía*, or the quality of being Cuban, in the context of Western culture. The *Cubanía* was a field where different classes, races, and cultural projects waged battle. Porset's lectures not only aimed to harness the potential of the tropics to develop a new design vision but also sought to control, civilize, and transform social reality. Searching for the *Cubanía* was also a way to contest the backdrop of US neocolonialism, which simultaneously provided Cuba with economic advantages. Between 1930 and 1959, Cuba experienced massive economic growth matched with a sophisticated modern movement in architecture, urbanism, and art. Architects such as Walter Gropius, Josef Albers, Richard Neutra, Ludwig Mies van der Rohe, and Josep Luis Sert visited Cuba or had projects on the island. Local architects such as Mario Romañach, Antonio Quintana Simonetti, Frank Martínez, and Max Borges Recio, among many others, developed a vast body of work that is still the core of modern architecture in Havana—from affordable housing in popular neighborhoods to high-end modern mansions and apartment buildings. American design intermingled with Cuban architecture and life: Knoll furniture company had a showroom in Vedado, and Herman Miller's objects were sold and advertised in the pages of Cuban architecture magazines (fig. 3). According to scholar Abigail McEwen, American culture and especially its "cars were undoubtedly a ubiquitous presence in republican Cuba, from the Model Ts that first appeared in the 1910s to the Cadillac Fleetwoods, Buick Roadmasters, Dodge Coronets, and ubiquitous Chevrolets in later years. Over eleven thousand new American cars were sold in Cuba in 1956," and there was "fanfare over the arrival of the 1957 models from Detroit."[11]

However, in 1950s Cuba, social inequality expanded. The vitrines of fancy department stores were places where poor Cuban people accumulated the desire for change, and vanguard artists like Clara Porset and others sought a radical social transformation in which design would lead to a new society. Two critical facts embarrassed Cuban intellectual elites at that time: the anti-constitutional coup d'état conducted by General Fulgencio Batista to overthrow the democratically elected government of Carlos Prío Socarrás in 1952 and the extreme corruption of mafioso and gangster culture, where Meyer Lansky, Lucky Luciano, and Santo Traficante ran significant operations for their problematic businesses. To this situation, the Cuban artistic

Fig. 4 Interior of Cafeteria Kimbo in Havana with interior design by Gonzalo Córdoba, including the *Jaialai Chair*, 1950s. Courtesy Laura Córdoba

class answered with abstract painting, Concrete Art, women's clubs, modern architecture, and a solid, modern ideology to engage with art as a mode of social correction. In the words of Jorge Mañach, the author of the essential essay "An Inquiry into Choteo,"[12] *choteo* is the predisposition of the Cuban people to satirize everything. The Concrete Art movement in the Havana of the 1950s was "a happy discipline in the Caribbean chaos, a ballet on the edge of an abyss."[13] Modernity and its forms were synonyms of labor power, civilization, development, radical change, industrialization, seriousness, austerity, and an array of terms shaping the Caribbean political reality and nature.

Under the coexistence of two authoritarian governments, Gerardo Machado (1925–1933) and Fulgencio Batista (1952–1959), what was at stake at the political and artistic level was a "correct" idea of progress for Cuban mid-century designers and artists. It was in the avant-garde circles of Havana, and other international cities like Paris and New York, that Cuban intellectuals found the space to be inspired and improve their understanding of a society deeply afflicted by colonialism and other social conflicts such as repression, freedom of speech, and economic disparities related to the politics of authoritarian governments.

One of these progressive designers was Gonzalo Córdoba. Born in Argentina in 1924, Córdoba moved to Havana as a young man and worked as a draftsman for the French furniture firm Maison Jansen in 1943 at nineteen years old; later in the same decade, he worked for the Cuban venue of the Theodor Bailey furniture company. In the early 1950s, Córdoba was hired as the designer for the popular furniture store in Havana Vieja, Decor, which was run by three upper-middle-class women, Isis Ortiz (daughter of distinguished Cuban scholar Fernando Ortiz), Hilda Sarrá, and Silvia Aróstegui. In 1952, Córdoba traveled to New York and returned to Havana with the exclusive rights to sell Herman Miller furniture through his new firm, Contempor. After his second trip to New York, inspired by the work of the American designer Raymond Loewy, Córdoba conducted several projects that catered to the elite of Havana's entrepreneurial class. Created out of Cuban wood and natural rattan fiber, his furniture for the Miramar Yacht Club (1955) premiered his signature style: elegant curves in armchairs, triangular frames reminiscent of Jean Prouvé-style chairs, and a slight inclination of the chair back influenced by Gio Ponti.

He soon received the commissions that would shape the interiors of the most emblematic and modern places of Havana's nightlife. The angular shapes and tropical geometries of the venues summed up the influence of diverse Latin American cultures. The materials (straw, jacaranda, mahogany) and designs were inspired by the local landscape, as well as by the "sunny" Tiki-style modernism of places like California, Hawai'i, or Mexico. The pinnacle of the Cuban Tiki style were the interiors for Wakamba and Kimbo (fig. 4), American-style cafeterias that Córdoba designed in La Rampa, the modern center of the Vedado district in Havana.
The cafeterias displayed different materials and anachronistic objects; some looked futuristic, with spider-like lamps and counters, and others referenced organic shapes and materials of the tropics. From this period, Córdoba's *Jaialai* dining chair emerged as a simple and sober seat made of wicker and featuring a painted black iron frame.

Revolution's Utopic Idea

In 1959, when Fidel Castro entered the streets of Havana with armed forces, a considerable number of vanguard artists and designers saw an opportunity. They perceived the chance to advance their progressive beliefs, produce social architecture and design, build an organized and publicly supported modernist regime, and control nature and politics through the forms of design. Following art critic and theorist Boris Groys's thoughts about the Russian vanguard, the radicality of the new political project in Cuba had been cultivated during the preceding Republican period. According to the Caribbean poet Aimé Césaire's metaphor of the colonial boomerang, the Cuban vanguard generation, educated mainly in the US, hit American neocolonialism back in the face. Clara Porset, known for her progressive ideas, returned to Havana in 1960 to work for the revolutionary government. In the same year, Fidel Castro hired Porset to design and create the school town of Camilo Cienfuegos,[14] projected to serve more than four thousand students in the Sierra Maestra, the mountains where Fidel Castro successfully waged war against Batista.

Recovered in Cuba and presented in the accompanying exhibition is some of the furniture that Porset designed for resident faculty housing, including a dining table for six, slatted dining chairs, two slatted accent chairs, a rocking chair, and a coffee table (see pages 42–47). In addition, Porset included a particular version of her iconic *butaque*, with and without arms, called on this occasion *Miguelito* (see page 33)—a smaller version adapted to the scale of more humble homes. Honoring her proposal to MoMA in 1940, Porset used carob wood, a tree local to the Sierra Maestra area with a unique green patina, to make the furniture. Again avoiding cushions, the designer employed slatted pieces of wood and added leather to the *butaque*, combining only two materials to create the whole. For his part, Córdoba became an inveterate supporter of the Revolution and the favorite designer of the Cuban government. Supported by an entire industry willing to produce his designs, he developed his most extensive body of work.

The Era of Dujo and EMPROVA

Córdoba was championed by Celia Sánchez, an intimate friend of Fidel Castro and one of the most powerful women in the upper echelons of the revolutionary government. Córdoba became instrumental in designing the offices and residences of high-ranking officials, hotels for tourism, and spaces to entertain foreign dignitaries—the outward face of the new Cuba. Marked by an intimate relationship with power, the materials chosen were expensive and elegant: precious woods, leather, marble, and rattan. Sánchez paired Córdoba with a business partner, María Victoria Caignet, who designed textiles and undertook executive roles in their collaborative endeavors for the next three decades. Caignet had studied architecture in France and specialized in textile design, although she also produced some furniture and became a partner in the design and cultural

Fig. 5 Dujo Muebles showroom at the fourth *Salon International de Meubles de Paris*, 1967. Courtesy Laura Córdoba

management of the operation alongside Córdoba. They began by producing projects for the Interior and Furniture Design Workshop of the Tourism Projects Commission and the Central Planning Board.

For instance, an architectural project underway during the Revolution was Guamá, a hotel retreat with thatched-roof wooden cabins in the middle of a swampy lagoon (see pages 92–95). Inspired by the Taíno culture, Guamá would serve as the precursor to ecological tourism, embodying the exoticism of Cuba's tropical geography but through a modernist lens. After 1959, it was reassigned as a retreat for the new working class. The furniture project (1960–1961) was entrusted to Gonzalo Córdoba, who, in the context of an indigenous Taíno village, decided to demonstrate the *Cubanía* through the natural landscape and indigenous references. The *Guamá* collection is still one of the island's most fascinating design products. The *Guamá Lounge Chair* (see pages 60–64), Dujo's flagship furniture product, is a perfect combination of mid-century modern simplicity, inspired by designer Finn Juhl, and Cuban indigenous influence, featuring a curved one-piece seat influenced by the shape of a *dujo* (see page 94), a ceremonial chair used by the Taínos. Variations of the chair come with leather, rattan, and mahogany seats. In the series, Córdoba also references natural forms for inspiration, as seen in the *Laguna Chair* (see page 99), and Taíno tools, like the functional ax that informs the design of the *Petaloide Chair* (see page 76).

In 1964, Córdoba began designing the furniture for the new government palace in collaboration with the architects Antonio Quintana Simonetti (one of the most influential architects of the Cuban Republican period, who decided to stay in Cuba), Rodolfo Fernández,[15] and Joaquín Galván. Córdoba designed furniture for the offices of Fidel and Raúl Castro, the reception hall of the palace, and the offices of several vice ministers. During this period, Córdoba created the refined *Havana Lounge Chair* (see page 65), a mahogany chair with a seat made of a single piece of leather; the *Isla Table*, an exquisitely simple structure made with marble or wood tops and leather slats for magazines; and the *Turiguanó Sofa* (see page 6), exclusively designed for Fidel Castro's office, which features a combination of cylindrical mahogany pieces and cushions of polished leather from Turiguanó, a type of Cuban cow.

In 1966, Córdoba and Caignet traveled to Paris to present the collection of Dujo Muebles, a government-owned company, with a mission to promote furniture and handicraft exports of new Cuban state-owned companies. At Galerie Steph Simon in Paris, they commercially tested furniture from the *Guamá* collection and those produced for the Castro brothers. It was successful, and the gallery, which also exhibited designers such as Isamu Noguchi, Charlotte Perriand, and Jean Prouvé, began to work with Cuban designers, especially Córdoba and others at Dujo. An export plan was organized around Dujo Muebles, whose catalog exhibits formidable pieces by several designers, including three about whom little is known, A. Peralta, María Victoria Caignet, and L. Rosado, and Gonzalo Córdoba, who is credited with more than eighty percent of the designs (see pages 96–113).

According to Córdoba, it was essentially a secret that some of Fidel Castro's office furniture was being sold in Europe. The Dujo brand would soon be prominently featured in several exhibitions, including the *Salon International de Meubles de Paris* (fig. 5) in 1967, the *Triennale di Milano* in May 1968, the *Salone Internazionale del Mobile* in Milan in 1969, and at the Liljevalchs Konsthall in Stockholm in 1972. Italian architect Agnoldomenico Pica described the room as follows:

> The section occupies a part of the semicircular gallery on the ground floor. The floor is covered with a tobacco-colored coconut mat. . . . The section is separated from that of France by a wall painted blue. The lighting is resolved by a series of chandeliers that hang from the ceiling in several groups of four. . . . In the room there are seven wooden platforms, with a square or rectangular plane of various sizes and

heights, completely covered with a coconut mat like the floor. Several objects are arranged on the platforms, from vases and plates in colored Cuban marble to wooden and leather armchairs. Against the blue wall at the bottom, a wooden table with a magazine rack made of leather strips, a stuffed rocking armchair, and a wooden-framed armchair with braided leather strips are displayed on the floor.[16]

This descriptive paragraph and Córdoba's reference to Che Guevara reveal the meaning of these objects in the world at the time: the Dujo collection depicts a tropical Revolution whose modern buildings and progressive ideas survived in craftsmanship, a fiction firmly rooted in the belief in a utopian coexistence between the political and natural landscapes. On the other side of the coin, censorship and intense propaganda surrounded the furniture in its Cuban context: this included enlarged photos of Fidel Castro and his military elite, the graphics of agitation by the radical left, and the exclusivity of the furniture's placement, as it did not exist in the homes of any ordinary citizen. After completing jobs for the government, architects and designers sometimes suffered reprisals and were accused of being bourgeois—the Castro regime has never been a safe place for the artistic community.

The export program would last only for a few years. In 1974, Córdoba and Caignet founded the Various Productions Company (EMPROVA), where they embarked on creating textiles, furniture, office supplies, and other design objects primarily dedicated to tourism, senior officials' offices, Cuban embassies in allied countries, and government public works projects. The designs from this era integrate all kinds of materials—ranging from the luxurious to the inexpensive—and feature modularity for serial production. Furniture designs were based on square or rectangular mahogany frames, whose voids were covered with rattan to achieve an elegant and standardized aesthetic (see pages 78–84). This distinctive structural appearance continues to serve as a recognizable marker of EMPROVA-designed furniture. EMPROVA consolidated the biggest and most ambitious furniture industry of the revolutionary period, producing hundreds of original designs. The company furnished government offices, art centers, hospitals, hotels, and many other spaces in which socialist life was being enacted. Like the modernist grid in design and the latest technologies used for daily life in an industrial society, EMPROVA shaped national life to expand bureaucracy, socialist welfare, and totalitarian power.

Light Industry Group

In 1963, after a disagreement over the organization of Cuba's first industrial design school, for which Clara Porset had been selected as director, she decided to leave Cuba for the last time. The school was an initiative by the recently created *El Ministerio de la Industria* (Ministry of Light Industry), an institution in charge of developing a national industry beyond the strategic macro-economic sectors of Cuban economy, such as sugarcane, mining, energy, and so on. Porset was replaced by the brother of Raúl Castro's wife, Iván Espín. A guerrilla fighter in the Revolution, Espín came from a very wealthy family of lawyers from the Bacardí rum family, which allowed him to study architecture at Massachusetts Institute of Technology (MIT) in the 1950s.

Through his attachment to the Castro family, Espín also formed the Light Industry Group (1968–1971), a design collective, which included Reinaldo Togores, Heriberto Duverger, María Teresa Muñiz Riva, and Eva Björklund, a Swedish designer who came to work in post-revolutionary Cuba and took the group on a trip to Sweden to study IKEA and their modular methodologies. The collective produced some of Cuba's most pioneering modern designs of the era. It was created with an ambitious design-for-all ethos in anticipation of the increased need for housing for a growing society. In an interview with Espín in 1971, his colleague Oscar Ruiz de la Tejera explains the mission of the group and its intention:

> In contrast to the Bauhaus, we start from a very concrete analysis of our own reality. From the need for a special kind of creator, linked to our future industrial development.... They did not define their criteria from social pressure, as is our case, that is to consider meeting the needs of large populations at the best quality level our manufacturing facilities allow in the coming years (for which the handcraft conception is not valid). There is therefore, at school, an awareness of social responsibility, that of the designer as an individual immersed within a social group, which forms him and to which he must provide his services. At school it arises even in its composition, that is, its structure and organic composition that correspond to our country's social structure.[17]

The initiative from the government to invest time and funds in prototypes by the Light Industry Group was linked to the iconic campaign by Fidel Castro to produce ten million tons of sugar to grow the country's economy significantly. The idea was that the epic-sized sugar harvest would result in an abundant fiber derived from processed sugarcane husks that could be converted into particleboard, material for mass-produced furniture commonly found at IKEA today. As Togores explains:

> We were asked to carry out a series of prototypes that demonstrated the fundamental principles proposed: development of furniture production using particleboards made from sugarcane bagasse as raw material and manufactured by continuous automated lines of high productivity, conception of furniture as a system of standardized modular elements with multiple combinatory possibilities, use of furniture as an element to divide and articulate the interior space of the house, replacing the heavy and expensive "large panels" of concrete then in use.[18]

In 1968, the Cuban government championed the "revolutionary offensive," a second wave of radical expropriation of small- and medium-sized private businesses that took over the entire Cuban furniture industry. The government planned to use the confiscated infrastructure to develop its plans and ensure complete control. Seeking to "resolve the problem of housing," one of the Revolution's strategic social plans, the Light Industry Group produced furniture prototypes for massive housing projects that would never happen. The group's most prolific architect, Reinaldo Togores, designed a series of plastic cord armchairs (see pages 201 and 204), with frames of either painted pinewood imported from the Soviet Union or metal, in the spirit of the famed *Wassily* chair by Marcel Breuer from the Bauhaus era. *La Roja* (*The Red*, 1969) and *La Verde* (*The Green*, 1969), named after the colors of the cords, are emblematic objects of the period. Although these chairs were not extensively produced, a cheap rocking chair version made of metal and plastic cord remains popular in many Cuban backyards today.

Within the new social scheme, utopian privilege originated in proximity to power. For instance, María Teresa Muñiz Riva, architect and partner to Reinaldo Togores, was given the task of designing children's furniture and interiors for a kindergarten and primary school in Havana housed in an old church officiated by Padre Sardiñas, a "priest who supported Fidel Castro fighting" in the guerrilla army. The school hosted the children of mothers working in a plastic sandal factory, popularly called *kikos*, a symbol of the standardized material culture of Cuban mid-century socialism. Múñiz's furniture for the school, known as the *Jigsaw* series (1969; see pages 180–181), consisted of a modular system of parts cut from a single plywood board (imported from the Soviet Union) with a tab-and-slot design. Children could interchange parts to build small chairs, desks, rocking chairs, and doll cradles, stimulating their learning skills and senses. For a different project of the same group, also produced from a single plywood board, the Swedish designer Eva Björklund designed her *Little Monster* series (1969, see page 197), composed of a tab-and-slot coffee table and an armchair with a foam cushion covered in a geometric blue and yellow patterned textile.

Plywood and particleboard were the preferred materials of these designers, and puzzle pieces cut from a single board were their favorite techniques. In 1970, Heriberto Duverger designed the *Yab-Yum Lounge Chair*, inspired by one of the sexual postures of the Kama Sutra (fig. 6). Under the motto of the "chair that 'constantly makes love,'" the *Yab-Yum* reflected the zeitgeist in Cuba, a mix of hippie spirituality, progressivism, radical leftist ideas, sexual repression, and design, in the words of Duverger: "Yab-Yum is Father-Mother. It is also Ying-Yang. The tongue-and-groove joint suggested that the encounter between the female seat and male backrest fit into the emptiness of two side frames to reach the definition of its use. *Ananga Ranga*, *Kama Sutra*, *One Hundred Years of Solitude*, and other books, filled the flowery years of *make love not war*, with many ways to the discovery of *Yab-Yum*."[19] Again, the chair is jointless and uses Soviet-supplied plywood instead of the unrealized sugarcane fiberboard.

Fig. 6 *Taller de Experimental Diseños* fashion show with Heriberto Duverger's *Yab-Yum Lounge Chair*, Havana, 1970. Courtesy Reinaldo N. Togores and María Teresa Muñiz Riva. Photo: Jesús García Saavedra (Kuko)

The *Yab-Yum* was designed as part of a modular and affordable interior project undertaken in the same year by Togores, Duverger, and Muñiz, in 1970. The project was called the Furniture Industry Prototype Workshop and proposed a series of folding, modular, and interactive furniture, including closets and shelves, all made from plywood, metal, and wood for small interior spaces. The workshop merged different levels of design, spanning from graphic design to interior architecture. It presented a distinct alternative to the prevalent Soviet-style construction dominating Cuban architecture. The dominant approach favored concrete panels, aligning with the Castro regime's ambitious dream of constructing 100,000 houses annually. However, this architectural method did not adapt well to the tropical climate. In the words of Togores: "These buildings were originally considered in the USSR as a temporary solution until the housing shortage was definitively resolved with what was expected to be the impetuous development of the socialist economy." They "were inadequate because of [the design's] rigidity and high cost, as it used heavy panels of reinforced concrete not only for external closures but also for all of the interior partitions."[20]

In Havana, the Furniture Industry Prototype Workshop was presented to Cuban government functionaries to seek its approval for mass production in a show entitled *MueblePared* (*Furniture Wall*, 1971) (see page 185). The theoretical tenets of the show attempted to solve the problem of storage in tiny houses, "the distinction between storage furniture and other furnishings, and the contribution of lamps—illumination—and industrially produced graphics—color—in the characterization of the housing environment and its

Fig. 7 Interior of Fernando Salinas's *Modular Multiflex Housing System* at Wajay with furniture designed by the Ministry of Light Industry, 1971. Courtesy Reinaldo N. Togores and María Teresa Muñiz Riva. Photo: Paolo Grasparini

possible variations."[21] The exhibition was a survey of more than two years of research. The group traveled to Eastern European communist allied countries and Sweden to gain experience with the materials and the industrial machinery used for production. However, this proposal was discarded by the administration. The same fate befell other proposals in Cuban architecture, such as the *Modular Multiflex Housing System* (1967) designed by Fernando Salinas as a residential housing prototype (fig. 7), and another modular house popularly known as the "caterpillar house" designed by Mercedes Álvarez and Hugo D'Acosta in 1969 (see pages 222–227).

Conclusion

Cuba's furniture and design industry steadily declined from the 1960s to the 1990s, when it finally disappeared. Some projects were canceled in 1972 due to the Cuban government's preference for imported Soviet solutions, while others were abandoned because of clashes with governing authorities, as exemplified by Clara Porset's case in 1961. In a conversation with Gladis Bidot, a design assistant at EMPROVA, she alleges that the company not only fell apart because of the economic crisis that followed the fall of communism in Europe in the 1990s but also because EMPROVA had abandoned its original commitment to crafting Cuban-designed and locally produced furniture. Instead, the company began importing "ugly" furniture from corrupt foreign vendors who offered financial inducements.[23]

The history of these objects is that of a lost generation that proposed radical ideas about politics and design and was simultaneously an active participant and a victim of its social consequences. Imagine that we are at the end of the 1960s. At this time the Cuban Revolution as presented as a perfectly geared machine of economic and social progress, with architecture as one of its mechanisms, led by the principle of modernity and stripped of superfluous embellishments and ornamental elements. The end justifies the means in this machine. Everything that does not fit its parameters is rejected and excluded. Thus, the authoritarian culture prevails; the machine generates products, contents, and stories, while every "defect" is relentlessly discarded. The Cuban government became a machine of exclusions, which slowly took over the lives and everyday stories of these designers. It began to overshadow their different perspectives on democracy and socialism, treating their individual subjectivity as a flaw. The machine's products are the objects, the components of socialist material culture. The friction between product and defect is the history of contemporary Cuba: violence, denial, excellence, enthusiasm, and the successive loss of generations of Cuba's creative class. These stories are increasingly urgent as the machine continues, generating more defects than products. Restoring the humanity of these objects is the most important aim of this research, which is also a history of defects.

1 "Mayor Approves Cuban's Caricature," *New York Times*, June 7, 1939, 12.

2 The work of Clara Porset in Mexico has been studied by the Mexican curator and scholar Ana Elena Mallet and the designer Oscar Salinas Flores in *El diseño de Clara Porset: Inventando un México moderno* (Madrid: Turner, 2016).

3 For an extensive chronology, consult Jorge R. Bermúdez, *Clara Porset: Diseño y cultura* (Havana: Letras Cubanas, 2005).

4 Clara Porset, *La decoración interior contemporánea: Su adaptación al trópico* (Havana: Úcar, García y Co., 1931), 3.

5 Clara Porset, "Interiores norteamericanos: Los de ahora," 1931, in Bermúdez, *Clara Porset*, 59–61.

6 Adolf Loos and Adolf Opel, *Ornament and Crime: Selected Essays* (Riverside, CA: Ariadne Press, 1998).

7 Porset was not recognized at the time of the MoMA exhibition, but her authorship has been credited for the design alongside Guerrero.

8 Eliot F. Noyes, *Organic Design in Home Furnishings* (New York: Museum of Modern Art, 1941), 40.

9 Noyes, 11.

10 In 1948, Clara Porset taught the class "Interior Space for Living in Cuba" in the architecture program of the University of Havana and gave a series of lectures about design at the Lyceum y Lawn Tennis Club, a democratic cultural institution managed and founded by women that became one of the centers of vanguard art before the Revolution.

11 Abigail McEwen, *Revolutionary Horizons: Art and Polemics in 1950s Cuba* (New Haven: Yale University Press, 2016), 16.

12 Jorge Mañach, *An Inquiry into Choteo*, trans. Jaqueline Loss (Barcelona: Linkgua Ediciones, 2021).

13 Jorge Mañach, quoted in Beatriz Gago, *"El espacio cualificado: Mapa para una isla concreta,"* in *Más que 10 pintores concretos* (Madrid: Fundación Mariano Rodríguez, 2020), 29.

14 Camilo Cienfuegos was one of the most charismatic commanders of the Cuban Revolution's guerrilla fighters. In 1959, Cienfuegos lost his life in doubtful circumstances. While the Cuban government claims that Cienfuegos disappeared in a plane that crashed into the ocean and was lost, credible Cuban historians and witnesses of the political turmoil affirm that Camilo Cienfuegos was killed following an order from Fidel Castro, due to his anti-communist ideas.

15 Rodolfo Fernández was the grandfather of the author.

16 Agnoldomenico Pica, "Sezione di Cuba," *Quattordicesima Triennale di Milano: Esposizione internazionale delle arti decorative e industriali modern e dell' architettura modern*, (Milan: Arti grafiche Crespi & Occhipinti, 1968), 93.

17 Nils Castro, Iván Espín, and Oscar Ruiz de la Tejera, "Conversaciones sobre la nueva Escuela de Diseño Industrial de La Habana," *Cuadernos de arquitectura y urbanismo*, no. 82 (May–June, 1971): 63.

18 Reinaldo Togores, "1969–1972: El olvidado diseño industrial cubano de fines de los sesenta," in *Formas y funciones*, accessed at: http://www.togores.net/arquitectura-y-diseno/premisas.html.

19 Heriberto Duverger, "Una historia plus: Bauhaus Tropihaus," email to the author, February 27, 2017.

20 Reinaldo Togores, "MueblePared: Una Propuesta (1971)," in *Formas y funciones*, accessed at: http://www.togores.net/arquitectura-y-diseno/premisas/mueblepared.html.

21 Togores, "MueblePared."

22 Togores, "MueblePared."

23 Interview with Gladis Bidot, April 17, 2017.

CLARA PORSET

In the wake of the Cuban Revolution, Clara Porset y Dumás returned to the country of her birth. For the previous two decades, Porset had had a flourishing career as a furniture designer in Mexico while circulating within leftist intellectual and artistic circles. She was excited by the prospect of designing for the masses instead of high-end clients, and believed that the successful reconstruction of a more equitable Cuba could be achieved through applying modernist design principles and harnessing local craft industries. To help achieve these goals, she welcomed an opportunity to create a new industrial design school. However, despite her revolutionary hopes, the removal of Fulgencio Batista did not lead to her permanent resettlement in Cuba. She left Castro's Cuba after only a few years, never to return.

Porset was born on May 25, 1895, in the early days of the Cuban War of Independence against the Spanish Empire, a date that coincided with the passing of writer and Cuban nationalist José Martí. As a designer, she would continue Martí's fight for Cuban liberation from colonialism and imperialism by promoting the cause of working people in the Republic of Cuba. Porset believed that design could be instrumental in leveling economic inequality and social differences by promoting shared social and cultural values, especially if spaces, buildings, and furniture were designed with the masses in mind.

Clara Porset (at the top of the stairs) disembarking from an airplane after arriving in Cuba. Courtesy Archivo Clara Porset. CIDI. FA. UNAM

Despite her political leanings, Porset was the daughter of a conservative Spanish politician who grew up in a wealthy family from Matanzas, a port city east of Havana, where her father was a provincial governor.[1] She benefitted from an international education, studying at the Manhattanville Academy of the Sacred Heart in New York City before attending Columbia University's School of Fine Art and the New York School of Interior Decoration.[2]

Porset continued her studies in Paris, notably apprenticing with Henri Rapin, a leading figure in the Art Deco movement that had transfixed Europe. Rapin—who worked as a painter, illustrator, and designer—had made a name for himself by building multiple pavilions for the 1925 International Exposition of Modern Decorative and Industrial Arts hosted in Paris.[3] Additionally, Porset took classes on the history of art and design at the École des Beaux-Arts and the Sorbonne as well as drawing lessons at the Louvre.

When she returned to Havana, Porset began to introduce European approaches to the fields of architecture and design that were previously unseen in Cuba, especially advocating for what would become known as modernism, a style deemed to be rational through attention to clean, sleek lines; the minimalization of embellishment and ornamentation; and the rejection of historical references. In the magazine *Social*, she wrote about the execution of these concepts by various European designers such as Walter Gropius and Le Corbusier.[4]

In a speech at the University of Havana on May 22, 1931(see pages 34–41), Porset spoke about the application of modernist principles to a tropical context when constructing buildings in Cuba. Championing local materials, Porset instructed aspiring Cuban architects to embrace the formal elements of colonial Spanish homes, including *persianas* (blinds), *patios* (courtyards), and *portales* (arcades) to keep buildings cool throughout the year. These "three Ps" of Cuban architecture would be echoed and first used that very decade in Cuba by architect Eugenio Batista, who would become a chief influence for the new generation of Cuban architects.[5]

Instead of rejecting colonial architecture, Porset's approach synthesized modernism with traditional Spanish construction on the island and rejected the popular modes of architecture at the time that were referential and decorative. The diversity and lack of uniformity of construction at the beginning of the twentieth century had caused Havana to be known then as the "ante-chamber of the Americas."[6] Porset demonstrated that forward-thinking design could also incorporate traditional elements, even of a despised imperial past.

Porset also sought to expand her own knowledge and tried to study at the Bauhaus in Germany. However, she was referred to former Bauhaus professor Josef Albers at Black Mountain College in North Carolina after the German design school was threatened with closure by the Nazis. Porset's time at Black Mountain in the summer of 1934 led Albers to travel to Havana to give lectures at the Havana Lyceum and Lawn Tennis Club, a social club for women, in December 1934.

Porset never sustained a substantial career in Cuba before or after the Revolution. Exiled twice by dictators in the 1930s, she was first forced to flee after joining the revolutionary movement against Gerardo Machado but was allowed to return when he was overthrown in 1933. She secured employment as a professor of industrial design for the Rosalía Abreu Foundation, a technical school for women from rural, disadvantaged backgrounds, but in May 1935, Porset participated in a workers' strike against the Carlos Mendieta government, causing her to lose clientele and eventually forcing her to leave Cuba and settle in Mexico City.[7]

While in Mexico, Porset joined *La Liga de Escritores y Artistas Revolucionarios* (The League of Revolutionary Writers and Artists), a network of intellectuals promoting communism, and married one of its members, Xavier Guerrero, a Mexican artist of indigenous heritage. In 1940, Guerrero was awarded one of four prizes at the Museum of Modern Art's *Organic Design in Home Furnishings* competition in the Latin American category. The design for a set of low-cost furniture for use by Mexican farming families, denoted as "rural furniture," was a collaboration with Porset even though she was not credited at the time. Despite the lack of recognition, Porset's career blossomed in Mexico as she was supported by leading Mexican architects, including Mario Pani, Enrique Yáñez, and Luis Barragán, who furnished their buildings with her designs.[8] Seeking broader social good, Porset believed her work was not optimized to appeal to people beyond wealthy clients, writing in a letter to her husband that she had "left behind the simplicity and purity of the early times due to the need to make furniture splendorous so that the bourgeois will accept it. A genuinely damaging concession."[9]

Porset's most recognizable work—an interpretation of the *butaque*, a synthesis of a Spanish colonial x-framed chair and the sling-like seating position of an indigenous Taíno *dujo* (see page 94)—was first manufactured in 1948. Emphasizing its vernacular identity, the *butaque* (see pages 32–33) would go through many iterations, manufactured with a variety of local materials such as oak, mahogany, wicker, and leather.

The victory of Castro's guerrilla army in 1959 finally appeared to be the opportunity for Porset to return home permanently for the first time since 1935. In April 1961, Porset proposed to the revolutionary government a department of design "to investigate Cuban folklore, increase the value of artisan craft, and stimulate industrial design."[10] After traveling to Stockholm, Moscow, Prague, Weimar, Halle, and Warsaw, Porset lectured about the state of industrial design in Central and Eastern Europe in the spring of 1965; however, conflict over the supervision of an industrial design school led to her leaving Cuba.[11] Instead of an independent institution, a design school was incorporated into the *Escuelas Nacionales de Arte* (National Schools of Art) (see pages 166–169).

Before she left Cuba, Porset had completed three design projects, all educational commissions, including two thousand pieces of furniture for *La*

Clara Porset (left) with unidentified guerrilla revolutionary at Ciudad Libertad Airport near Havana, c. 1960. Courtesy Archivo Clara Porset. CIDI. FA. UNAM

***Ciudad Escolar Camilo Cienfuegos*, later transformed into the University of Matanzas; furniture for the administrative buildings of the University of Havana; and chairs for the National Schools of Arts, particularly for the buildings designed by Ricardo Porro, which included the schools of plastic art and modern dance.[12] An educator as well as a designer, Porset continued to teach for the rest of her life in Mexico, notably at the *Escuela Nacional de Arquitectura* (National Architecture School). Although her dream of a communist Cuba had been achieved, she never returned, passing away in 1981. ARDP**

1 Randal Sheppard, "Clara Porset in Mid Twentieth-Century Mexico: The Politics of Designing, Producing, and Consuming Revolutionary Nationalist Modernity," *The Americas* 75, no. 2 (April 2018): 352.

2 Jorge R. Bermúdez, *Clara Porset: Diseño y cultura* (Havana: Instituto Cubano del Libro, 2005), 10.

3 Bermúdez, 11.

4 Sheppard, "Clara Porset in Mid Twentieth-Century Mexico," 353.

5 Victor Deupi and Jean-François Lejeune, *Cuban Modernism: Mid-Century Architecture,1940–1970* (Basel: Birkhauser, 2021), 42.

6 Gabriel Fuentes, "Between History and Modernity: Searching for *Lo Cubano* in Modern Cuban Architecture," Design Action Studio for Research, Architecture, and Urbanism, 2011, published online at: https://www.designactionstudio.com /between-history-and-modernity.

7 Bermúdez, 13.

8 Louise Noelle, "Clara Porset: A Modern Designer for Mexico," *Docomomo Journal*, no. 46 (January 2012): 56.

9 Clara Porset to Xavier Guerrero, June 19, 1955, UNAM, Facultad de Arquitectura, Centro de Investigaciones de Diseño Industrial, Archivo Clara Porset. Sheppard, "Clara Porset in Mid Twentieth-Century Mexico," 377.

10 *Borrador del Proyecto de Desarrollo del diseño industrial*, presentado por Clara Porset al gobienro revolutonario, 12 de abril, 1971. (*Draft of the Industrial Design Development Project*, presented by Clara Porset to the revolutionary government, April 12, 1971).

11 Bermúdez, 18–20.

12 Bermúdez, 19.

Clara Porset, *Cuban Butaque*, 1960, linden tree wood and leather. Collection Cuban Modern. Photo: David Avilés

Clara Porset, *Miguelito Armchair*, 1960, linden tree wood and leather. Collection Cuban Modern. Photo: David Avilés

CONTEMPORARY INTERIOR DECORATION: ITS ADAPTATION TO THE TROPICS

LECTURE READ BY CLARA PORSET IN THE AUDITORIUM OF THE UNIVERSITY OF HAVANA ON MAY 22, 1931. TRANSLATED BY DR. MARK EVAN DAVIS. PUBLISHED WITH PERMISSION FROM ARCHIVO CLARA PORSET. CIDI. FA. UNAM.

I would like to clarify before anything else that I use the term "Interior Decoration" because of its common usage among us, but I am aware of its inadequacy; moreover, to be frank, I am hostile to it.

To decorate means to adorn, that is to say, to add ornamental forms for the sole purpose of producing a decorative effect. This concept cannot be reconciled with the requirements of the contemporary spirit. We have risen to a higher level of discernment and have new spiritual needs, well above the sensations that ornament has to offer us. We are capable of perceiving and appreciating austere beauty, stripped of ornamentation.

For me, the art of the interior is about the perfection of forms and the relationships between objects, not superimposed material. And with this observation, we give clear evidence of spiritual improvement, since, as Adolf Loos says, the more cultured a people is, the more ornamentation drops out of sight.

For this reason, it is unsuitable to give the name "Interior Decoration" to a discipline whose excellence rests on foundations distinct from the purely ornamental and that aspires to much more worthy aims.

The English term "Interior Design" is much closer to the truth, and "Interior Architecture," commonly used in Europe, is even better, since issues are addressed following architectural principles.

More and more often, the Germans employ another meaningful term, which is excellent: "The Art of Organizing Enclosed Spaces."

So as not to seem pretentious, and for the reason stated earlier, that its use is most generalized, I will continue to call this art of ours "Interior Decoration," though truthfully, it not only lacks ornamental sentiment but is opposed to it.

Every creative era has produced its own corresponding cultural expression in Interior Decoration, representative of its mentality and its general trends. Ours has its own, strongly pronounced features that differentiate it clearly from those of previous eras. It has an intense dynamism and is full of social and technical revolution. How could one conceive then, that its form of artistic expression would be the same as in earlier periods?

This era of ours is one of outdoor living; a healthy, clean, quick, honest or brutal life, however you may choose to describe it. An era of wireless telegraphy, airplanes, and giant ocean liners by necessity had to produce a form of Interior Decoration logically derived from its special way of being and which expresses its way of thinking.

This form or concept of Interior Decoration, of perfect consistency with the powerful new spirit that drives our admirable century, has by now assumed a definitive direction, after the uncertainties and natural stumbling-blocks of its early days. But, before we consider this contemporary orientation, let us have a look back at these aforementioned setbacks.

At the end of the nineteenth century, an extremely interesting personality emerged in England, a forerunner to current ideas. I am referring to William Morris, whose artistic doctrine was so advanced it could be taken for a declaration of principles of today's German Werkbund.

Morris preached utilitarianism and simplicity in Interior Decoration, repudiating ornamentation, and came to have a great influence in England. But this influence ended at his death.

Nevertheless, the success of his work was a stimulus for Continental decorators at a restless time, in which a valiant but confused movement began in France: *art nouveau.*

The group promoting this movement tried vigorously to free themselves from the spirit of routine of the nineteenth century, to embark on a search for an original style. But, although conceived with great intentions and admirable courage, the movement failed for lack of foundation. They approached their task as if it were a question of ornamental form, forgetting structure, and the result was an unbearable style and immediate condemnation.

The same spirit of renewal sprang up in Germany and Austria, almost at the same time as in France.

Germany produced a black-and-white style, solemn and funereal, which, once industrialized, conferred supremacy on the German decorative arts in the first ten or twelve years of this century.

In Austria, Josef Hoffmann and his disciples gave impetus to the idea of renewal, creating a more fanciful style than that of the Germans.

But both styles failed for the same reason as *art nouveau* in France: neglect of the principles of structure.

With the Great War came the brutal shock that would free us from the last ties to the past, in art as in other things. The use of the machine for destructive ends had clearly proven its multiple possibilities. The point was to use machines in a constructive way. Mechanization, on the rise since the beginning of the century, was made possible by the industrial progress of the nineteenth century and was now well established.

Interior of the house of Orlando Álvarez, Havana, Cuba with furniture designed by Clara Porset, c. late 1950s. Courtesy Archivo Clara Porset. CIDI. FA. UNAM

A group of men of action addressed architectural matters in accordance with the new spirit of logic and integrity.

A great era of architecture began, and the birth of this era ended the hesitant period of Interior Decoration. It is no longer about addressing the question of interior spaces in a decorative way. Already it is about something higher. It is Interior Architecture: the art of organizing enclosed spaces.

However, we have yet to record the failure of the Paris Exhibition of the Decorative Arts of 1925, in the French sections, especially.

I have tried to make sense of this French insistence on ornamentation when as early as 1925 they had distinguished architects operating at the height of their powers, such as Le Corbusier, Tony Garnier, Robert Mallet-Stevens, et cetera, all of them enemies of ornamentation. It only becomes clear when one remembers the leadership group behind the Exposition was Ruhlmann's, made up of technically savvy men but who were antagonistic to the new spirit. Men who, due to the great influence that they enjoyed in government centers, managed to make themselves the organizers of the Exposition. Moreover, besides this group, the main exhibitors of interiors were the merchants Bon Marché, Louvre, et cetera, who more than anything else, were concerned with pleasing their bourgeois clientele with an excess of ornamentation and wealth.

It was Sweden, Germany, Denmark, and Austria that displayed the new style in their contributions.

France learned its lesson and, interpreting the new concept according to its national sensibility, has produced interiors comparable in artistic interest to those of any other nation in the past five years.

Four expositions of Interior Decoration, held in 1930, established the current climate. These were the Salon of Decorators of Paris, in its section of the Deutscher Werkbund; that of the United Artists—vanguard of French decorators; that of Stockholm—the most complete expression to date of the functionalist theory; and that of Monza, interesting for the effort invested in it by two eminently traditionalist nations: Italy and England.

This brings us to the present moment.

We were saying before that the contemporary form or concept of Interior Decoration had come to take a definite direction.

It might be objected that I am judging this concept at a time when it is still being developed, and that also I am also attributing a final character to early attempts while they were still being worked out, which did not prevent their later being judged failures. But the objection is immaterial because the contemporary concept is so strongly grounded, and its foundations are as logical as the previous attempts were unstable. Hence it does not seem risky to assert the permanence of this orientation.

It could be allowed, of course, that there are errors and imperfections in this moment, but that can be explained by the fact that it is only geniuses who are sorted from the chaff without suffering accidents; and we know of course that there are very few geniuses. We are living in a moment in which this new concept is being put into practice; so, we cannot attest yet to the elimination of the bad and the mediocre.

Now, Interior Decoration is a question of organizing simple forms, stripped of ornamentation, and of relating and balancing them in an expressive manner, using functional elements that correspond to the same spirit, in such a way that, with their combination, perfect unity is achieved.

Components of this perspective include the renewal of the very concept of structure, caused in turn by the use of new materials and the change in mentality corresponding to a new aesthetic sensibility.

The use of concrete allowed endless freedom in structure, which necessarily had to produce novelties of form. Walls, freed from their function of structural integrity, have become simple insulating membranes that can, therefore, be removed at will and which, when they are present, admit the use of different materials, with doors and windows placed wherever is most convenient and sized however desired.

Today, the exterior of a house is a logical extension of the interior, so that reasonable demands of the latter can be fully accommodated, because there is no need to make concessions to the facade. This renewal of the concept of structure has logically tended to lead to a new approach to the interior.

Moreover, we have to draw attention to another factor: a change of mentality corresponding to a new aesthetic sensibility.

It is undeniable that the Great War brought with it an entirely different attitude towards life, with a radical shift in values. A new spirit emerged from it, equally perceptible in all moral and artistic manifestations. A spirit of sincerity, of precision and logic, stripped of redundancy and artifice, that is evident daily, both in social manners—that of young people especially, raw and forthright—and in music, literature, and the fine arts: a spirit that reviles the picturesque and pretty, that seeks truth above all, in life as in art.

Hence, in today's Interior Decoration, one feels a positive unease when confronted with ornamentation that hides forms and distracts from them. It should not disguise structure nor its component elements. It should recognize beauty in usefulness and abhor everything that is imitation.

Incidentally, it is curious to note that this same era, so friendly to the truth, speaks out against realism in painting and sculpture, taking for granted that truth and realism are not only different, but antagonists.

Functionalism, integrity, simplicity, mechanization, standardization, unity. These are the terms we now hear often connected to Interior Decoration; they are the characteristics it embodies.

Functionalism is a new word for a very old concept. When we speak of the Parthenon or of the Gothic cathedrals, we refer to function as the characteristic that made them eternal, but in these cases we call it rationalism.

Functionalism is the use of elements whose utilitarian purpose is logically derived from their materiality. Its foundation is respect for the laws of materials and reason. Applied to Interior Decoration, it has led to the creation of forms that fulfill a function and that express it without misrepresentation of any kind. It has added to the mission of embellishing an interior, doing it with scientific precision. The eyes should be indulged only after reason has been satisfied.

Functionalism brings honesty in tow. Each thing represents itself just as it is and makes clear what it is good for. This open confession clothes our art in an extraordinary yet simple grandeur.

Simplicity is another characteristic that is evident in the form and general tone of the interior. Some prefer to see it as the imposition of a world in economic crisis, to which we are resigned because we have no choice. This idea is not acceptable. The simplicity of modern things is not a compromise but a preferred quality. We seek it out of spiritual necessity: precisely because we are so complex.

Moreover, it is quite debatable that simplicity means economy. As evidence of that, consider the difference in cost between a piece of furniture with large smooth surfaces, that by necessity requires perfection of materials and workmanship, and another with a carved inlay—camouflage in most cases, for defects in construction and materials.

There is an interesting opposition between the tendencies of morality and art in the nineteenth and twentieth centuries. In the first, exaggerated moral puritanism develops parallel to an absolute license in art; on the contrary, ours is characterized by an exaggerated permissiveness in morals, while aesthetically, it undoubtedly trends toward the austere.

Mechanization is an idea that frightens many, because they think it means making the interior into a replica of a factory floor with its mechanical gear assemblies, but this is not right, or is only partly so. Naturally, given the effectiveness of machinery, some of its elements have been brought indoors; like metal, used until now only in machines. But this does not mean we intend to use wheels instead of chairs; rather, we apply to the chair the same spirit of exactitude and logic that makes the wheel efficient.

Now, it is true that the standardization derived from mechanical production means economy. Creating a model that is aesthetically good and then reproducing it in large quantities considerably lowers unit cost. Mass production—of houses or objects—brings comfort, cleanliness and beauty to the middle class and the poor, when they were previously exclusively for the rich. This is what we seek at the present moment, societies more concerned with the wellbeing of the masses than of the individual.

But, alongside this tendency towards undeniable economic and social benefits, individual interpretation has to be developed, varying in each instance according to the personality of the artist and the specific conditions of the case. It is understandable that for anyone who is not worried about economy, custom-made is always preferable to the merely standard.

Unity is a salient characteristic of today's Interior Decoration. The same spirit inspires all of the industrial arts, so that, despite the fact that a number of them always combine to make up the interior, unity is established by a common creative spirit.

The results are better still if the group of artists and industrialists who collaborate on an interior already have the habit of working together for the same projects, as is the case with one famous Parisian group, whose members are already almost inseparable. In an interior created by Francis Jourdain or Djo-Bourgeois, it is very difficult to find fabrics other than those of Héléne Henri or Elise Djo-Bourgeois; a lamp not made by Jean Perzel; stained glass windows that are not by Barillet, or rugs that do not come from the workshop of [Ivan] da Silva Bruhns.

It is common to object to our kind of decoration, saying it gives an impression of coldness. The criticism is apt only if sparing is considered synonymous with cold. Today's interior is sparse, but to keep the cold out, it has enormous windows that let in as much light as desired during the day; and artificial light at night, used for emotional purposes in addition to functional ones.

Color is used intelligently—in walls, floors, and fabrics—to counteract the cold sensation that the use of metal might produce; it has the general tone of informality characteristic of all modern life; and, finally, the use of natural flowers—a warm element—as they have never been used before.

The modern ease of communications has brought with it a constant exchange of people and ideas, tending to weaken purely regional characteristics.

With a community of similar concepts and necessities of life, it is natural that in architecture the nationalistic sense is relative. Moreover, the intense rationalism present in all contemporary expression forces concessions to the climate of each area, concessions that taken together are a factor leading to differentiation.

That is to say, a house in the tropics will have the same characteristics as another in a different area, and it must be their communities that establish each as genuine products of the contemporary spirit. But, while the first has excess light and heat as a problem to resolve, the other lacks those things, and this must logically produce some difference between the two.

We have previously seen contemporary criteria, whose development gives a universal nuance to architecture, both exterior and interior.

Let us do the same with the adaptation of these criteria to our terrain, which will give occasion to consider particular aspects of those criteria; but without considering them national, since they would be similar in any other country whose climatic conditions were comparable. The tropical perspective is not uniquely Cuban.

I see the living space of the tropics in the future as a marvelous adaptation of contemporary architecture to our climate. Of the typical colonial house, it would take only what has been proven effective to offset the excessive heat—our greatest problem for three seasons of the year. Mainly, these are the three "p"s: patio, portal, and pillar.[1]

The patio has been used in all hot-climate construction since long ago. It was found in the Egypt of the Pharaohs and pagan Rome, in Renaissance Italy; in Spain since Roman times and, brought by Spain to Hispanic America, from colonial settlement on.

The patio increases considerably the flow of air into the surrounding rooms. Moreover, it creates an area of strong light in opposition to the half-lit interior, which results in an interesting pattern of variations from full light to shadow, and it does this in a private way that heightens its value. Everyone is aware of the importance of the patio in the development of social life in the south of Spain.

The incorporation of a patio into a floor plan naturally requires more land, consequently increasing the total cost of the building. And that creates an issue that, being economic in nature, is of great importance today. The lower cost of the land in the suburbs of the city reduces this problem to some extent and explains, among other factors, the tendency to locate residences far from the urban center. In addition, standardization reduces the cost of construction materials, thereby offsetting the increase for land acquisition.

And, since I am stating my personal vision of a house in any hot country, I would like to clarify, although it seems unnecessary since I speak of contemporary architecture, that I suggest reintegrating the patio into a house in these climes simply because I consider it an advantageous element, one with emotional possibilities, within the general composition. I am not saying in any way that I mean to use it as a picturesque form of decoration drawn from Spanish cinematography.

The absence or smallness of the main entrance [portal] in the type of home imported from the United States and built in Cuba recently has made us acutely aware of how necessary it is in our climate. Without a portal, the tropical house produces a disagreeable sensation of a lack of air, of suffocation. It is an essential element for summer. And our summer is almost permanent.

The entryway itself has a dual utility, because it protects the rooms it surrounds from the direct effects of the sun, keeping them in the shade, which is both cool and a comfort to the eyes. Also, with the protection against the sun and rain provided by substantial eaves –an element that our climate requires—when extended by awnings, the main entrance become the most pleasant and livable place in the house, especially in the months of great heat.

The entryway as terrace has been the most wasted of spaces. But in the house of the future, it will be placed at different heights and on different planes, and could become a hanging garden, as so delightfully presented in contemporary homes in Europe and North America.

So an entryway—whenever possible and as large as can be—has to be the most essential element in the house of the tropics, adding a room to the exterior, habitable during the hours of daylight if covered, and if not—as a terrace garden—another room that will be a favorite place after nightfall.

The cost of land may limit the construction of main entrances, terraces, and patios and may even eliminate the latter. But it does not influence the use of pillars at all, because they extend themselves in vertical lines.

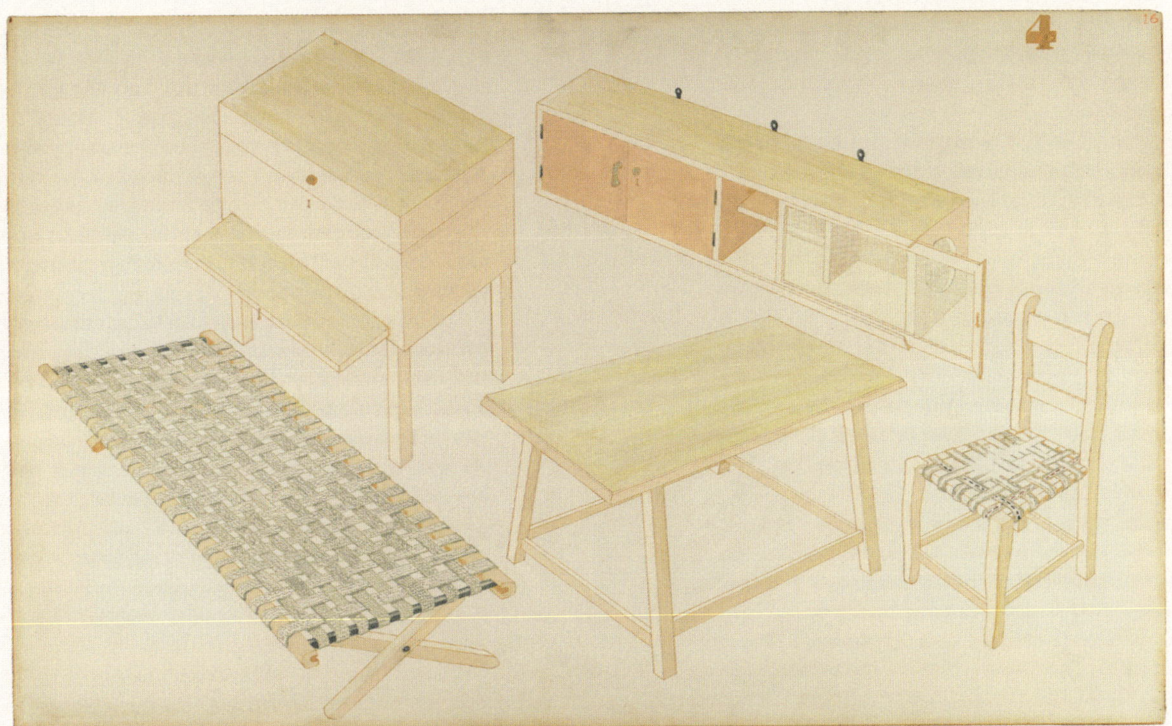

Clara Porset and Xavier Guerrero, *Entry Panel for the Museum of Modern Art's Latin American Competition for Organic Design in Home Furnishings*, c. 1940, gouache and ink on board. Collection the Museum of Modern Art, New York, NY. Courtesy Art Resource, NY

Pillars are so important for increasing air circulation—the primary purpose that all construction in the tropics seeks—that they must be adopted regardless of any associated cost increase they entail, even if higher walls mean higher costs due to the use of more materials.

And this is where I situate myself within my true subject matter: the interior, out of which I have just dared to trespass onto someone else's property. Functionally, a tall pillar provides ease of aeration to the interior. But how can we not mention also the emotional possibilities it offers us?

The height of the pillar establishes an upward movement, creates spirituality, and must be accentuated by the inevitably horizontal line of the furniture. Let us think about the subtle effect of the different areas of light and shadow produced by the light that passes through the great openings of a room with high pillars, especially when contemplated from a very low seat. Let us also think about the magical effects of electric lighting that vertical development allows.

Today, as life becomes ever more tiresome and damaging to the nervous system, it is more necessary than ever to respond with a peaceful and effortless interior environment.[2] To achieve this, it is necessary that each component element be studied and defined, and that it take its place with mathematical precision. In providing its usefulness, the element takes on spiritual and artistic value and contributes to creating an environment of consoling tranquility and satisfaction.

Further, it is in this polished and exact state that we now discover the three principal elements of interior decoration: shape, light and color. If we are to give preponderance to one of the three, it must be shape, as the interior is now essentially sculptural.

An enclosed space has to be organized with simple shapes. As this space is generally limited today, and we seek order and effortlessness, it follows that we must eliminate any non-essential form. Therefore, furniture—the principal form of the interior, as well as a structural one—is limited to functional use and takes advantage of available space to let traffic move freely in the room, however small it maybe.

"A room can be arranged very luxuriously by de-furnishing it rather than furnishing it," says Francis Jourdain; and he adds: "the great decorator of the future must limit himself to strictly necessary elements, while establishing such an exact proportion and a balance so perfect, that no gap remains, nor any lacunae, so the room where they are placed does not appear naked."

This is the same concept that Djo-Bourgeois invokes when he says, "the room forms a broad rectilinear volume where pieces of furniture are inserted in turn, as additional rectilinear volumes: harmony results, as in architecture, from the relationship between one and the other."

So furniture has become an integral part of architecture. Furniture has fused with the building.[3] It has become a utilitarian and non-decorative element—although this does not mean it has stopped being expressive, since this quality is obtained through the relationship and equilibrium between elements, taken as objects.

With this principle, to the extent it relates to the rest of the architectural composition, a piece of furniture ceases to be of interest as an isolated unit to be acquired only for its functional value—as it has been up to now.

The horizontal line, the most prevalent in furniture, is the most logical. Most elements of nature are presented horizontally. A landscape rarely develops vertically. Human beings likewise move in that way, just like almost all the means of locomotion they have invented.

In the tropics, the horizontal direction of furniture, combined with the verticality of the walls, provides interiors with an ideal balance of spirituality and rationality.

Two new materials have been added to wood, the commonly used material for furniture to date: concrete and chrome-plated metal.

Djo-Bourgeois has used concrete with the idea of making the incorporation of the furniture into the wall more evident, thus accenting its architectural value. But, until now, he has always done it sparingly; on the back and arms of a sofa, or in a bookcase that comes out of the wall.

By contrast, metal furniture—a typical product of the industrial arts of our era—is already broadly espoused, not only by progressive decorators, but also by the majority of the more conservative ones.

Metal furniture is sturdy and light and, although it does not present the same appearance of voluptuous wealth and comfort that fine wood furniture does, it has appeal because of its good proportions, clean lines, and ingenious construction.

Djo-Bourgeois's attempts to use concrete furniture are singular and controversial. Hence I do not connect them to our climate.

But I do see the relevance of metal furniture; it has great possibilities among us, due to its lightness and coldness, both in appearance and in fact. Some object to the use of metal in Cuba, due to its likely oxidation, especially in places close to the sea. In my personal experience with different nickel-plated and chrome-plated pieces manufactured here, to date they have not shown any deterioration. I must say, nevertheless, that they have only recently come into use. In addition, I am familiar with a group of chromed furniture pieces—chairs, armchairs and tables—imported from Germany in 1929, that are in perfect condition, despite their constant use and placement in houses close to the sea.

The airplane, with its need to employ light and strong materials, embraced wood veneer techniques—gluing very thin sheets of wood together and placing them on top of one another while alternating the grain to avoid weak spots—to produce a material that is lightweight and unyielding, even in abrupt changes of temperature.

This system makes possible the large bare surfaces in furniture, where the natural beauty of the wood is highlighted as never before.

In Cuba we have an abundance of them: 126 distinct kinds of wood have been classified. Consequently, their combination makes it possible to obtain infinite possibilities of color and design on the surface of furniture.

Once the cutting of wood into fine veneers is perfected among us, it will not be necessary to import them from abroad, as we do now, which is absurd, given our natural riches.

Reed and wicker furniture in fact feels as cool as it looks. This has always made it popular in the tropics. But, to add comfort and convenience, cushions are put on it that generate heat, because they are stuffed with fibers and wool and covered with relatively thick fabrics. In this way, the cool effect is neutralized and its special effectiveness is nullified. Now, if the cushions were made of straw, even of Panama weave, stuffing them with asbestos, we would make this characteristic coolness both apparent and real, which makes wicker furniture an essential element in our climate.

Wicker furniture should be given the simplicity of line and horizontal movement that harmonizes it with the rest of the set. And as in our era—which condemns pomp—logic takes precedence over formality, in the tropics wicker must be permitted in all rooms, even in reception rooms, from which it has almost always been excluded until now.

Interior lighting is part of the basic plan of a room and coordinates with its overall design. Its importance is so overarching and requires such careful study that it has given birth to a new specialty: that of architectural lighting design.

Light has two aspects: the functional, or the purpose of the illumination, whether by natural or artificial light, and the expressive, also achieved by both types of lighting.

During the day, large glass windows—made possible by contemporary architecture and which, sometimes substitute glass for an entire wall—let in the maximum amount of sunlight. But here we have to consider again the differences that accompany the distinct climates. Professor Bruno Taut of Berlin, in a recent work about contemporary architecture, says that the window is to a house what the eye is to a person, and that, just as it dilates when there is a lack of light and contracts when there is an excess of it, the window must be larger or smaller depending on whether it is in a country with a little or too much of sunlight.

Professor Taut's theory is good for those countries where the interior of the house is maintained, not cooler but less hot, by avoiding admission of sunlight, bearer of heat, as much as possible. But this would not be acceptable in Cuba, where we have the privilege of the sea breeze. We cannot completely insulate the interior from the exterior to avoid the heat, as is done in other countries. We need to resolve the problem in a way that keeps the light out as much as possible, at the least by filtering it to counter its temperature, but at the same time allowing the breeze in. Therefore, our openings have to be just as big as one could wish, but, unfortunately, without windowpanes, which produce the opposite of the effect we are looking for, since they prevent the passage of air and intensify the heat. I say "unfortunately" because in hot climates the logical substitute for glass until now has been blinds. Blinds prevent us from taking advantage of exterior space and connecting it to the interior. Blinds remain the most suitable option for our windows, which have to open from the floor up to allow air to flow from that level.

The surprising progress of electric light in recent years has made it possible to prolong the day's activities into the night. Indirect general light is established in each room, which is what gives the impression of natural light, complemented by patches of light arranged according to one's tastes or needs.

With the transformation of the principles of lighting, the pendant and applique lamps have been dispensed with and walls and ceilings have become light-producing areas. Chromed metal and opaque glass are mainly used in this technique. The expressive aspect of this light is no less important than the utilitarian one. A pattern, white or colored, can be used in place of a picture, with a still subtler emotional effect. On a sculpture, it raises its expressive value. It can also serve to accent architecture, intensifying the play of light and shadow, or even apart from that, through the unforeseen patterns produced when designs are projected onto the wall and floor.

Color is inseparable from interior architecture, as a complement to form, just like light. It reveals outlines, reinforces or fine-tunes volumes, decreases or increases real distances through visual effect; it counteracts the absence or the excess of luminosity that can be caused by the orientation of the room by means of the use of warm tones or cold ones, respectively. Its use is altogether a complex science, but it makes up for that with its profound emotional impact. That established, we come to the question of whether the interior walls of a tropical house should be white—as they were in colonial houses—or colored.

The white wall is a frank background, absolute, against which each thing stands out just as it is. There is a grandeur in a white wall because of its implied honesty. But if we come to it from the outside, where the sun is blinding, it certainly does not offer us the visual rest we hope for. Nor does it tend to bring together the elements of the interior. The same precision by which each thing stands out against it severs the relationships between one thing and the other and makes the sense of harmony impossible.

Colonial houses have always suffered from this defect, where the relationship between elements was not perceptible. Each thing seemed placed so as to be contemplated in isolation, as if it were in a shop.

Other temperate countries have had and still have white lime walls in the interior, but in almost all of them, the use of hangings compensates for the unifying color and the tendency of white to separate; in addition, they provide some variation for the eyes, giving them rest. In this way, if we are obliged to seek relationships in the interior, relationships that will produce the sense of harmony, we have to color our walls, either in a single-color tone, or in several, depending on the circumstances and desired effects.

The large bare surfaces of today's interiors invite a rebirth of the mural.

The contribution of the mural painter to our interiors—like that of the sculptor to the light-filled exterior—must be credited a tremendous value. In the one case as in the other, the purpose is not solely decorative, of course, but that of complementing the architecture, in the manner of Giotto's dramatic frescoes of the Church of Santa Croce in Florence, or the sculptors of Chartres.

Various fabrics and kinds of straw, used to upholster furniture, provide other means of introducing color, as do curtains. In cold countries, curtains are functional, but not in our country. Despite this, I find using them justifiable as a small concession of the rational to the sensorial, as long as they are kept within the simplicity of lines and are placed on the wall framing the window, so as not to obstruct the flow of air.

The floor offers another opportunity for color, of a singular interest, because it is here that the final unity is sought between the color of the walls, the fabrics, and the furniture.

Our long summer leaves a very short time for using rugs, so there is almost no reason to consider them. It is the material of the floor itself that interests us. Marble, terrazzo, mosaics, and ceramics are all cold materials and, as such, more suitable for our climate than wood. With any of these, combining colors creates designs that make the floor much more interesting than if it were monotone. Everything is a matter of following the same principles applied to rugs; that is, distributing the color in balanced volumes, so that the design does not make the floor overpower the whole.

This harmonizing and compensating mission of the floor color is perhaps what contributes the most to the feeling of rare orchestration that emanates from an accomplished interior.

Great cultural centers, like Paris, Stockholm, Vienna, and Berlin, are those that give warmth to new trends in art. We, in Cuba, always keep up with the vibrancy of these European cultural centers and welcome many of these trends before other countries, to which they arrive late or not at all.

My intention in composing this address has been to contribute to the accentuation of interest in theories about the interior as practiced in Europe in this moment, and for the special resonance that they could have among us. I hope that these intentions will suffice to justify my boldness in gathering such a select group of people to hear it.

1 Translator's note: the English word "portal," once roughly equivalent to the Spanish *portal* is now almost exclusively used in a technological sense. It is difficult to find another precise English equivalent to the Spanish term because the architectural feature Porset refers to is now rare in the English-speaking context. Here, I use "portal" to maintain Porset's "three Ps," but elsewhere I use the term "entryway" or "main entrance" to approximate the meaning, although these solutions are admittedly a little unsatisfactory. For *puntal,* which often refers to a post, especially a temporary one used during construction, the English word "post" is a fair equivalent. However, the author appears to be most concerned with larger, permanent architectural features, so I translate the word as "pillar."

2 "De economía de esfuerzo."

3 Porset's original Spanish makes a play on words which is as clever as it is resistant to translation: "De mueble se ha convertido en inmueble."

Cuban workshop fabricating Clara Porset's furniture designs for Ciudad Escolar Camilo Cienfuegos, 1960. Courtesy Archivo Clara Porset. CIDI. FA. UNAM

Clara Porset, *Rocking Chair*, 1961, for Ciudad Escolar Camilo Cienfuegos, carob tree wood. Collection Cuban Modern. Photo: David Avilés

Clara Porset, *Bench*, 1961, for Ciudad Escolar Camilo Cienfuegos, carob tree wood. Collection Cuban Modern. Photo: David Avilés

Clara Porset, *Dining Chair*, 1961, for Ciudad Escolar Camilo Cienfuegos, carob tree wood. Collection Cuban Modern. Photo: David Avilés

Clara Porset, *Armchair*, 1961, for Ciudad Escolar Camilo Cienfuegos, carob tree wood.
Collection Cuban Modern. Photo: David Avilés

LE JOURNAL DE LA MAISON

Nº 10/MARS 1969/MENSUEL/3,50 F/BELGIQUE : 35 FB/SUISSE : 3,50 FS/ESPAGNE : 52 PTAS.

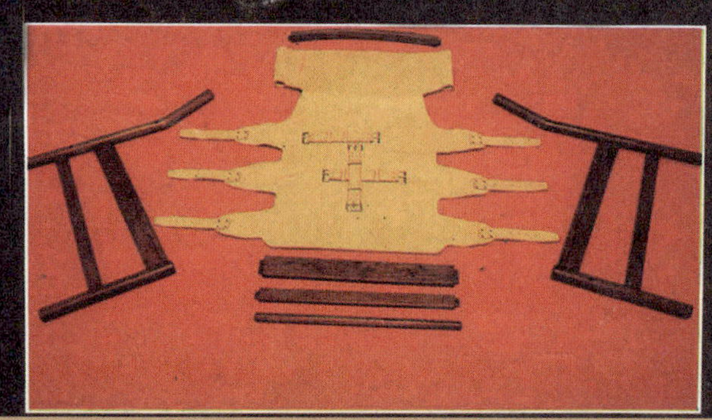

UN CUBAIN TOUT BLANC. Deux matières très nobles, le cuir et l'acajou, se sont réunies pour composer ce siège que nous devons au designer Cordoba. Pour reconstituer le corps, les morceaux d'acajou se fixent les uns aux autres à l'aide de vis. La peau se glisse sur les montants du dossier, et les petites ceintures qui se trouvent de chaque côté passent par des glissières percées dans le bois. Elles sont rattachées sous le siège par des sangles également en cuir blanc. (Modèle Havana, prix conseillé : 650 F. Sur demande Industria Cubana communique la liste de ses revendeurs.)

GONZALO CÓRDOBA: DUJO MUEBLES AND EMPROVA

Born in Argentina in 1924, Gonzalo A. Córdoba Vázquez (d. 2020) moved to Havana as a teenager, finding employment and training as a draftsman in the Cuban workshops of several international design companies. After working for Decor, a popular furniture store in Old Havana, the core of the original Spanish colonial city, his visibility in the design world rose by importing furniture to Cuba from large international design firms such as Herman Miller.

Notably, before the Revolution, Córdoba had designed spaces for bourgeoisie leisure and consumption, including the Miramar Yacht Club as well as Wakamba and Kimbo, eateries in Havana's commercial centers that had menus in Spanish and English. His designs oftentimes referenced tropicalism; emphasized elegantly curved, gradually inclined seats; and used local, precious woods such as mahogany and majagua—a flowering, shrub-like tree found along Caribbean shores. (continued on page 55)

Cover of *Le Journal de la Maison* with Gonzalo Córdoba and the *Habana Lounge Chair*, March 1969. Courtesy Laura Córdoba

Dujo Muebles showroom at the fourth *Salon International de Meubles de Paris* with *Mangrove Table* surrounded by *Petaloide Chairs* (front), and *Turquino Chair* (back, next to plant), 1967. Collection Laura Córdoba

Dujo Muebles showroom at the fifth *Salon International de Meubles de Paris* with the *Guamá Lounge Chairs* (left), *Turiguano Sofa* (back), *Turiguano Chairs* (right), *Isla Table* (Center), and *Banco Guanes* (front), 1969. Courtesy Laura Córdoba

Dujo Muebles showcase *Cuba à Lyon*, Lyon, France, 1968. Courtesy Laura Córdoba

Exterior advertisement of the Dujo Muebles showcase *Cuba à Lyon*, Lyon, France, 1968. Courtesy Laura Córdoba

Dujo Muebles advertisement in unidentified French magazine with *Guamá Lounge Chair*, c. late 1960s. Courtesy Laura Córdoba

Diez Ãnos de EMPROVA (Ten Years of EMPROVA) with *Lotus Tables*, Havana, 1984. Courtesy Laura Córdoba

Even after the Revolution, Córdoba continued to create furniture of comparative luxury for the hospitality sector. In 1960—while simultaneously designing furniture for hotels in Havana, Pinar del Río, Trinidad, and Isla de Pinos—Córdoba created outdoor seating for Havana's public beaches. Nonetheless, by 1962, he had begun work on more practical projects, most notably designing for the Plan Camagüey, which encompassed the construction of four thousand new homes.

By 1966, Fidel Castro's government developed the Plan Especial de Exportaciones de Muebles y Artesanías ("Special Plan for Exporting Furniture and Handicraft"), which included the exportation of luxury furniture to Europe designed by Córdoba under the name Dujo Muebles (Duho Furniture). The designs for this collection comprised an amalgamation of furniture from his previous projects, most notably the furniture he created for a resort in Guamá (see pages 92–95) on the southeastern coast of Cuba, as well as the furnishings he designed for the reception hall and offices of the Palace of the Revolution, the seat of Castro's government.

The furniture from Guamá, a swampy touristic retreat, referenced an indigenous Cuban past; precious Cuban woods were combined with materials such as leather, animal hair, and natural fibers. The furniture from the governmental palace represented another part of Cuban identity—this time not of a historic past, but rather the Cuban revolutionary present. In his own words, Córdoba described his designs as "*diseños Cubanos para Cuba*" ("Cuban designs for Cuba"). Ironically, these designs were marketed to Europeans in showrooms at both the 1967 and the 1969 *Salon International de Meubles* de Paris as well as the *Milan Triennial XIV* in 1968.

The designs by Córdoba that would be most used by Cubans comprise his work from 1974 to 1989 as director of the Departamento de Diseños y Proyectos de la Empresa de Producciones Varias (Department of Designs and Projects of the Various Productions Company, known as EMPROVA). Officially inaugurated on June 4, 1974, EMPROVA was an initiative supported by Celia Sánchez to create everyday furniture for Cubans. It was also a collaboration between Córdoba and his wife, María Victoria Caignet, who had trained as a textile and fashion designer. While Córdoba designed individual pieces of furniture, Caignet would develop the overall impression of the interior environments and settings. Supported by a team of up to seventeen designers, draftspeople, and craftspeople, EMPROVA featured multiple workshops organized around specific materials and processes, including upholstery, ceramics, woodworking, plastics, and stonemasonry.

EMPROVA's prolific output, evidenced by realized designs for more than one hundred hotels in Cuba, also included a material turn in Córdoba's work.

While still making examples of designs, such as the *Adria Lounge Chair* and *Flora Lounge Chair* (see page 84) in mahogany and leather, Córdoba embraced plywood versions of the same designs for wider distribution and use in a line of hotel furniture called the *Grupo Plania*. The *Lotus Tables* highlight this material change along with an embrace of brighter and unnatural colors. Another furniture line from EMPROVA—the *Grupo Libia*, which focused on guest houses instead of hotels—included a menagerie of wooden kitchen utensils as well as a modular sofa.

While leading EMPROVA, Córdoba was celebrated through design shows in Havana, including *Diseños de Gonzalo Córdoba* (*Designs of Gonzalo Córdoba*) at Galería Habana in 1979 and *Diez Años de la EMPROVA* (*Ten Years of EMPROVA*) at the Experimental Workshop at La Rampa in 1984. Although he had begun his career as an importer of American furniture and a designer of furnishings for bourgeoisie spaces, he had become the premier furniture designer in post-revolutionary Cuba. **ARDP**

Diez Años de EMPROVA (Ten Years of EMPROVA) with the *Grupo Libia* collection (left), Havana, 1984. Courtesy Laura Córdoba

Gonzalo Córdoba, kitchen menagerie for EMPROVA. Courtesy Laura Córdoba

Diez Años de EMPROVA (Ten Years of EMPROVA) with various chairs, Havana, 1984. Courtesy Laura Córdoba

EMPROVA design team, date unknown. Courtesy Laura Córdoba

Gonzalo Córdoba, *Guamá Lounge Chair*, 1959, for Dujo Muebles, mahogany and leather. Collection Cuban Modern. Photo: Denis Guerra

Gonzalo Córdoba, *Guamá Lounge Chair*, 1959, for Dujo Muebles, mahogany and yarey. Collection Cuban Modern. Photo: David Avilés

Gonzalo Córdoba, *Guamá Lounge Chair*, 1959, for Dujo Muebles, mahogany and wicker. Collection Cuban Modern. Photo: Daniel Martín Corona

Gonzalo Córdoba, *Habana Lounge Chair*, 1964, for Dujo Muebles, mahogany and leather. Collection Cuban Modern. Photo: David Avilés

Gonzalo Córdoba, *Isla Table*, 1964, for Dujo Muebles, mahogany and leather. Collection Cuban Modern. Photo: David Avilés

Gonzalo Córdoba, *Guanes Stool*, 1961, for Dujo Muebles, mahogany and sisal fiber. Collection Cuban Modern. Photo: Daniel Martín Corona

Gonzalo Córdoba, *Guanes Stool*, 1961, for Dujo Muebles, mahogany, foam, yarey, and leather. Collection Cuban Modern. Photo: Daniel Martín Corona

Gonzalo Córdoba, *Guanes Bench*, 1961, for Dujo Muebles, mahogany and paper cord. Collection Cuban Modern. Photo: David Avilés

Gonzalo Córdoba, *Banquito Santiago*, 1961, for Dujo Muebles, mahogany and leather. Collection Cuban Modern. Photo: Daniel Martín Corona

Gonzalo Córdoba and A. Peralta, *Coffee Table*, 1960s, for Dujo Muebles, Mahogany. Collection Cuban Modern. Photo: David Avilés

A. Peralta, *Taburete Chair*, mid-1960s, for Dujo Muebles, mahogany and goat hide. Collection Cuban Modern. Photo: Denise Guerra

Gonzalo Córdoba, *Petaloide Chair*, 1961, for Dujo Muebles, mahogany, foam, and leather. Collection Cuban Modern. Photo: Daniel Avilés

Gonzalo Córdoba, *Mangrove Table*, 1961, for Dujo Muebles, mahogany. Collection Cuban Modern. Photo: Daniel Avilés

Gonzalo Córdoba, unnamed armchair, 1970s, for EMPROVA, mahogany and rattan. Collection Cuban Modern. Photo: Denise Guerra

Gonzalo Córdoba, unnamed lounge armchair, 1970s, for EMPROVA, mahogany and rattan. Collection Cuban Modern. Photo: Denise Guerra

Gonzalo Córdoba, unnamed modular sofa, 1970s, for EMPROVA, mahogany and rattan. Collection Cuban Modern. Photo: Denise Guerra

Gonzalo Córdoba, unnamed coffee table, 1970s, for EMPROVA, mahogany and rattan. Collection Cuban Modern. Photo: Denise Guerra

Gonzalo Córdoba, *Flora Lounge Chair*, 1970s, for EMPROVA, mahogany, fabric, foam, and leather. Collection Cuban Modern. Photo: Daniel Martín Corona

Overleaf: Dujo Muebles showroom at the fourth *Salon International de Meubles de Paris* with *Mangrove Table* surrounded by *Petaloide Chairs* (front), and *Turquino Chair* (back, next to plant), 1967. Courtesy Laura Córdoba

Dujo Muebles showroom at the *Milan Triennial XIV* with *Turiguano Chair* (center) and *Habana Lounge Chair* (right), 1968. Courtesy Laura Córdoba

Dujo Muebles showroom at the *Milan Triennial XIV* with *Tambor Chair* (center), 1968. Courtesy Laura Córdoba

Dujo Muebles showroom at the fifth *Salon International de Meubles de Paris*, 1969. Courtesy Laura Córdoba

Dujo Muebles showroom at the fifth *Salon International de Meubles de Paris*, 1969. Courtesy Laura Córdoba

GUAMÁ

Interior view, Touristic Center Guamá, 1960s. © Archive Eduardo Luis Rodríguez. Photo: Alberto Korda

Soon after midnight on November 25, 1956, Fidel Castro set sail from Mexico to Cuba on a yacht called *Granma* with the goal of overthrowing Fulgencio Batista's regime. The landing in southeastern Cuba emulated José Martí's own in 1895 at Playa de Cajobabo in the Cuban War of Independence from Spain. The eighty-two-man contingent, including Fidel, his brother Raúl, and Che Guevara, made their way through the Sierra Maestra to the foot of Pico Turquino, the tallest mountain on the island, to begin life as guerrillas fighting against the dictatorship. Pico Turquino is located in the municipality of Guamá, named after an indigenous leader who fought against the Spanish in the sixteenth century. Even as the Revolution proceeded, a vacation resort with the same name—Boca de Guamá—was being developed on Laguna de Tesoro in Cuba's tropical wetland interior, with the goal of recreating an indigenous Taíno village for foreign visitors.

During the colonization of the Caribbean, Taíno was an identity the Spanish formulated for the indigenous people of the Greater Antilles, whom they deemed to be noble, generous, helpful, and generally

Exterior view, Touristic Center Guamá, 1960s. © Archive Eduardo Luis Rodríguez. Photo: Alberto Korda

receptive to Spanish conquest, in contrast to the Kalinago, the indigenous people of the Lesser Antilles, who were portrayed as violent, aggressive, and resistant to European colonization and referred to as "Caribs" by the Spanish.[1] Despite this moniker, Guamá is named after an indigenous *cacique*, a Taíno term for leader, who led an early rebellion against Spanish rule in Cuba in the 1530s. The Spanish had quickly developed the *encomienda* system upon their arrival to the Caribbean, which forced indigenous inhabitants to work on plantations and to convert to Christianity. The genocidal combination of forced labor and imported disease resulted in the widespread decimation of the Taíno.[2] In the nineteenth century, during movements to end Spanish colonization, independence seekers differentiated themselves from supporters of the Spanish Empire, known as *peninsulares*—the highest caste in the Spanish colonies, usually people born on the Iberian Peninsula—to embrace a more hybridized form of representation, emphasizing indigenous as well as Spanish heritage.[3]

Even after the Cuban Revolution in 1959, construction of the vacation site at Guamá did not halt. However, when the resort opened in 1961, it was not for foreigners but rather a destination for Cuban workers and revolutionaries. Alberto Korda, the Cuban photographer who photographed Castro and Che Guevara as guerrillas in the Sierra Maestra during the Revolution, took photographs of the resort.

Many of the chairs sold by Dujo Muebles in Europe were first designed for Guamá; they contain elements that reference indigenous technology and design as well as the natural features of southwestern Cuba. The name of the company, Dujo, references *dujos*, ceremonial Taíno seats that were influential in the development of the armchairs called *butacas*, which are also represented in Dujo's line of furniture. *Dujos* are low, curved seats linked to wealth and status or used for specific ceremonial functions, such as playing *batey*, a ritualized ball game, and in the *cohoba* ritual that involved the inhalation of hallucinogens.[4] Further Taíno references include Gonzalo Córdoba's *Petaloide Chair*, which evokes a Taíno axe used to clear land;[5] A. Perlata's *Tambor Chair* references a Taíno drum; the *Isla Table* and *Laguna Chair* by Córdoba speak to aspects of nature through the Spanish names for "island" and "lake"; and other designers, such as L. Rosado, titled furniture after Cuban locations, for example the *Turquino Chair*, a direct reference to the mountain Castro climbed as a guerrilla.

In 1958, one year before Castro's victory, architect Nicolás Quintana Simonetti was drawing up the Plan Regulador del Centro Turistico de Varadero (Master Plan for the Varadeo Tourist Center) to continue the development of a tourist center with condominiums and yacht clubs on a peninsula on the north shore of the island, near Matanzas.[6] This vision was more in line with the Batista government's

Artist unknown, *Ceremonial Chair (Duho)*, Haiti, Taíno People, 14th century, wood. Collection Musée du quai Branly–Jacques Chirac. Courtesy Art Resource, NY

Dujo Muebles showroom at the fourth *Salon International de Meubles de Paris* with *Guanes Stools* (left), *Isla Table* (center), and *Guamá Lounge Chairs* (right), 1967. Courtesy Laura Córdoba

original plan for utilizing Guamá as an alternative vacation destination for foreign visitors and foreign investment. As a vacation destination for workers, the resort in Guamá represented a new type of tourism, one centered on invoking Cuba's indigenous past. It exemplified a type of architecture that referenced Cuba's national identity and its historic past, going against the grain of the sleek, universalizing language of modernist architecture of the time. The location of this resort in Cuba's interior, far away from Havana, was distinctive and noteworthy, too, as most investment focused on destinations closer to the capital. ARDP

1 Arlene Dávila, "Local/Diasporic Taínos: Towards a Cultural Politics of Memory, Reality, and Imagery," in *Taíno Revival: Critical Perspectives*, ed. Gabriel Haslip-Viera (Princeton, NJ: Markus Weiner Publishers, 2001).

2 Dominican friars often opposed the *encomienda* system, believing it facilitated abuse. When the Taino were granted freedom in 1542, the population was so minuscule that a bishop recorded only sixty individuals left on Puerto Rico. (See Ricardo E. Alegría, "An Introduction to Taíno Culture and History," in *Taíno: Pre-Columbian Art and Culture from the Caribbean,* ed. Bercht et. al (New York: The Monacelli Press and El Museo del Barrio, 1997), 30–32.

3 Jorge Duany, "Making Indians Out of Blacks: The Revitalization of Taíno Identity in Contemporary Puerto Rico," in Haslip-Viera, *Taíno Revival.*

4 Joanna M. Ostapkowicz, "To Be Seated: 'Great Courtesy and Veneration:' Contextual Aspects of the Taíno Dujo," in Bercht et al., *Taíno*, 64.

5 Marcio Veloz Maggiolo, "The Daily Life of the Taíno People," in Bercht et al., *Taíno*, 41.

6 Victor Deupi and Jean-François Lejeune, *Cuban Modernism: Mid-Century Architecture 1940–1970* (Basel, Switzerland: Birkhauser, 2021), 231.

Title page from the Dujo Muebles catalog, 1960s.
Courtesy Laura Córdoba

The line of furniture presented in this catalogue is a fortunate convergence of several factors which have been evolving in Cuba for practically two hundred years: the rich inheritance of the fine Spanish craftmanship developed in Cuba during her long colonial past, is here influenced by the new trends inspired in genuine folkloric concepts and national traditions. These elements have contributed to the creation of a contemporary design which does not deviate too much from thc classical conceptions.

The traditional quality of Cuban fine woods -mahogany, majagua, "baría" and many others- is enhanced in the expert hands of veteran cabinetmakers who give each piece a distinctive seal of high craftmanship.

Only genuine leather under different tanning processes enter in the manufacture of this furniture, since no other material could properly harmonize with their skilled tooling. The ancient art of the weavers of Trinidad is present in the meshwork used in certain pieces where the "yarey" fiber is carefelly balanced into the overall style conception.

The finished surface is the culmination of a highly specialized technique which strains to preserve intact the personality of the fine woods employed.

The influence of the robust aboriginal element attains a sophisticated air as it blends with the baroque colonial style. Our designers have found the critical point where the aboriginal concept is brought to its highest expression without interfering with the characteristics demanded by contemporary comfort.

With genuine pride, we offer to architects, decorators and interior designers, this source of novel ideas which we hope shall be useful to the conception of their projects.

7

English introduction from the Dujo Muebles catalog, 1960s. Courtesy Laura Córdoba

Gonzalo Córdoba and A. Peralta, *Balance Chair* from the Dujo Muebles catalog, 1960s. Courtesy Laura Córdoba

Gonzalo Córdoba, *Laguna Chair* from the Dujo Muebles catalog, 1960s. Courtesy Laura Córdoba

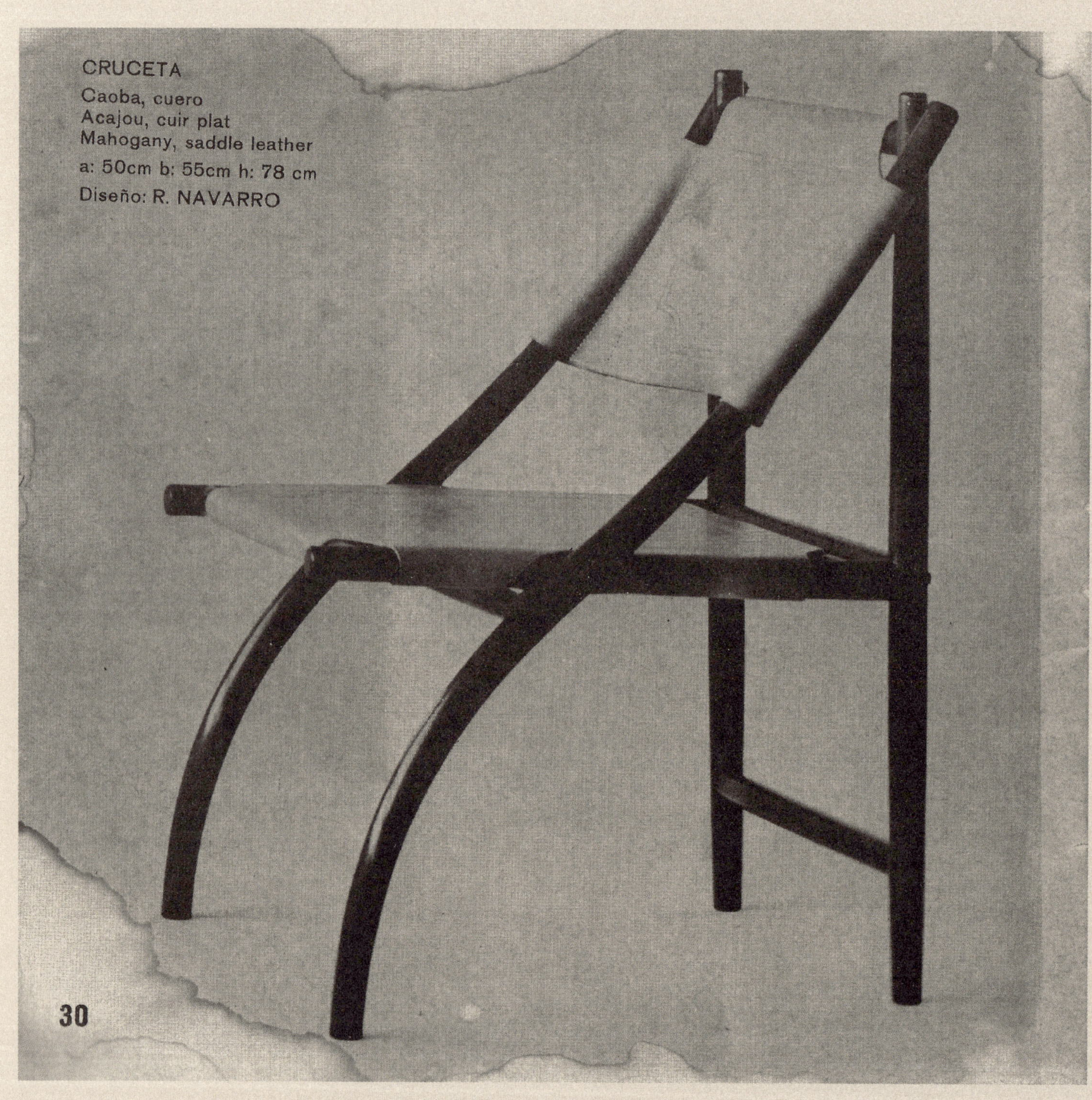

R. Navarro, *Cruceta Chair* from the Dujo Muebles catalog, 1960s. Courtesy Laura Córdoba

L. Rosado, *Turquino Chair* from the Dujo Muebles catalog, 1960s. Courtesy Laura Córdoba

A. Peralta, *Tambor Chair* from the Dujo Muebles catalog, 1960s. Courtesy Laura Córdoba

Gonzalo Córdoba, *Turiguano Chair* from the Dujo Muebles catalog, 1960s. Courtesy Laura Córdoba

María Victoria Caignet, unnamed chair from the Dujo Muebles catalog, 1960s. Courtesy Laura Córdoba

Gonzalo Córdoba, unnamed chair from the Dujo Muebles catalog, 1960s. Courtesy Laura Córdoba

Gonzalo Córdoba, *Guamá Lounge Chair* from the Dujo Muebles catalog, 1960s. Courtesy Laura Córdoba

Gonzalo Córdoba, *Banquito Santiago* from the Dujo Muebles catalog, 1960s. Courtesy Laura Córdoba

Gonzalo Córdoba, *Guanes Bench* from the Dujo Muebles catalog, 1960s. Courtesy Laura Córdoba

Gonzalo Córdoba, *Guanes Stool* from the Dujo Muebles catalog, 1960s. Courtesy Laura Córdoba

Gonzalo Córdoba, *Habana Lounge Chair* from the Dujo Muebles catalog, 1960s. Courtesy Laura Córdoba

L. Rosado, unidentified rocking chair from the Dujo Muebles catalog, 1960s. Courtesy Laura Córdoba

A. Peralta, *Taburete Chair* from the Dujo Muebles catalog, 1960s. Courtesy Laura Córdoba

Gonzalo Córdoba, *Petaloide Chair* from the Dujo Muebles catalog, 1960s. Courtesy Laura Córdoba

IMPORTING MODERNISM,
EXPORTING REVOLUTION

BECO
INTERN

ANDREW SATAKE BLAUVELT

MING
ATIONAL

The history of design has been so closely aligned with industrialization and capitalism that thinking about design beyond this particularly Western economic framework is both rare and difficult. Cuba in the mid-twentieth century, as it transitioned from capitalism to communism, offers us a unique opportunity to better understand how modern design was used by the new nation-state as a form of soft power in navigating the Cold War.

The term "soft power" was coined in the late 1980s by political scientist Joseph Nye within the context of the waning of the Cold War and the diminishing influence of its two superpowers, the Soviet Union and the United States. Soft power is an exercise not of coercion and retribution (e.g., the hard power of war, economic sanctions, or military coups) but rather of attraction and persuasion. Exercises in soft power often rely on a country's culture, societal values, political ideals, and foreign policies to make itself attractive to advance its own positions and to influence others.

Mid-century design, emerging fully as it did after the Second World War, was already implicated in the politics of the Cold War—that period of geopolitical tension between the United States and the Soviet Union when direct conflict was replaced by a series of strategic alliances, proxy wars, and propaganda campaigns by each country. As a dominant superpower, the United States enjoyed a privileged position in exercising its own forms of soft power, particularly in the realm of arts and culture.[1] This was true as it leveraged modernism by rescripting its once socially transgressive, egalitarian aspirations rooted in the betterment of society as a whole into a narrative about individual freedom, marketplace choice, and artistic autonomy as a way of underscoring the aspirational values of American capitalist democracy. This version of what critics have labeled "Cold War modernism"[2] could be found in the US and its allies through, for instance, the championing of postwar abstraction over traditional figuration in art, especially in contrast to the more blatant propagandistic styles of Socialist Realism instituted by Joseph Stalin in the Soviet Union or during Mao Tse-tung's Cultural Revolution in China. It would also manifest in design, for example, by using modern architecture for US embassies or the many international expositions that would feature the latest technological advances, such as color television and computers or multitudinous displays of consumer goods, including the latest Detroit automobiles or the newest domestic appliances.

Perhaps the most famous of these international cultural exchanges debuted in the summer of 1959 in Moscow at the American National Exhibition, which hosted the famous televised "kitchen debates," between Soviet premier Nikita Khrushchev and US vice president Richard Nixon. The two leaders would argue the relative merits of capitalism and communism inside one of four contemporary and futuristic kitchens on display, replete with automated meal preparation and robotic cleaning gadgets (fig. 1). A film about daily life in America—*Glimpses of the USA* by Charles and Ray Eames—was split into seven large film screens, all suspended inside a geodesic dome by Buckminster Fuller (fig. 2). The dome also contained an IBM computer programmed to answer up to four thousand questions about America for the fair's mainly Russian visitors. A separate glass-walled pavilion contained the "Jungle Gym," a vast structural grid displaying thousands of examples of consumer goods chosen by designer George Nelson and donated by numerous companies, as well as the aforementioned kitchens and an exhibition of abstract and representational art. The Soviet Union was still focused on increasing its industrial production and capacity, and thus it had expected more displays from the US about advances in engineering and technology—how to make things rather than the things themselves. The plethora of consumer goods on display foreshadowed, however, the impending shift in the American economy from one based on production to one reliant on consumption. If early twentieth-century modernism was a tool for solving basic societal needs, then mid-century American modernism became an instrument for feeding consumer desire. This and other exhibitions were organized by the United States Information Agency (USIA),[3] which was formed in 1953 by President Eisenhower to counter Soviet propaganda during the Cold War, effectively becoming the world's largest public relations firm. Ostensibly created to foster better relations with other nations, increase cultural and business exchanges, and advance mutual understanding between the two superpowers, the American National Exhibition in Moscow did manage to illuminate the ideological divide between nations while reducing tensions, if only temporarily.

Six months earlier in Cuba, an anti-imperialist revolution led by Fidel Castro had overthrown the government of US-backed dictator Fulgencio Batista, an event which would bring seismic changes to the island and would usher in a new realignment in global geopolitics. Although initially interested in recognizing the new regime in Havana after Castro's government nationalized all American assets on the island in 1960, the US instead

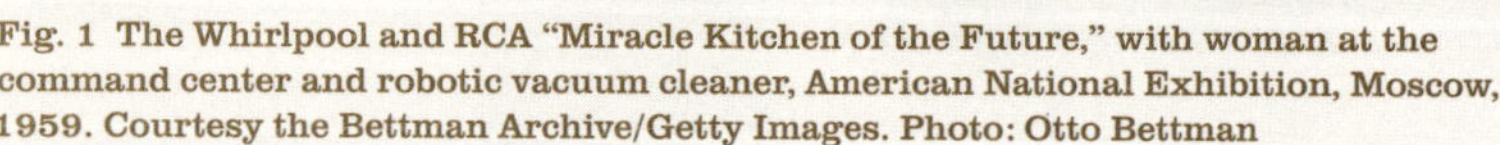

Fig. 1 The Whirlpool and RCA "Miracle Kitchen of the Future," with woman at the command center and robotic vacuum cleaner, American National Exhibition, Moscow, 1959. Courtesy the Bettman Archive/Getty Images. Photo: Otto Bettman

Fig. 2 The Charles and Ray Eames film *Glimpses of the USA* as installed at the American National Exhibition, Moscow, 1959. © The Eames Office, LLC

froze Cuban assets in the US, severed diplomatic relations, and tightened its embargo. Relations between the two countries steadily worsened, culminating in the failed US-backed coup at the Bay of Pigs (1961) and the Cuban Missile Crisis (1962), which saw the introduction and eventual withdrawal of Soviet nuclear weapons to the island. Not surprisingly, US-imposed sanctions served to push Cuba further into the orbit of Soviet influence in the coming decades—a relationship of economic dependence that would end in 1991 with the fall of the Soviet Union and its Eastern Bloc allies and the beginning of the Special Period in Cuba, a decade-long economic crisis marked by material shortages, employment precarity, and food and energy scarcity.

In all these machinations, Cuba was viewed through the lenses of the US and USSR as simply another proxy battle in the Cold War. The US feared that Cuba's revolution would spread to other countries in Latin America (an extension of the "domino theory" used to justify intervention in Vietnam), threatening American assets and interests in the region. The Soviet Union relished the opportunity to support Cuba in what was essentially an anti-American revolt against capitalist exploitation, neocolonial policies, and political interference in America's own backyard. While the US adopted the conventional means of hard power in its dealings with Cuba, the Soviet Union deployed its own forms of soft power in its allyship with Castro's regime.

I Am Cuba

One such anomalous example is the 1964 film *Soy Cuba* (*I Am Cuba*), a joint production between the countries' two main film production entities, the Soviet Mosfilm and the Instituto Cubano del Arte e Industria Cinematográficos (Cuban Institute of Cinematographic Art and Industry, ICAIC), directed by Mikhail Kalatozov. It began production in Cuba in 1962, just weeks after the Cuban Missile Crisis and at the height of the Cold War. Russian poet Yevgeny Yevtushenko and Cuban novelist Enrique Pineda Barnet wrote the screenplay, while filmmaking crews consisted of both Russian and Cuban members. The film anthologized four discrete characters in the period leading up to the Revolution: María, who is forced into a life of prostitution catering to the island's casino-hopping American tourists; Pedro, a sharecropper working and living on a sugar plantation, who destroys his livelihood when he discovers that his life's work is being sold to an American conglomerate; Enrique, a university student and activist against police brutality and corruption, who is shot during an uprising and dies a martyr; and Mariano, a farmer whose family dies in a military attack on insurgents in the countryside and who enlists in the Revolutionary army and arrives triumphantly in Havana. The stories are joined by what is essentially a fifth character, the island itself, which narrates its history through poetic verse.

Soy Cuba is a dazzling and dizzying sequence of contrasting realities and tropes: the decadent world of hedonistic American tourists luxuriating in casinos, nightclubs, and mid-century hotels; impoverished Afro-Cubans in rural villages and inner cities; the exploited working classes toiling under an extractive capitalism; the corrupt and violently repressive imperialism of the ruling class; and the revolutionary, nationalist fervor of an educated elite joining forces with the downtrodden and disenfranchised masses.

Ostensibly, the film sketches the contours of the genesis of the Cuban Revolution and the societal ills and exploitation afflicting Cubans at the time—albeit in a rather heavy-handed, melodramatic fashion. Despite the lavish resources devoted to its production, the film did not find much support in either Moscow or Havana. Critics in Cuba viewed the film as too stereotypical, and their counterparts in the Soviet Union deemed the work not sufficiently revolutionary and too sympathetic to the bourgeois lifestyles of pre-revolutionary Cuba. Perhaps this fate is not surprising given the ambiguous nature of its role as propaganda jointly produced by two previously unacquainted cultures. Traditionally propaganda is most effective when it is directed at a specific audience. Who was this film for exactly, Cubans or Russians? Cuban audiences would have been intimately familiar with the impetus for the Revolution and the lived reality of the country's exploitation, and it's quite possible that Castro did not find the allegorical treatment of the Revolution that he and his comrades had personally undertaken sufficiently specific and ingratiating—after all, it was Castro, and he alone, who could confidently claim, "I Am Cuba." Without much knowledge or experience of the country, the Soviets had harbored early suspicions about the Cuban Revolution, and the film's very specific treatment through its artistry identifies its subject through a distinctly and literally Soviet lens trained on this strange and exotic island.

Award-winning cinematographers Mikhail Kalatozov and Sergei Urusevsky filmed *Soy Cuba* in black and white, contributing innovative camera shots and memorable mise-en-scènes that are now recognized as advances in filmmaking.[4] Perhaps not surprisingly the film shares more in common aesthetically with the innovative techniques of early Soviet avant-garde cinema, however, substituting montage and jump cuts for exceedingly long single takes with a continuously smooth field of camera vision that glides the viewer to and through the action. Two remarkable scenes adopt this approach. In the first, the camera looks out high across the rooftops of Havana's casino hotels and descends to a rooftop swimming pool that hosts a swimsuit pageant and a raucous band of musicians and revelers deckside, before the camera seamlessly plunges into the pool to record the bodies of swimmers underwater. In an even more protracted single-take sequence, the camera follows a funeral procession for Enrique through the streets of Havana, starting some four stories above the action before descending and seamlessly passing through an open window of a cigar-making factory, through a group of workers who fly a flag in solidarity, before exiting out a back window for a long aerial view of the hordes of assembled mourners lining the streets. Shot before the invention of Steadicam technology, the results are astonishing. Handheld camera scenes and the use of diagonal camera angles, another reference to early Soviet cinema, bring a heightened dynamism to the action scenes, whether the violence of the once tranquil countryside or the pulsating rhythms and bodies inside urban nightclubs.

While these techniques bring the viewer into the scene in a direct way, erasing the usual distance between the subject and cinema's detached viewer, *Soy Cuba* also deploys a defamiliarizing use of infrared film to record certain outdoor scenes—rendering nature itself unnatural. One such instance is the opening sequence of the film that brings the viewer to the island from the ocean with an aerial view taken from a helicopter and recorded on infrared film, sometimes used in cinema to record "day for night," nighttime scenes recorded in daylight. The eerie effect renders a forest of palm trees blowing in the winds on an otherwise bright, sunny day—a glowing lightness against darkened skies and waters. The same technique is used in the scenes with Pedro destroying his sugarcane fields in protest (fig. 3). The sugarcane plants are transformed into a glowing white, chosen by the filmmakers to underscore the whiteness of processed sugar, which, in addition to tobacco, was one of Cuba's major export crops dating back to the days of colonial occupation and slavery. Sugar would also become a lucrative export crop to the Soviet Union and its Eastern Bloc allies during the Cold War. These filmic techniques as well as the aforementioned voice-over personify the island and the history it narrates: "It sometimes seems to me that the sap of my palm trees are full of blood. Sometimes it seems to me that the murmuring sounds around us are not the ocean but choked-back tears of the people."[5]

The idea that a country's history and values could be embodied in otherwise inanimate materials recalls the work of the Cuban anthropologist Fernando Ortiz (1881–1969), who published his seminal book, *Contrapunteo cubano del tabaco y el azúcar* (*Cuban Counterpoint: Tobacco and Sugar*), in 1940.[6] In *Cuban Counterpoint*, Ortiz offers a personified, allegorical tale—a point-counterpoint—between these two important crops so entwined in the island's history. For Ortiz, tobacco, which is native to Cuba, represents the country's indigeneity and creative artistry through its handcrafted production, while sugar, introduced by the Spanish along with slavery, comes to represent the extractive legacy of colonialism and imperialism. In *Cuban Counterpoint* Ortiz coins the neologism "transculturation" to express the complex, entwined histories of the Cuban people—the native Taíno culture, the Spanish colonial influence, and those of African,

Afro-Caribbean, and Afro-Cuban descent.[7] Ortiz sought to counter the then-prevailing concept of acculturation in anthropology, which emphasized the assimilation of one culture by another dominant one. Rather than being wholly subsumed or integrated into the culture of an oppressor, a new cultural condition arises influenced by such strategies as adaptation, negotiation, inversion, and resistance.

Fig. 3 José Gallardo as Pedro destroying his sugarcane crop, still from the film *Soy Cuba* (*I Am Cuba*), 1964. Directed by Mikhail Kalatozov. Produced by Mosfilm and ICAIC. Courtesy Milestone Films

More attuned with later concepts such as creolization and hybridization, Ortiz and his concept of transculturation redirects the White, Western, anthropological gaze in the study of other cultures to a subject much closer to home—a self-reflexive examination signaling the birth of Latin American studies.[8]

The concept of transculturation provides a useful lens with which to better understand the manifestations of Cuban culture at mid-century in areas such as architecture and interior, furniture, and graphic design. Influences from American and European forms of modernism were transformed and transfigured not only by the intrinsic hybridity of the pre-existing Cuban culture and the country's unique material circumstances and tropical environment, but also by the ideological shifts as Cuba moved from capitalism to communism. But just as the principle of transculturation does not presume a wholesale replacement of one set of cultural values for another, the complexities of Cuban culture and history offer a more nuanced and imbricated relationship to the country's importations and exportations of modernism.

Cuba at Expo 67

If *Soy Cuba* offered an outsider's view of the Cuban Revolution in film, a new opportunity to tell this story would emerge with the country's decision to participate in Expo 67 in Montréal. In 1965, architects Vittorio Garatti,[9] Hugo D'Acosta,[10] and Sergio Beroni were selected to design what would be the new Cuban regime's first entry into an international exposition since the Revolution. The resulting structure (fig. 4) was a striking exercise in elemental geometries—a highly graphic stacking of rectilinear and triangular volumes punctuated by a series of round convex windows and all of it set atop a series of concrete footings. The pavilion was assembled from prefabricated panels and components, taking advantage of modern manufactured building technologies that began to be deployed in Cuba before the Revolution.

The fact that the structure rested lightly on the ground atop pylon footings enhanced its rather alien, spacecraft appearance. It would not be alone in its evocation of the cosmos at the Expo, however, as the Cold War battle to colonize space raged. The US pavilion featured actual lunar landing and command modules from the Apollo program housed inside a vast geodesic dome designed by Buckminster Fuller and Shoji Sadao and pierced by a monorail.[11] The Soviet Union's pavilion, notable for its huge glass walls and soaring roof line that resembled a ski jump, offered a replica of Yuri Gagarin's space capsule and a theater where simulated lift-off rides on a journey to Mars enticed visitors.

Inside the Cuban pavilion, visitors were confronted by a barrage of propaganda in the form of large photomurals, typographic panels, and a series of films projected on various surfaces, even the windows, and set amid music, all the while extolling the transformations of post-revolutionary life.[12] In essence, the Cuban pavilion was an immersive, multimedia environment, which Garatti would later describe as a giant "projection machine."[13]

The exhibition design for the pavilion[14] would also draw upon early Soviet avant-garde design strategies. Curated by Enrique Fuentes, the dynamic graphic presentation draws an immediate comparison to El Lissitzky's pioneering design of the Soviet entry to the 1928 *Pressa* exhibition in Cologne, Germany. Dedicated to exploring the role of journalism in building a literate and engaged citizenry in the nascent communist state, Lissitzky's innovative graphic display featured a 78-foot-long, nearly 12-foot-high photomontage wall and used tall, inclined, conveyor-belt-like structures mimicking those of newspaper printing presses to highlight the achievements of the Soviet press through texts and images (fig. 5). A popular success, the novel design of the *Pressa* exhibition seemed to transcend any hesitations about its clearly propagandistic content, drawing exuberant praise from other nations' critics.[15] In an era in which visual communication and marketing were just beginning to be understood as potentially powerful

Fig. 4 Vittorio Garatti, Hugo D'Acosta, and Sergio Baroni, aerial view of the Cuba Pavilion at the 1967 International and Universal Exposition (Expo 67), Montréal, Canada, 1967. Courtesy Università Iuav di Venezia, Archivo Progetti, Vittorio Garatti archive

influences, Lissitzky's creation was seen as an exemplary object lesson useful to ideologies of all kinds, not just communism.

Bold and graphic, the content of the exhibition inside the Cuban pavilion offered a multivalent history of the island, from its native Taíno inhabitants, its "discovery" by Christopher Columbus, and the long colonization by the Spanish and their introduction of slavery—illustrated by the famously horrific diagram of a ship's hold depicting the number and placement of enslaved bodies—to the country's struggle for independence and its ultimate liberation from American imperialism via the Revolution. These stories were told through large photomontages that lined the walls and were also made dimensional, wrapped around cubes and wedges mimicking the exterior architecture. Statements and slogans punctuated the displays, rendered in English and French with the urgency of all capital letters: "FIGHT," "VICTORY," "THIS IS OUR LIFE, OUR HISTORY" (figs. 6, 7, 8). While the first floor of the exhibition served as an orientation to Cuba's history of struggle for its largely Western visitors, the second level told the story of post-revolutionary Cuba with its advances in education, medicine, industry, and agriculture.

Given the opportunity for Cuba to make its case to an international audience, which included neighboring Americans to whom the island nation and its products were now off-limits, it did not hold back. The United States had expected the onslaught of propaganda from the Castro regime, which had come to master international media relations during the Revolution. While the

Fig. 5 El Lissitzky, entrance hall of the pavilion for the Soviet Union at the *Pressa* exhibition, Cologne, Germany, 1928. Collection Fostin Cotchen (www.fostinum.org). © 2023 Artists Rights Society (ARS), New York

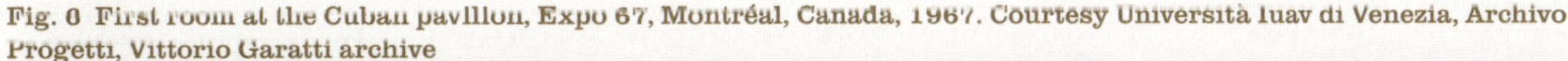

Fig. 6 First room at the Cuban pavilion, Expo 67, Montréal, Canada, 1967. Courtesy Università Iuav di Venezia, Archivo Progetti, Vittorio Garatti archive

Fig. 7 Visitors at the Cuban pavilion, Expo 67, Montréal, Canada, 1967. Courtesy Università Iuav di Venezia, Archivo Progetti, Vittorio Garatti archive

explicit content of the pavilion embraced the didacticism of propaganda, another element of cultural soft power was being deployed at the structure's periphery. Interestingly, the pavilion included a terrace café and bar overlooking a canal that harkened back to pre-revolutionary days, replete with white-shirted waiters once again serving mostly Western tourists. A clear contrast to and respite from the multimedia bombardment of the rest of the pavilion, the café offered something familiar and nostalgic to visitors, namely the smells, sounds, and tastes of Old Havana. Perhaps not surprisingly, this kind of experience—immersive and multisensory in its own way—proved to be most popular among the pavilion's visitors. The design of the space also drew upon elements of pre-revolutionary design with the dining room featuring mahogany and rattan folding café chairs (see page 173) that eschewed the modern geometric simplicity and modularity of forms found in contemporaneous designs also emanating from the state-operated Dujo brand in favor of more symbolic, intricate, and articulated chair components.[16] The dichotomous or hybrid nature of the Cuban pavilion combined the design-forward look of 1960s modularity and geometric abstraction with a certain *Cubanía,* or Cubanness.[17]

As the Soviet and American pavilions jockeyed for international attention and Cold War bragging rights, the Cuban pavilion offered a third way by aligning its own struggle with other liberation movements around the world. Inside the pavilion, visitors would have encountered portraits of Nguyen Van Troi, a martyred member of the Vietcong who had planned to assassinate US secretary of state Robert McNamara and US ambassador Henry Cabot Lodge Jr. and was captured and executed by the South Vietnamese in 1964; Patrice Lumumba, the first prime minister of the newly independent Democratic Republic of Congo, who was killed in 1961 after a successful coup facilitated by its former colonial occupier, Belgium, and the United States; and Augusto César Sandino, the revolutionary leader who led a successful rebellion against the US occupation of Nicaragua but was assassinated shortly thereafter in 1934, ushering in a nearly forty-year period of dictatorship in the country. These portraits would be joined by another unplanned one, that of Cuban revolutionary hero Ernesto "Che" Guevara, after he was captured and executed

Fig. 8 Carlos Fuentes et al., photographic mural installations at the Cuban Pavilion, Expo 67, Montréal, Canada, 1967. Courtesy Università Iuav di Venezia, Archivo Progetti, Vittorio Garatti archive

while leading resistance fighters in Bolivia in October 1967. The geography of these choices was no accident, as they represented historic anti-imperialist struggles in what we now call the Global South and what was then termed the "Third World"—the supermajority of the international community not represented in either the "First World" of the US and its Western allies or the "Second World" of the Soviet Union and Eastern Bloc countries.

While the US and USSR divided the world into friend or foe, the majority of the international community sought to distance itself from this Cold War binarism. Instead, countries newly independent from colonial rule and those struggling for emancipation were joined by another set of nations seeking self-determination free of Soviet and American installed or backed governments. As a recent successful example of such emancipation, Cuba would position itself to play a leading role in the effort to reorder the geopolitical landscape.

The Tricontinental Solidarity Poster

In 1966, a year before the pavilion opened, the Organization of Solidarity with the Peoples of Asia, Africa, and Latin America (OSPAAAL) was formed during the Tricontinental Conference held in Havana, which included five hundred attendees representing eighty-two countries. The gathering was the successor to an earlier conference held in Bandung, Indonesia, in 1955 with twenty-nine Asian and African delegations, many representing countries just emerging from colonial rule or still struggling against it.[18] The Bandung Conference promoted the right of national self-determination and peaceful coexistence, economic and cultural cooperation between members, the protection of human rights, and an end to racial discrimination. By contrast, the tone of the Tricontinental Conference, while espousing similar values to those in Bandung, was decidedly more militant in its call for revolutionary actions to counter Western and specifically "Yankee" imperialism. This sentiment was expressed in what became the conference's tagline: "This great mass of humanity has said, 'enough!,' and has begun to march,"[19] or Guevara's communique from Bolivia to the delegates, where he speculates about the creation of "two, three, or many Viet Nams"[20] to undermine US hegemony. OSPAAAL's logo (see page 133), designed by Renilde Suárez, effectively distilled the organization's militancy and worldwide ambitions through an outstretched arm grasping a rifle against the simplified lines indicating longitude and latitude on the globe.

Having extended its geographic reach across the Global South, OSPAAAL under the leadership of Castro's Cuba represented a major threat to US geopolitical interests. The ever-escalating American military presence in Vietnam, which spread to other parts of Southeast Asia, became a touchstone for the delegates as a prime example of US intervention in the struggle for a country's right to self-determination and national independence. Equally concerning to the US was OSPAAAL's support of Black Americans and their struggle for civil rights at home and their advocacy of Puerto Rican independence (fig. 9).

As a way of spreading its message and connecting its far-flung constituencies, OSPAAAL produced both a bulletin and a magazine called *Tricontinental*, which published essays and reported on numerous revolutionary activities in hot spots around the world. At its inception in 1967, fifty thousand copies of the magazine were printed in Spanish, English, and French. Folded and inserted inside each addition of the magazine was a colorful poster advocating tricontinental solidarity and commemorating a specific country's revolutionary causes. Although brief messages appeared on each poster in up to four languages—English, Spanish, French, and Arabic—it was the posters' image-dominated designs that transcended linguistic and literacy barriers. Like other state-sponsored productions, which tended to eschew the individual in favor of the collective, many early posters were not signed by individual designers, although their complete attribution would eventually be ascribed.[21]

Despite this anonymity, the posters nevertheless displayed a surprising degree of individuality. In fact, what is particularly remarkable about these posters is their extreme variety in terms of graphic styles and approaches. Alfredo Rostgaard, who directed the poster program, ascribes this phenomenon to a by-any-means-necessary approach: "We wanted to create a means of communication that was immediate, directly or indirectly, but at the same time original, and we did not reject any method or technique that would make our posters more effective or modern."[22]

Among the three-hundred-plus posters that were produced over the course of OSPAAAL's existence (see pages 134–155), a range of influences that chart larger artistic or graphic movements, both historic and contemporaneous, can be discerned. For instance, artist René Mederos's 1971 untitled poster (fig. 10) depicting US president Richard Nixon's vampiric head collaged atop an eagle's body, its claws drawing blood from a map of Indochina, recalls the acclaimed work of Dada artist John Heartfield, best known for his satirical photomontages of Adolf Hitler and the subversion of Nazi symbols against fascism during the Second World War. Mederos also traveled to Vietnam, and embedded with the Vietcong at the behest of Cuba's propaganda office to capture that country's revolution, to which Cubans found a particularly strong affinity.[23] Elena Serrano, one of the few women among the OSPAAAL designers,[24] created *Day of the Heroic Guerrilla (October 8)* (see page 12) commemorating the one-year anniversary of the last day of life for Che Guevara in the style of contemporaneous Op Art—the iconic visage of the revolutionary leader, taken from the famous photograph by Alberto Korda—radiating out like infinity across the continent of South America. Combining offset lithography, which the magazine used, and silkscreen printing, OSPAAAL poster designs employed both photographic images utilizing the former and hand-drawn illustrations using the latter. Félix Beltrán, who was born in Havana but studied in the US at the School of Visual Arts in New York in the 1950s, produced *Freedom for Angela Davis* (see page 174), an iconic illustrated portrait of the activist after her arrest in 1971, rendered in a simplified and influential graphic style.[25]

It is important to note that the Cuban poster that has become so well-known and critically acclaimed around the world—which includes not only the

Fig. 9 Jane Norling, *Day of World Solidarity with the Struggle of the People of Puerto Rico (September 23)*, 1972, poster for OSPAAL, offset lithography on paper. The Lindsay Webster Collection of Cuban Posters, Wofford College. Courtesy Lincoln Cushing/Docs Populi

work of OSPAAAL but also the country's revered film posters and those produced by the central propaganda office—was formed in the immediate post-revolutionary period and invented practically ex-nihilo, from nothing that existed before it. The posters that would have been found on the streets of Havana before the Revolution were largely produced by and for the varied capitalist interests and targeted at American businessmen and tourists, such as the kind of clichéd travel posters depicting swaying palm trees, sunset beaches, and sevillana-clad women. This blank slate meant that invention was not only possible, but necessary. While Western poster art was invented precisely to differentiate and advertise the latest consumer goods—think of the early twentieth-century *Sachplakat*, or German object poster—Cuba's needs under a communist economic model meant that messages would now emanate from the government instead of businesses. Posters with messages reorienting society to revolutionary goals were now directed towards its citizens, not its tourists. If pre-revolutionary messages compelled consumption, the revolutionary poster served a more explicit pedagogical function, turning the streets into schools for re-education.

The work of OSPAAAL would add another important dimension to such messaging as it brought into alignment the revolutionary struggles of Cubans with other similarly disenfranchised peoples around the world. The grossly simplified, exclusionary, and distorted reflection of Cuba found in pre-revolutionary billboards and the alienation experienced from messages addressed to foreigners could be supplanted by an international communion selling not things but common cause. The anti-imperialist struggle espoused by OSPAAAL was conflated by the US and much of the West into simply an expansion of the communist revolution across three or four continents instead of a broader global emancipatory struggle to free countries from colonial legacies of control and exclusionary Cold War allegiances with superpowers that only created new forms of dependence. Working against this global emancipatory struggle of non-aligned nations, however, was the slide of Cuba further into the orbit of the Soviet Union and the establishment of a dictatorial regime rather than a social democratic reform of government.

The OSPAAAL solidarity posters offered yet another unique context for designers to operate. The posters' messages were only occasionally about events in Cuba and more often about actions taking place elsewhere in the world: conflicts in Palestine, Angola, Vietnam, or Guatemala; apartheid in South Africa; and racism in America, for instance. Such far-flung places presented a cultural gap that had to be bridged by Cuban designers. In the early years, designers favored the use of folkloric or indigenous elements of the subject country as a way of connecting revolutionaries and resisters alike to pre-colonial lives and histories. Heroic figures from a country's struggle, past or present, or the use of newly adopted partisan colors or flags were invoked to instill feelings of patriotism. In this way, OSPAAAL as a form of Cuban poster art is unique because it traded in an internationalism and stylistic eclecticism that a truly global anti-imperialist struggle demanded, and did not lapse into a static, uniform, and, ultimately, dogmatic national aesthetic—the kind that seemed to befall other communist revolutions. In other words, the revolutionary poster became *the* Cuban poster aesthetic because it was able to synthesize any number of modern influences from beyond its shores and export a wholly new cultural aesthetic designed and destined for other cultures and countries with whose causes the designer could express an authentic, empathetic solidarity.

That said, it is precisely this problem of representation, however, which the OSPAAAL poster navigates: who is speaking for whom? Not really knowing the culture of other peoples, the designers risked alienating their intended audience—a problem neatly summarized by the late art critic Craig Owens as "the indignity of speaking for others."[26] As Owens points out, even Karl Marx once insisted that there are those people, among the most dispossessed and therefore lacking sufficient class consciousness, who "cannot represent themselves, they must be represented."[27] But Owens points out the inherent problem behind this statement: Marx presumes the traditional role of the artist in bourgeois society, a right to speak for others. However, as Owens concludes: "to represent is to subjugate."[28] The ultimate question is what is the role of the artist (or better yet the designer) in a revolutionary society? Author and critic Susan Sontag, in an early essay about the Cuban poster, tackles this very question, but without definitive resolution.[29] In post-revolutionary Cuba, the artists were afforded an opportunity to become designers, perhaps not permanently but through assignment—to take their artistic skills and put them to a more social and public use. Of course, designers are almost always asked to speak on behalf of others, just as others, most notably commissioners, speak through the designer. In the case of the OSPAAAL poster, it is the collective experience of subjugation under colonialism and imperialism that is shared by all parties, not an absence of class consciousness among people without cultural connections. This shared exploitation—first under colonialism and then under imperialism—becomes the basis of allyship and solidarity. It is also important to note that OSPAAAL designers have said that their work was welcomed by its intended audiences, occasionally serving as inspiration for other designers.[30]

Becoming International

As early as 1970 the Cuban poster was celebrated in *The Art of Revolution*, a book by the American illustrator and designer Dugald Stermer, who was art director of the left-wing magazine *Ramparts*. The large-format book was accompanied by the aforementioned essay from Sontag, who recognized that a defining quality of Cuban posters was their eclectic range of styles and influences. Sontag noted among the influences were the personal styles of American designers Saul Bass and Milton Glaser, Czech film posters, and psychedelic rock posters of the 1960s, as well as American Pop Art of the period.[31] Over time, there would be other influences: contemporary designers, such as those outside Cuba who visited the island, or the work of Emory Douglas, who designed the posters for the Black Panther Party newspaper, through collaboration (see page 153). This is not to suggest that Cuban poster art lacks originality,

Fig. 10 René Mederos Pazos, *Untitled ("Nixon tearing the heart out of Indochina")*, 1971, poster for OSPAAL, offset lithography on paper. Collection Lincoln Cushing/Docs Populi

which is, after all, a Western concept whose values are steeped in bourgeois sensibilities. Rather, the OSPAAAL posters gain their unique qualities through their collective synthesis of various cultural influences, which is not distilled into a unified whole but rather remains eclectic and expansive, in other words, diverse and inclusive. This accomplishment, at this historical moment, might be a particularly Cuban feat, one that goes against the grain of the kind of international graphic modernism that was conquering so much of the rest of the Western world.[32]

Diversity of style, however, is but one factor in the success of the Cuban revolutionary poster. The very internationalism that the Tricontinental poster served found its roots in the country itself. Ortiz's description of the inherent qualities of *Cubanía* as rooted in the unique ethnic and racial matrix of Cuba—the mix of indigenous, European, African, and Asian peoples[33] who were brought to the island either voluntarily or through force—is an echo of the geographic reach of OSPAAAL itself. Perhaps in the cultural and racial inheritances of Cuba, incubated through centuries-long struggles, and able to resist a hegemonic acculturation, lies another factor in the global resonance of OSPAAAL.

It is the accumulation and transculturation of such modern influences in furniture, graphic design, and architecture from around the world that post-revolutionary Cuba harnessed so well in the moment before global idealism became national realpolitik. During that time, Cuba exported not a monolithic national or even regional identity in the classic sense (think of postwar Italian or Scandinavian design, for instance), but rather a reflection of a diverse global sensibility that was liberated, in part or in whole, through the seemingly never-ending processes of decolonization. As Sontag concluded: "Becoming international is then Cuba's indigenous path to cultural revolution."[34]

1 For an examination of how US governmental agencies such as the CIA and the State Department deployed American modernism in literature and the visual arts during the Cold War, see: Greg Barnhisel, *Cold War Modernists: Art, Literature, and American Cultural Diplomacy* (New York: Columbia University Press, 2015).

2 For one of the first comprehensive examinations of modern design in the Cold War era, see: David Crowley and Jane Pavitt, eds., *Cold War Modern: Design 1945–1970*, exh. cat. (London: Victoria and Albert Museum, 2008).

3 For a comprehensive account of the United States Information Agency's design-related activities, see: Jack Masey and Conway Lloyd Morgan, *Cold War Confrontations: US Exhibitions and Their Role in the Cultural Cold War* (Baden, Switzerland: Lars Muller Publishers, 2008).

4 George E. Turner, "The Astonishing Images of *I Am Cuba*," *American Cinematographer*, May 17, 2019, published online at: https://theasc.com/articles/flashback-soy-cuba.

5 Subtitled translation from *Soy Cuba* (*I Am Cuba*). Mikhail Kalatozov, director (Moscow: Mosfilm and Havana: Instituto Cubano del Arte e Industria Cinematográficos, 1964; Milestone Films, 1995).

6 See Fernando Ortiz, *Cuban Counterpoint: Tobacco and Sugar* (Durham, NC: Duke University Press, 1995).

7 Ortiz, 102–103.

8 For an analysis of the history of the concept of transculturation, see Miguel Arnedo-Gómez, "Fernando Ortiz's Transculturation: Applied Anthropology, Acculturation, and Mestizaje," *Journal of Latin American and Caribbean Anthropology*, May 18, 2022, published online at https://doi.org/10.1111/jlca.12590.

9 In 1961, Garatti and Roberto Gottardi were invited by Ricardo Porro to design the National Schools of Art in a park that contained a pre-revolutionary golf course in Havana. Considered among the most important architectural projects of the immediate post-revolutionary period, five schools were either completely or partially constructed before the project lost the support of the regime and the entire complex fell into disuse and disrepair. See pages 166–169 for more information about the project.

10 Hugo D'Acosta and Mercedes Álvarez would design a prototype for a futuristic, asbestos cement prefabricated housing system between 1964 and 1968 in Havana, informally referred to as the "Caterpillar House." See pages 222–227 for more about this project.

11 For a detailed analysis of the US pavilion at Expo 67, see: Daniela Sheinin, "Kookie Thoughts: Imagining the United States Pavilion at Expo 67 (or How I Learned to Stop Worrying and Love the Bubble)," *Journal of Transnational American Studies* 5:1 (2013), published online at https://doi.org/10.5070/T851012648.

12 For a comprehensive account and analysis of the Cuban pavilion at Expo 67, see: Guillermo S. Arsuaga, "Exporting the Revolution: The Cuban Revolution at Expo 67, Montreal," in Ruben Gallo, ed., *Havana Modern: Critical Readings in Cuban Architecture* (Mexico City: Arquine, 2023), 146–69.

13 Garatti describes the pavilion in a 2020 video created by artists Florian Zeyfang, Alexander Schmoeger, and Lisa Schmidt-Colinet, "Pavilion in Parts," accessed at: https://www.florian-zeyfang.de/pavilion-in-parts/movie.

14 The design team of the pavilion included architects Vittorio Garrati, Sergio Baroni, and Hugo D'Acosta; art direction and photographic murals by Mayito, in collaboration with Raúl Martínez, María Eugenia Haya (Marucha), and Enrique Fuentes; films by Jorge Fraga; music by Juan Blanco; *Cosmoramas* by Sandu Darie; fashion design by Fernando Ayuso; and graphic design by Félix Beltrán. Gerardo Mosquera, René Francisco Rodríguez, and Elsa Vega, eds., *Adiós Utopia: Dreams and Deceptions in Cuban Art Since 1950* (Miami: The Cisneros Fontanals Art Foundation / This Side Up Publishers, 2017), 89.

15 Sophie Lissitzky-Küppers, *El Lissitzky: Life, Letters, Texts* (London: Thames and Hudson, 1992), 84–88.

16 For the Dujo furniture program, see Abel González Fernández's essay in this volume, pages 16–27.

17 For one explanation of *Cubanidad*, see Fernando Ortiz, "The Human Factors of Cubanidad," lecture at the University of Havana, 1939, translated by João Felipe Gonçalves and Gregory Duff Morton, *HAU: Journal of Ethnographic Theory*, 4:3 (Chicago: University of Chicago Press Journals, 2014) at: https://www.journals.uchicago.edu/doi/full/10.14318/hau4.3.031b.

18 For a history of OSPAAAL, its precedents, and for the contemporary relevance of tricontinentalism for our understanding of the Global South, see: Anne Garland Mahler, *From the Tricontinental to the Global South* (Durham, NC: Duke University Press, 2018).

19 The sentiment was first expressed by Fidel Castro on the occasion of the expulsion of Cuba from the Organization of American States and distributed as the "Second Declaration of Havana" (Havana: National General Assembly of the People of Cuba, 1962), published online at: http://www.walterlippmann.com/fc-02-04-1962.pdf.

20 Ernesto Che Guevara, "Message to the Tricontinental" (Havana: Executive Secretariat of the Organization of Solidarity with the Peoples of Asia, Africa, and Latin America, 1967), published online at: https://www.marxists.org/archive/guevara/1967/04/16.htm.

21 The most comprehensive accounts of the OSPAAAL poster are Richard Frick, *The Tricontinental Solidarity Poster* (Bern, Switzerland: comedia-Verlag, 2003), and Lincoln Cushing, *¡Revolucion! Cuban Poster Art* (San Francisco: Chronicle Books, 2003). View Cushing's online archive of OSPAAAL posters at: https://www.docspopuli.org/CubaWebCat/gallery-01.html.

22 Richard Frick quoting Rostgaard in Luigino Bardellotto, ed., *¡Mira Cuba!: Manifesti cinematografici, politici e sociali = carteles de cine, políticos y sociales* (Milan: Silvana Editoriale, 2013), 181.

23 For more on this episode, see: Tings Chak, "René Merderos and Ho Chi Minh's Sandals," *Hyperallergic*, April 3, 2023, at: https://hyperallergic.com/799671/rene-mederos-and-ho-chi-minhs-sandals.

24 Eight women designed twenty-two of OSPAAAL's known posters, which number more than three hundred. Cushing, *¡Revolucion!: Cuban Poster Art*, 12.

25 The poster design utilizes a hand-drawn, high-contrast, graphic translation technique that produces a stylized image, one frequently derived from photographs. Such a technique was a mainstay exercise at many schools of modern graphic design in Europe, the US, and Japan. For more on Beltrán, see: Sonia Díaz and Gabriel Martínez, *Félix Beltrán: Visual Intelligence: Graphic Design in a Social Sense* (Düsseldorf: Optik Books, 2022).

26 Craig Owens, "'The Indignity of Speaking for Others:' An Imaginary Interview," *Beyond Recognition: Representation, Power, and Culture* (Berkeley: University of California Press, 1992), 261.

27 Karl Marx, *The Eighteenth Brumaire of Louis Bonaparte*, 1852, published online at: https://www.marxists.org/archive/marx/works/1852/18th-brumaire/ch07.htm.

28 Owens, 261.

29 See Susan Sontag, "Posters: Advertisement, Art, Political Artifact, Commodity," in Dugald Stermer, *The Art of Revolution* (New York: McGraw-Hill Book Company, 1970).

30 See Olivio Martínez in Frick, *The Tricontinental Solidarity Poster*, 92–93.

31 Sontag, xv.

32 Graphic design historian Philip B. Meggs termed this movement the International Typographic Style in reference to the International Style in architectural modernism. Although rooted in early twentieth-century European modernism's quest for a transcendent universalism, this graphic approach, also known as the Swiss Style, became the default look for transnational corporate culture.

33 Ortiz, "The Human Factors of Cubanidad."

34 Sontag, xix.

OSPAAL
15 AÑOS DE SOLIDARIDAD TRICONTINENTAL
15 YEARS OF TRICONTINENTAL SOLIDARITY
15 ANS DE SOLIDARITE TRICONTINENTALE
اوسبال - ١٥ عاما من التضامن مع القارات الثلاث
DISENO: RAFAEL ENRIQUEZ
FOTO: MANUEL KAMPOS

OSPAAAL (ORGANIZATION OF SOLIDARITY WITH THE PEOPLES OF ASIA, AFRICA, AND LATIN AMERICA)

The Organization of Solidarity with the Peoples of Asia, Africa, and Latin America (OSPAAAL) was founded in 1966 in Havana, Cuba, to foster awareness and allyship among activists struggling against imperialism around the world. OSPAAAL was technically a non-governmental organization; however, it was led and supported by the Cuban government.

OSPAAAL was created during the Tricontinental Conference held January 3–16, 1966, in Havana, where more than five hundred delegates from Asia, Africa, and Latin America had gathered at what was once the city's Hilton hotel. The Tricontinental Conference was an outgrowth and geographic expansion of previous alliances such as the Afro-Asian Peoples' Solidarity Organization (AAPSO), which had convened in Cairo in 1957, and the Bandung Conference held in Indonesia in 1955. Not only did OSPAAAL include Central and South American liberation movements, but it also threw its support behind the Civil Rights Movement in the United

Rafael Enríquez Vega, *15 Years of Tricontinental Solidarity*, 1981, poster for OSPAAAL, offset lithography on paper. Collection Lincoln Cushing/ Docs Populi

States, the Anti-Apartheid Movement (AAM) against South Africa, and the Palestinian cause in the Middle East, underscoring a more fluid interpretation of imperialism unbounded by the discrete borders of nation-states. Like its predecessor organizations, OSPAAL was born out of anti-colonial and anti-imperialist sentiments among countries not aligned with either the US or the USSR—nations once referred to as the "Third World" that now form much of the Global South.

OSPAAL published the *Tricontinental Bulletin* (1966–1988) and the *Tricontinental* magazine (1967–1990),[1] which, at its height, was translated into multiple languages, including English, French, Spanish, and occasionally Arabic, and reached eighty-seven countries[2] in total estimated runs of fifty-thousand copies.[3] The contents of the magazine and the bulletin brought awareness to international struggles against imperialism and colonialism with a mission to build connections and understanding across geographic boundaries. Included inside these publications was a colorful poster about a liberation movement, revolutionary action, or historic event, each measuring about 21.5 × 13 inches unfolded. The publications and posters were printed in Cuba until production was suspended due to material shortages, particularly of ink and paper, when an economic crisis befell the island after the Soviet Union collapsed. In 1995, the publications resumed production but at a different pace and eventually appeared in digital form until OSPAAL itself ceased operations in 2019.

The more than three hundred posters of OSPAAL were instrumental in building Cuba's modern graphic design legacy and rich tradition of poster art.[4] Forty-five artists and designers created the posters between 1967 and 1999,[5] including a handful of women such as Gladys Acosta, Estela Díaz, Daysi Garcia, Asela Pérez, Elena Serrano, and Jane Norling, an American who traveled to Cuba in 1973 to work with OSPAAL.[6] From its inception until 1975, the program was directed by Alfredo Rostgaard (1943–2004), one of Cuba's leading graphic designers. OSPAAL posters were mostly offset printed and utilized a wide variety of design techniques, including hand-drawn illustrations, photographic collages, graphic translations, photographic solarizations, and geometric abstraction. The posters reflect a broad range of contemporary art influences, such as Pop Art, Op Art, and psychedelia, as well as idioms of modern graphic design from American, Swiss, Czech, Polish, and Japanese sources.

OSPAAL posters also reflected an equally broad range of visual communication strategies. Alfredo Rostgaard's *Day of Solidarity with the Congo February 13* (1972; see page 140) performs like a visual synecdoche, turning a profile view of the martyred Patrice Lumumba, Congo's first democratically elected prime minister, into the face of Africa, suggesting a decolonizing pan-African solidarity. Another visually clever work by Rostgaard is an untitled poster (1969) depicting Jesus as a guerrilla fighter (see page 150), a rifle slung over his shoulder. Undoubtedly this was a reference to Camilo Torres Restrepo, a Jesuit priest and member of Colombia's National Liberation Army who was killed in 1966. An exponent of liberation theology, Torres once claimed: "If Jesus were alive today, He would be a guerrillero."[7] Faustino Pérez Organero's *Day of Solidarity with Zimbabwe March 17* (1970; see page 142), depicts a Colonial-era pith helmet shot through with an arrow, a strategy that harkened back to traditional forms of weaponry—a common motif of OSPAAL posters—but rendered in a thoroughly modern idiom. Along with many others, these OSPAAL posters represented the highest levels of technical, conceptual, and graphic sophistication. Given the government's support and investment in printed materials and the kinds of freedoms enjoyed by designers during this period, the Cuban post-revolutionary poster of the 1960s and 1970s represents some of the most remarkable output of visual art in the country.

The lack of a prescriptive state style in Cuba and the aesthetic diversity of the OSPAAL posters themselves have been attributed to the permissiveness of the new regime when it came to cultural and artistic matters. Castro, in this oft-quoted line from his 1961 speech, "Words to Intellectuals," states: "This means that within the Revolution, everything; against the Revolution, nothing."[8] Granted, Castro did seem less concerned about issues of style than content—he was attributed as once saying, "Our enemy is imperialism, not abstract art"[9]—but it must be remembered that OSPAAL was an extension of the Cuban government, meaning that all creation and production was, in essence, sanctioned and thus clearly within the realm of the Revolution's overseas ambitions.

There was no shortage of possible topics for posters, especially in the early years. From the mid-1950s to the mid-1970s, fifty-five new sovereign states came into existence, mainly former colonies in Asia and Africa. At the same time, many countries in Latin America were struggling to overthrow autocratic governments installed or backed by the US. Not surprisingly, OSPAAL posters were produced for conflicts in places such as Guatemala, Nicaragua, Chile, Venezuela, Uruguay, the Congo, Guinea-Bissau, Angola, Zimbabwe, Namibia, Palestine, Korea, Cambodia, Vietnam, Laos, Puerto Rico, Mozambique, Bolivia, Colombia, and the Dominican Republic, as well as for movements against apartheid in South Africa and racism in the United States. While Cuba was eager to align itself with causes of anti-Black racism around the world, the country itself has struggled with its own histories of racial discrimination at home.[10]

International in scope, OSPAAL posters famously relied almost solely on imagery to communicate their messages across different languages and cultures. Like the magazines in which they arrived, the posters' minimal text was translated into English, Spanish, French, and Arabic. The posters—sometimes individually, often as a whole—combine both foreign and indigenous elements to create a collectively unique expression, one that links internationalism with anti-imperialist struggles worldwide:

> The art of Revolution is to be internationalist. At the same time it is to be closely linked to national roots. We will encourage valid and combative forms of cultural expression in Latin America, Africa, and Asia, those that attempt to destroy imperialism. Our cultural institutions will be the agencies of the real artists of these continents, of the ignored, of the persecuted and of those who have not let themselves be domesticated by cultural colonialism and are fighting with their nations against imperialism.[11]

The tricontinental solidarity posters produced by OSPAAAL managed to be globally distributed and representative without lapsing into the kind of universalism that a Eurocentric modernism offered. Certain poster designs embraced but always transcended the minimalist uniformity of modern Swiss-style graphic design that was being rapidly adopted around the world at the time by transnational corporations—becoming a kind of graphic lingua franca of capitalism. At the same time, OSPAAAL posters offered an inventive and vibrant example to counter the clichés and limitations of Socialist Realism—the house style of autocrats—that had been dictated as an official state aesthetic by other communist regimes, such as those in the USSR and China. The stylistic eclecticism of tricontinental solidarity posters fostered individual expression—albeit within the framework of the Revolution itself—while reflecting a more collective sense of inclusivity and global diversity. **ASB**

Renilde Suárez, logo for OSPAAAL, 1966

1 Anne Garland Mahler, *From the Tricontinental to the Global South: Race, Radicalism, and Transnational Solidarity* (Durham, NC: Duke University Press, 2018), 82–83.

2 Lincoln Cushing, *¡Revolucion! Cuban Poster Art* (San Francisco: Chronicle Books, 2003), 10.

3 Richard Frick, *The Transcontinental Solidary Poster* (Bern, Switzerland: Comedia-Verlag, 2003), Reinaldo Morales Campos, "Indice," 81.

4 Cushing identified 326 distinct OSPAAAL poster designs; Cushing, 12.

5 Frick, 81.

6 Cushing identified eight female designers who designed twenty-two posters for OSPAAAL. Cushing, 12.

7 Fiorella López Jiménez, "'If Jesus Were Alive Today, He Would be a Guerrillero': The Impact of Liberation Theology Movements in Latin American Politics," PhD diss., Lake Forest College, 2011.

8 Fidel Castro, speech, "Palabras a los Intelectuales" ("Words to Intellectuals"), (Havana, National Cultural Council, 1961), 32.

9 Cushing, 8.

10 The Revolution positioned itself, in part, as a culmination of the island's history of Black struggle as it would usher in a new era of racial equality through social and economic reforms. The Castro regime ended many overt forms of racial segregation in public life, for instance by opening up formerly private parks, beaches, and clubs, and expanding access to employment opportunities, education, and health-care. By the early 1960s, the government's official position reinforced the notion of a colorblind Cuban society. Because racial discrimination was decreed to be ended via the Revolution, however, it tended to curtail Black political activism and criticisms of ongoing issues of racial discrimination faced on the island that could be labeled as counterrevolutionary. For more on this complex history, both before and after the Revolution, see: Anne Garland Mahler, *From the Tricontinental to the Global South: Race, Radicalism, and Transnational Solidarity* (Durham, NC: Duke University Press, 2018).

11 From *Cuba International* (Havana: Culture and Education Congress, July 1971) as quoted in Frick, *The Tricontential Solidarity Poster*, 72.

Lázaro Abreu Padrón, *Nixon's Peace*, 1972, poster for OSPAAAL, offset lithography on paper. Collection Lincoln Cushing/Docs Populi

Ernesto Padrón Blanco, *Together with Viet Nam (March 13–19)*, 1971, poster for OSPAAAL, offset lithography on paper. Collection Lincoln Cushing/Docs Populi

Raúl Martínez, *Day of Solidarity with the Cuban Revolution (July 26)*, 1968, poster for OSPAAAL, offset lithography on paper. Collection Lincoln Cushing/Docs Populi

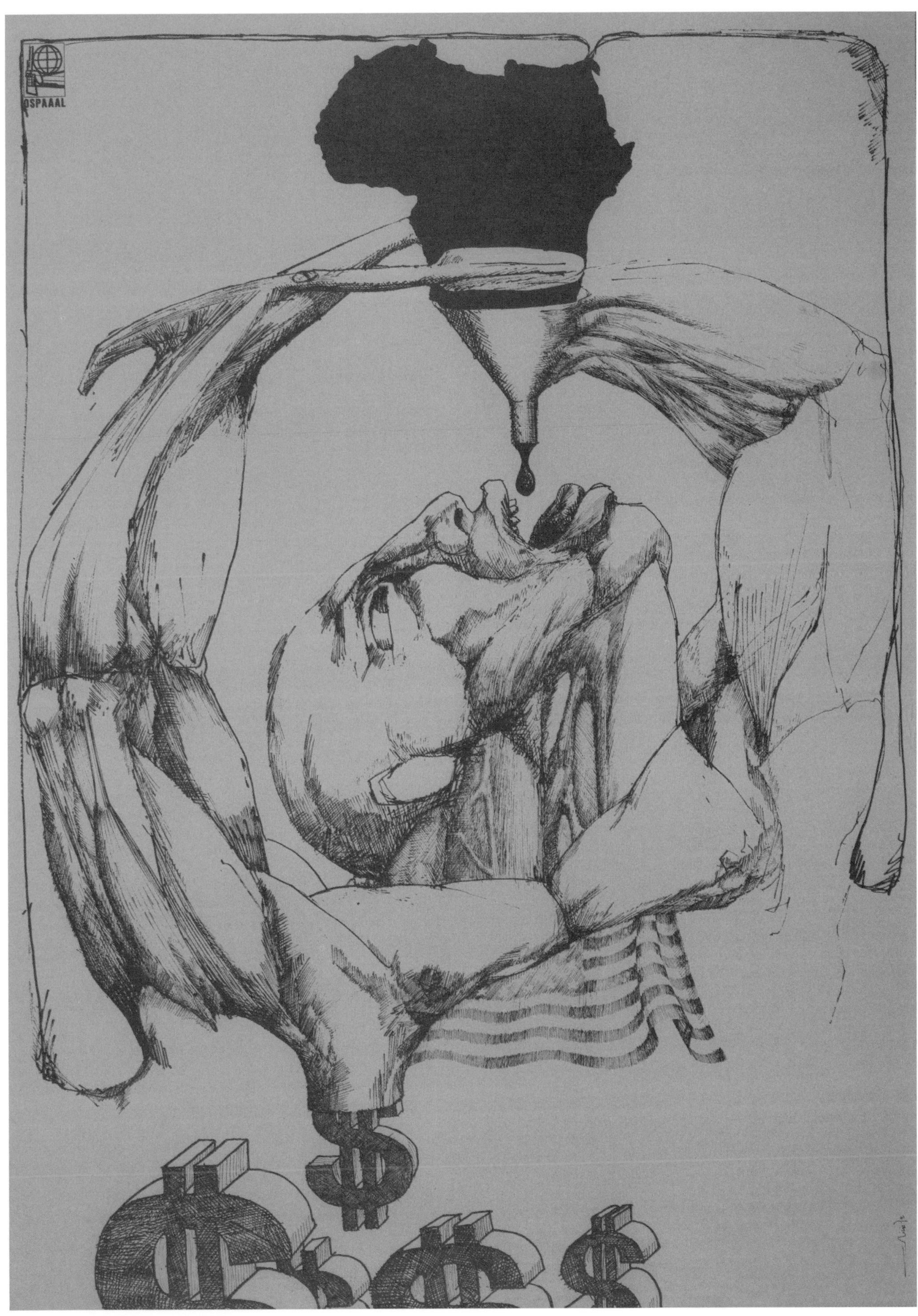

Olivio Martínez Viera, *Untitled ("Every Last Drop of Africa")*, 1975, poster for OSPAAAL, offset lithography on paper. Collection Lincoln Cushing/ Docs Populi

Gladys Acosta, *International Week of Solidarity with the Peoples of Africa (May 22–28)*, 1970, poster for OSPAAL, offset lithography on paper. Collection Lincoln Cushing/Docs Populi

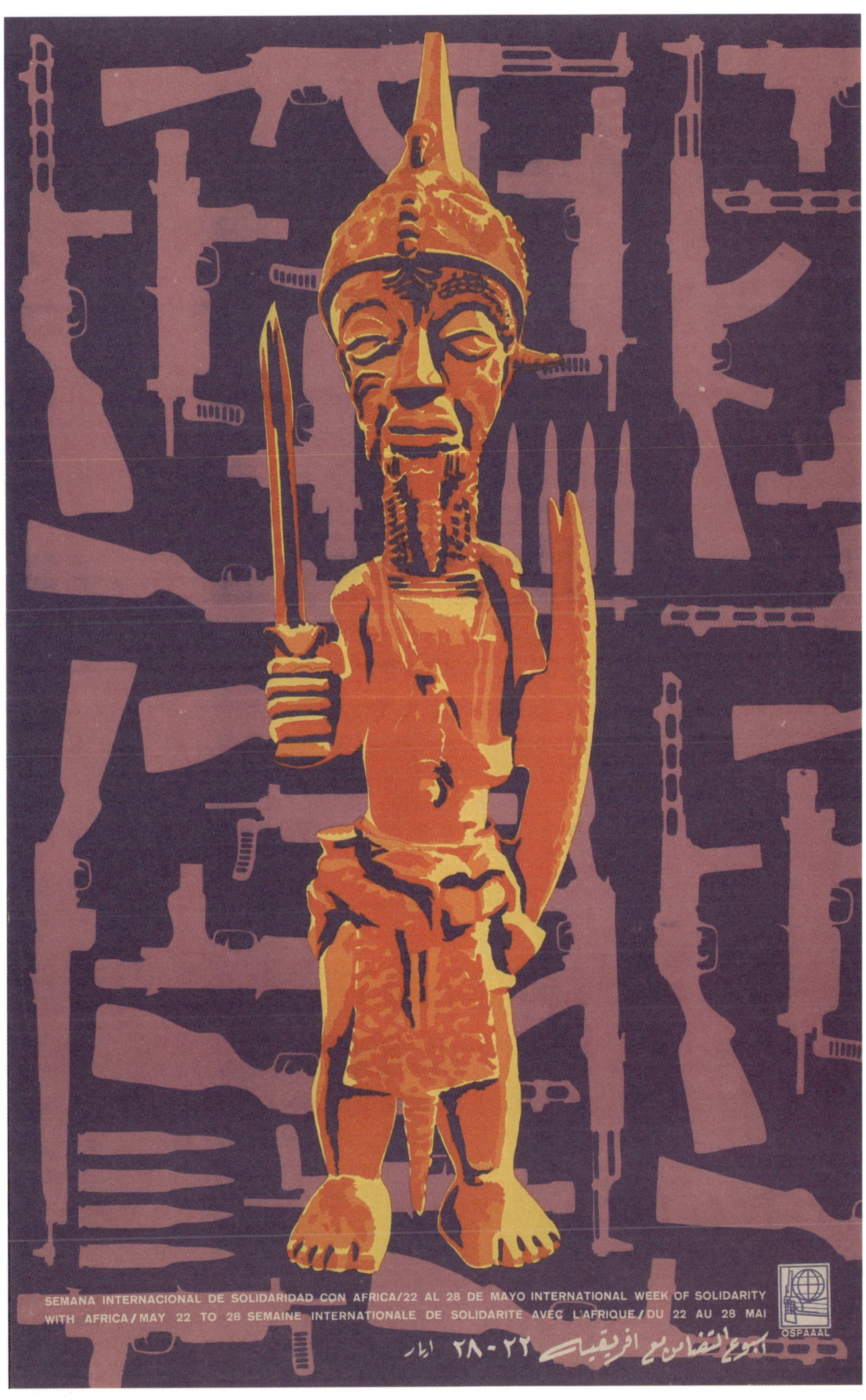

Jesús Forjans Boade, *International Week of Solidarity with Africa (May 22–28)*, 1969, poster for OSPAAAL, offset lithography on paper. Collection Lincoln Cushing/Docs Populi

Alfredo G. Rostgaard, *Day of Solidarity with the Congo (February 13)*, 1972, poster for OSPAAAL, offset lithography on paper. The Lindsay Webster Collection of Cuban Posters, Wofford College. Courtesy Lincoln Cushing/Docs Populi

René Mederos Pazos, *Day of Solidarity with the Struggle of the People of South Africa (June 26)*, 1970, poster for OSPAAAL, offset lithography on paper. Collection Lincoln Cushing/Docs Populi

Faustino Pérez Organero, *Day of Solidarity with Zimbabwe (March 17)*, 1970, poster for OSPAAAL, offset lithography on paper. Collection Lincoln Cushing/Docs Populi

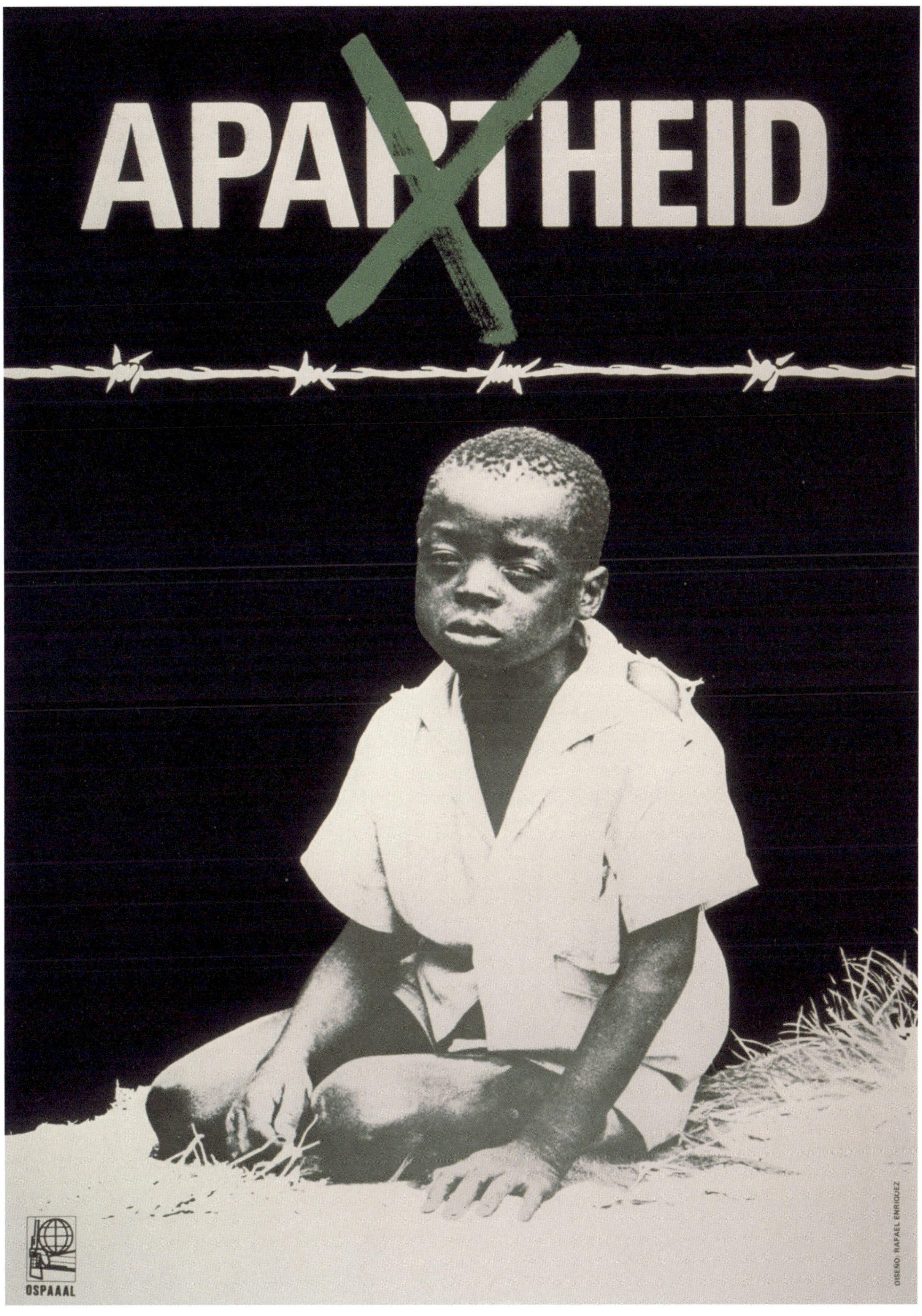

Rafael Enríquez Vega, *Apartheid*, 1987, poster for OSPAAAL, offset lithography on paper. Collection Lincoln Cushing/Docs Populi

José Luciano Martínez, *Day of Solidarity with Angola (February 4)*, 1972, poster for OSPAAAL, offset lithography on paper. Collection Lincoln Cushing/Docs Populi

Elena Serrano, *Day of the Heroic Guerrilla (October 8)*, 1968, poster for OSPAAAL, offset lithography and screenprint on paper. Collection Lincoln Cushing/Docs Populi

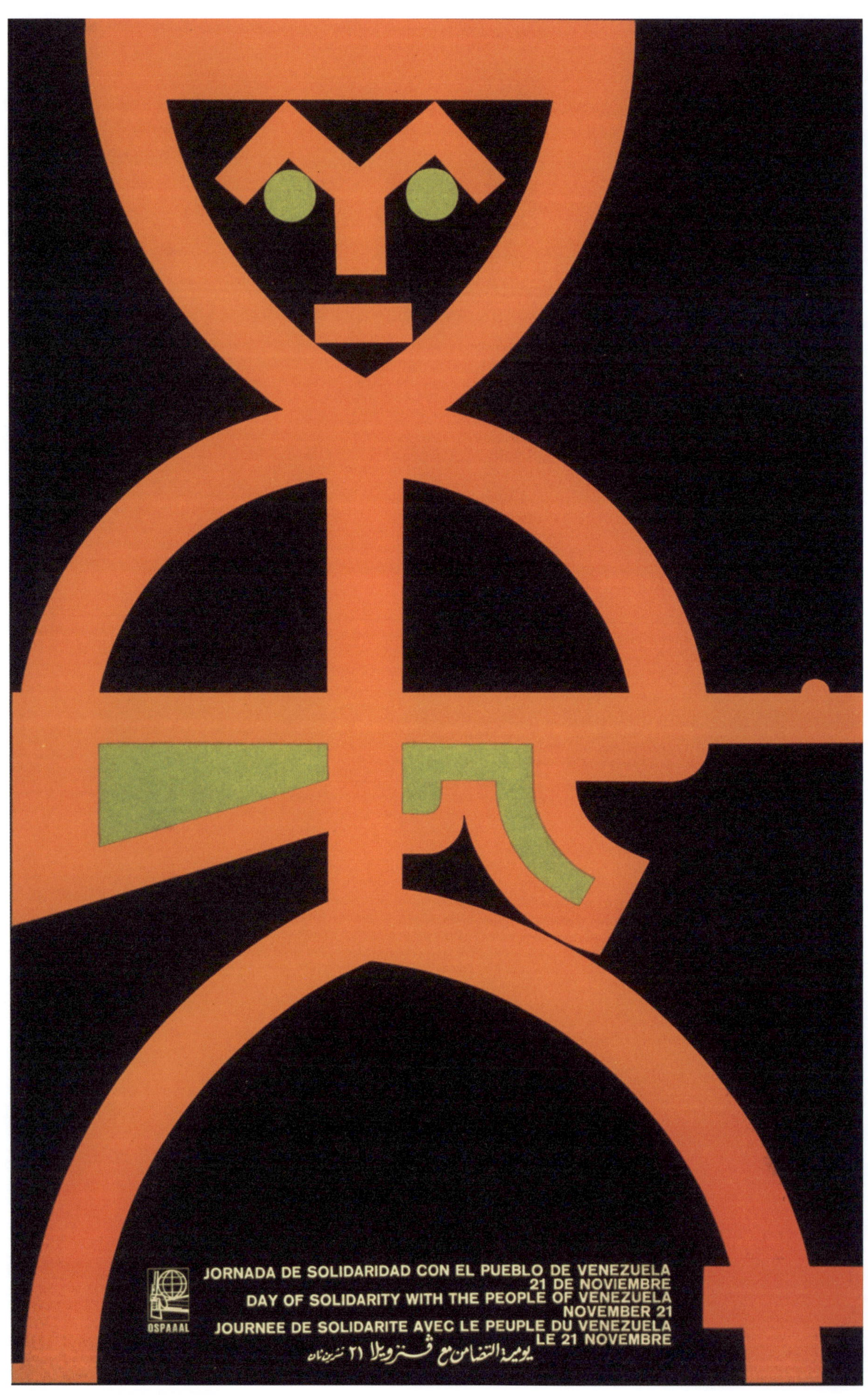

Faustino Pérez Organero, *Day of Solidarity with Venezuela (November 21)*, 1969, poster for OSPAAAL, offset lithography on paper. Collection Lincoln Cushing/Docs Populi

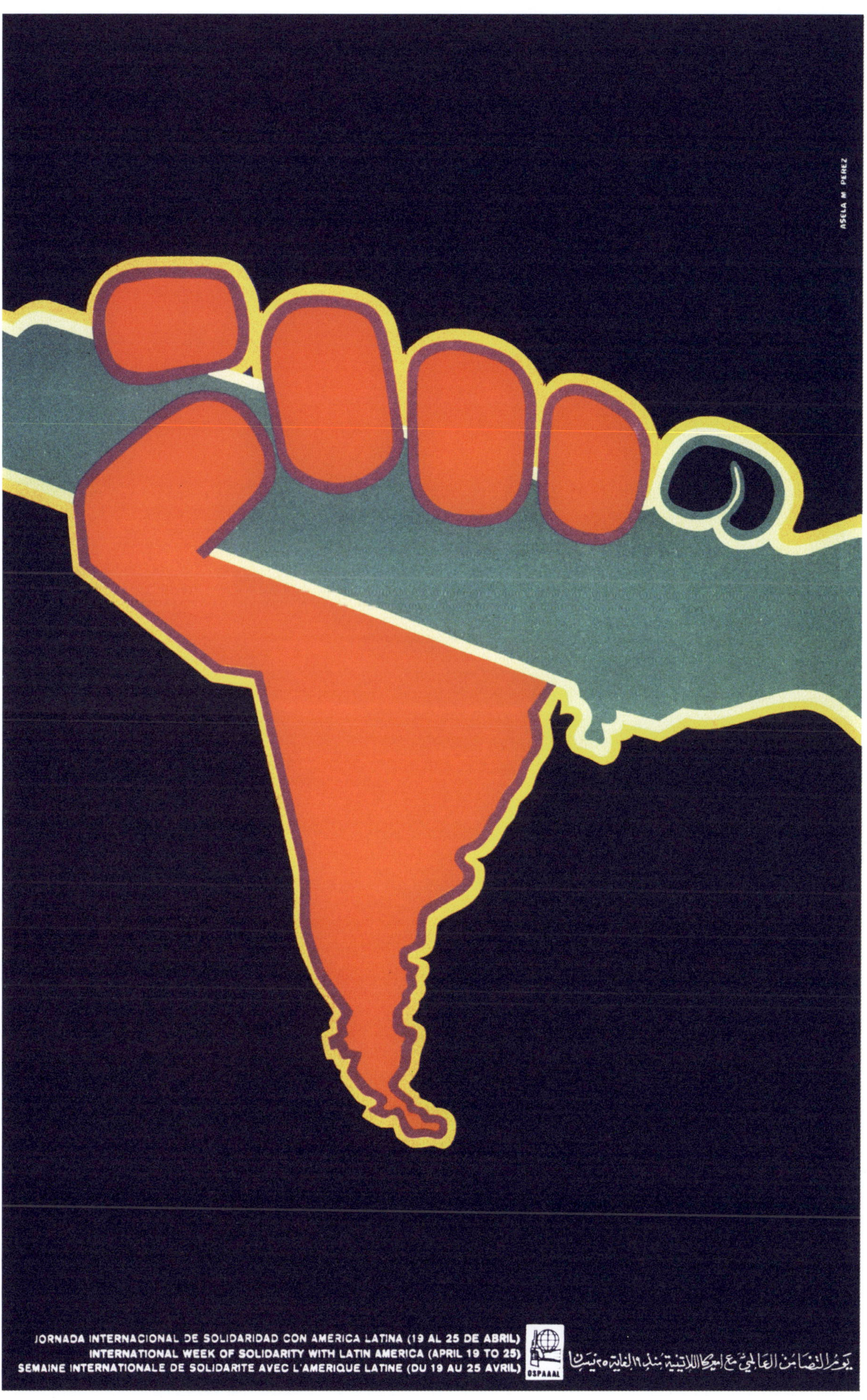

Asela M. Pérez Bolado, *International Week of Solidarity with Latin America (April 19 to 25)*, 1970, poster for OSPAAAL, offset lithography on paper. The Lindsay Webster Collection of Cuban Posters, Wofford College. Courtesy Lincoln Cushing/Docs Populi

Alfredo G. Rostgaard, *Untitled ("Radiant One")*, **1969**, poster for OSPAAAL, offset lithography on paper. The Lindsay Webster Collection of Cuban Posters, Wofford College. Courtesy Lincoln Cushing/Docs Populi

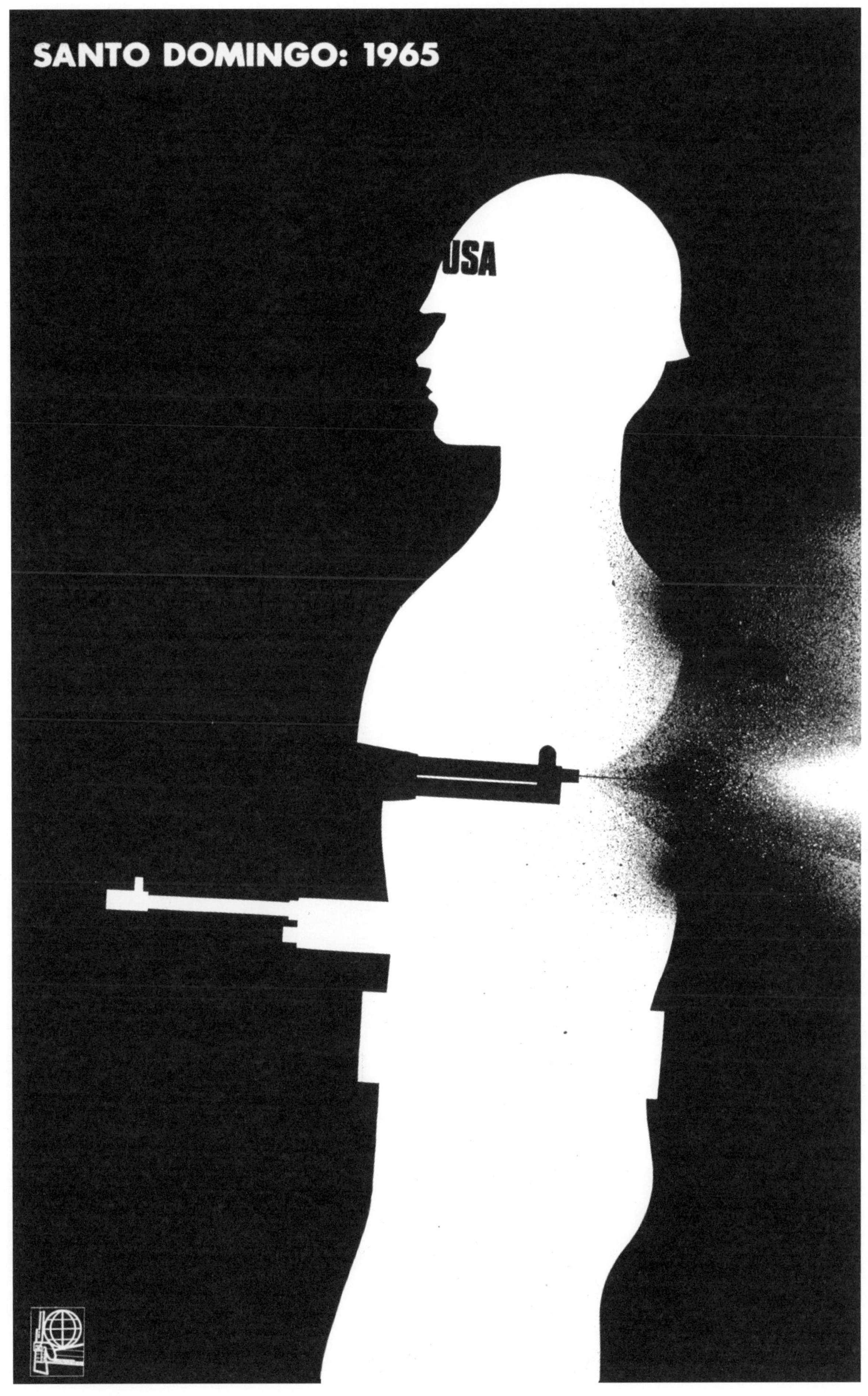

Alfredo G. Rostgaard, *Santo Domingo: 1965*, 1970, poster for OSPAAAL, offset lithography on paper. Collection Lincoln Cushing/Docs Populi

Alfredo G. Rostgaard, *Untitled ("Guerrilla Jesus")*, 1969, poster for OSPAAAL, offset lithography on paper. Collection Lincoln Cushing/Docs Populi

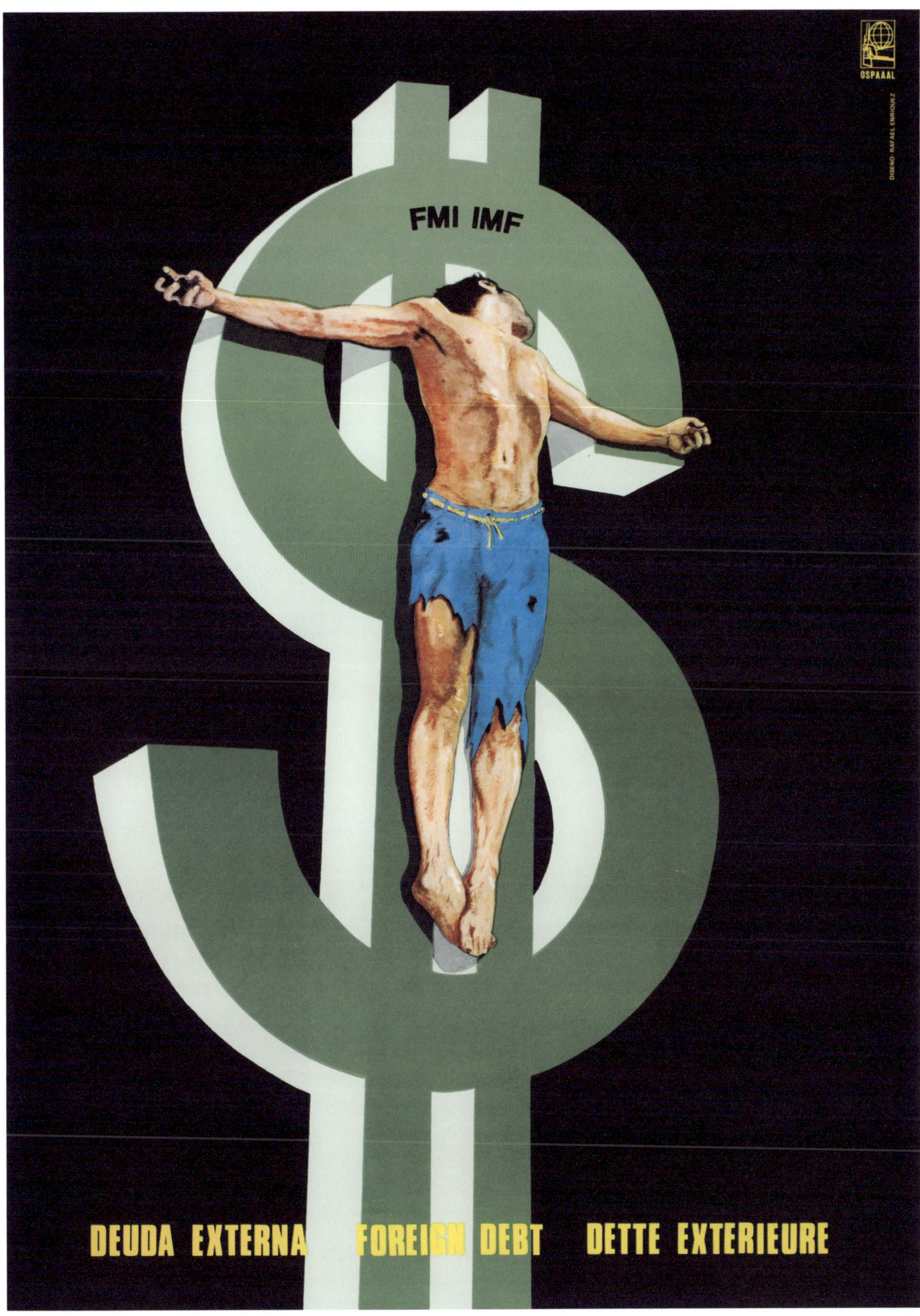

Rafael Enríquez Vega, *Foreign Debt*, 1983, poster for OSPAAAL, offset lithography in paper. The Lindsay Webster Collection of Cuban Posters, Wofford College. Courtesy Lincoln Cushing/Docs Populi

Daysi García, *Day of Solidarity with the Afro-American People (August 18),* 1969, poster for OSPAAAL, offset lithography on paper. Collection Lincoln Cushing/Docs Populi

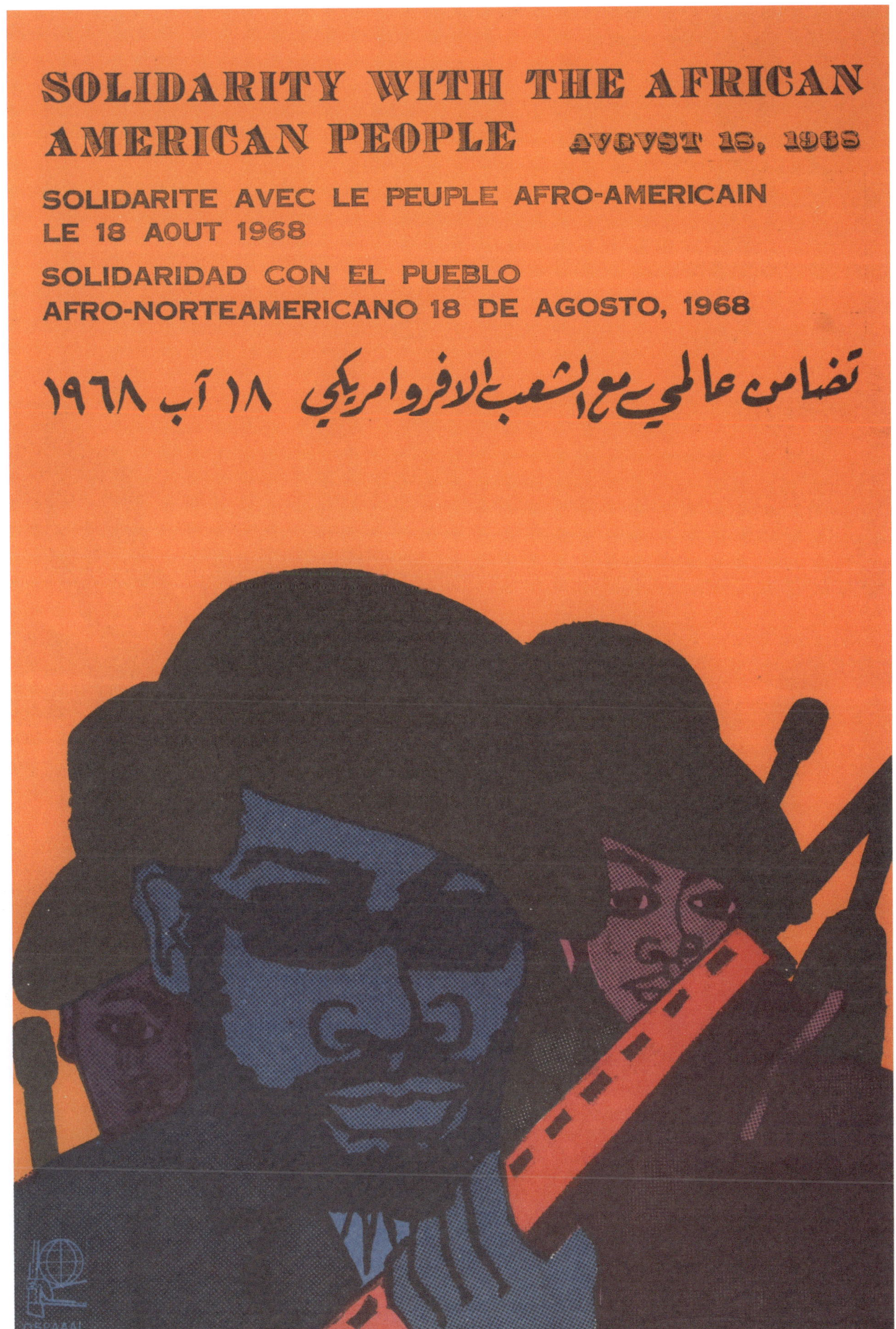

Lázaro Abreu Padrón and Emory Douglas, *Solidarity with the African American People (August 18)*, 1968, poster for OSPAAAL, offset lithography on paper. Collection Lincoln Cushing/Docs Populi

Rafael Morante Boyerizo, *Power to the People: George* [Jackson], 1971, poster for OSPAAAL, offset lithography on paper. The Lindsay Webster Collection of Cuban Posters, Wofford College. Courtesy Lincoln Cushing/Docs Populi

Power to the People
George
el poder para el pueblo
tout le pouvoir au peuple
ان السلطة هي للشعب

CUBA
CUBA

RAÚL MARTÍNEZ: QUIET QUEERNESS IN THE REVOLUTIONARY ROAR

The life of Cuban artist and designer Raúl Martínez did not follow a predictable, or straight, path. His conflicting identities were many: he was a classically trained artist who embraced modernist techniques; an abstract painter who turned to representation for social impact; a definer of the Cuban revolutionary aesthetic whose own personal life as a gay man was deemed to be incompatible with the Revolution; and a man once rejected and shunned in Cuba, now lauded as an exemplary artist.

Although a fervent supporter of Castro's deposition of Batista, Martínez's homosexuality eventually sullied his reputation in the 1970s, even after a decade of dedicated work for the new government. His contributions during the first decade of Castro's government, designing for domestic magazines and newspapers that promoted Castro's message around the country and drafting posters for the Organization of Solidarity with the People of Asia, Africa, and Latin America (OSPAAAL) to promote anti-imperialism internationally, would not protect him from political repercussions.

Raúl Martínez working on the painting *Cuba* in his home studio, 1969. Photo: Iván Cañas

Raúl Martínez, *Rosas y Estrellas (Roses and Stars)* or *Martí y la Libertad (Martí and Freedom)*, 1972, oil on canvas. Collection the Howard and Patricia Farber Foundation. The painting depicts José Martí (center) flanked from left to right by Simón Bolívar, Fidel Castro, Camilo Cienfuegos, Máximo Gómez, Che Guevara, and Antonio Maceo.

Martínez was born in Camagüey in central Cuba in 1927 to a large family of eight children. Tragedy frequently struck, as four of his seven siblings would not reach adulthood. After moving to Matanzas, a city on Cuba's northern coast, so that his father could gain employment in the boiler room of a sugar-processing facility, the family lost their house when it was destroyed by a hurricane.

When he was thirteen, in 1940, Martínez moved with his family to Havana, where he was enrolled in the Escuela Elemental de Artes Plásticas (Elementary School of Plastic Arts), an institute that prepared students to enter the Academia San Alejandro, then the National School of Fine Arts. Martínez's arrival in Havana also allowed him to see traveling exhibitions for the first time, and his exposure to Mexican muralists—José Clemente Orozco in particular—left a lasting impact on the young artist. Martínez recalled his first encounter with Orozco's works: "I didn't know that figures could be painted with such little detail and power, not just for its obvious expressionism but also for its dynamic composition."[1]

By 1946, his family's income was stable enough that he was able to attend Academia Nacional de Belles Artes San Alejandro in Marianao, a suburb of Havana. He also joined Sociedad Nuestro Tiempo (Society of Our Time), an artistic group devoted to leftist politics and supporting non-academic art, which was directed by Servando Cabrera Moreno, a painter who would also go on to be shunned for his sexuality. Nonetheless, despite being drawn towards modernist principles—he particularly admired the somber, monochromatic palette of Fidelio Ponce de León's atmospheric works and the geometric abstraction of José María Mijares—Martínez did not at first embrace the avant-garde in his own practice and remained uncertain about what subject he should paint. After two solo shows in 1950, he turned to abstraction to resolve this anxiety.

Inspired by the book *The New Vision: Fundamentals of Bauhaus Design, Painting, Sculpture, and Architecture*, by Hungarian artist and former Bauhaus professor László Moholy-Nagy, Martínez decided to enroll in the Institute of Design, created by Moholy-Nagy as the "New Bauhaus" in Chicago, as a non-degree-seeking student in 1952. The book, although published in 1931, contained ideas about aesthetic production different from anything Martínez had learned at Academia San Alejandro; most importantly, it synthesized and incorporated subjects such as architecture, social production, and photography into art, and further considered the artist as someone with a societal role related to both art and industry.[2] His time in Chicago exposed him to the works of Georges Braque, Paul Klee, Auguste Rodin, Fernand Léger, and Georges Seurat, artists who would be influential in his stylistic development. He also took courses in printing, typography, photography, and design, which supplemented his previous, more normative course of study at the academy.

When he returned to Cuba, Martínez worked as a designer for news publications, advertising agencies, and theaters as well as creating billboards and murals to support himself. He also joined the group Los Once (The Eleven), an artistic circle that included Guido Llinás, Hugo Consuegra, and Mario Carreño. The Eleven wished to free themselves from the highly structured academic art of Havana and believed that painting could be manipulated for political ends, a charge that they leveled at the Batista dictatorship. The group was controversial and prominent art critics even decried the members of the circle as jokes whose works were insulting to art.[3] As part of Los Once, Martínez exhibited in the 1954 "anti-biennale" called *Plástica Cubana Contemporanea: Homenaje a José Martí* (*Contemporary Cuban Visual Art: Tribute to José Martí*), against the official version organized by the Batista regime.

After the successful deposition of Batista, Martínez utilized his skills to support the new government, including contributing to the magazine *Lunes de Revolución* (*Mondays of the Revolution*) and the newspaper *Revolución* while completing graphic design work for the new Cuban diplomatic organization Casa de las Américas. He was a central member of the Unión de Escritores y Artists de Cuba (UNEAC, or Union of Artists and Writers in Cuba), designing mass communications to spread Castro's message throughout the country. As a leader in the Cuban poster movement, Martínez intertwined typography, photography, and illustration for a new graphic tradition. He also participated as an international ambassador, promoting Cuba abroad at certain events, including at Expo 67 in Montréal (see pages 170–173).

The emphasis on design in promoting political messages and conveying social change led Martínez to turn to representational work in his painting after 1964. The repeated portraits he created have been compared with Pop Art as they appropriate the movement's aesthetic, but instead of focusing on a culture based on consumption and mass media they promote socio-political transformations. Martínez considers his portraits of these leaders to be "landscapes of the revolution"[4] and linked figures such as Castro, Che Guevara, and Camilo Cienfuegos, a revolutionary leader who had died in the first year of Castro's rule, with historical revolutionary figures such as Simon Bolivar and José Martí, who had led revolutions against colonial Spanish rules—tying together anti-colonialist and communist messages. However, the point of the paintings was not to deify these figures. Martínez often combined ordinary people and anonymous revolutionaries with portrayals of Che Guevara and José Martí.

In 1971, Martínez began to feel unwelcome in UNEAC due to his sexuality, and work opportunities began to dry up. He was living with his partner, the playwright Alberado Estronio. After he lost a position at the National Schools of Art during a purge of

Raúl Martínez (left) in his home studio with his partner, Abelardo Estorino, c. 1972.

counterrevolutionaries, including homosexuals (see pages 166–169), he would take jobs working in printing and typography at the Instituto Cubano del Libro (Cuban Book Institute) to support himself.

As harsher economic realities set in with the continued United States embargo of Cuba, queer identities were attacked as anti-revolutionary, as they were associated with overconsumption and decadence.[5] Martínez was not as harshly persecuted as some artists, such as Servando Cabrera Moreno, who prominently featured homoerotic themes and a sensual exploration of the male body in his work and, therefore, was removed from his teaching position in 1965 and put under surveillance for five years.[6] Other queer artists such as René Portocarrero were spared from purges of the so-called *quinquenio gris* (five gray years) in the early 1970s—even while he lived with his partner and fellow artist Raúl Milián—as his work never explicitly contained homosexual themes. By the late 1970s, Cuba decriminalized homosexuality and thus began the slow process of rehabilitating the tarnished reputations of so many citizens and artists, such as Martínez, who had been fired, imprisoned, or sent to re-education camps.

The intertwined trajectory of Raúl Martínez's personal life and artistic career underscores the complex, and often conflicting, realities of life in Castro's Cuba, where one's private life and political stance become impossible to untangle. **ARDP**

1 Corina Matamoros, *Raúl Martínez: La gran familia* (Havana: Ediciones Vanguardia Cubana, 2012), 187.

2 Raúl Martínez, *Yo Publio* (Havana: Letras Cubanas y Artecubano Ediciones, 2007), 335–36.

3 Matamoros, *Raúl Martínez*, 33.

4 Matamoros, *Raúl Martínez*, 64.

5 Rudi C. Bleys, *Images of Ambiente: Homotextuality and Latin American Art 1810–Today* (London: Continuum, 2000), 72–73.

6 https://cubanartnewsarchive.org/2013/08/06/servando-cabrera-moreno-the-erotic-drawings.

COPPELIA ICE CREAM PARLOR

Fidel Castro eating ice cream at the Bronx Zoo, New York City, 1959. Courtesy Meyer Liebowitz/*The New York Times* via Redux Pictures. Photo: Meyer Liebowitz

On a diplomatic visit to the United States after overthrowing Fulgencio Batista's dictatorship, Fidel Castro was captured by a photographer for the *New York Times* eating an ice cream cone at the Bronx Zoo while sitting between two American officials. This light-hearted scene would be in stark contrast to his next visit to the city, in 1960, when he gave a more than four-hour-long speech to the United Nations General Assembly, in which he lambasted US foreign policy toward Cuba. The image would be prescient, however, as the development of an ice cream industry became an important facet of Cuba's post-revolutionary culture, identity, and economy—one best seen in the establishment and continued prominence of the Coppelia Ice Cream Parlor.

Castro's love of ice cream was so renowned that writer Gabriel García Márquez claimed he witnessed the Cuban leader consume eighteen scoops after eating lunch, and the CIA was even rumored to have attempted to assassinate him by contaminating a milkshake with poison.[1] In fact, Castro was photographed many other times indulging in ice cream, including by Cuban photographer Alberto Korda, whose iconic images of Cuban guerrillas were distributed widely around the world.

In the *New York Times*' image, Castro wears a revolutionary uniform yet appears relaxed, fully enjoying his cone in New York City. The photograph reflects a moment of positive American-Cuban contact before the United States' implementation of an embargo against Cuba in February 1962 and the eventual deterioration of relations between the two countries. The embargo, of course, included dairy products, which disrupted the island's supply of milk from the US. Undeterred, Castro was determined to prove the capabilities of a socialist system to produce a superior product. He ordered the construction of the world's largest ice cream parlor,

Mario Girona et al., aerial view of Coppelia Ice Cream Parlor, Havana, Cuba, 1966. © Archive Eduardo Luis Rodríguez

which grew into a chain, and facilitated the development of a special cow, Ubre Blanca (white udder), known for its prodigious milk production and ability to withstand the country's warm climate.

Seeking to create a competitive ice cream product for state-subsidized consumption in Cuba, Castro had an ambassador in Canada send him twenty-eight flavors of ice cream from Howard Johnson's, a US chain restaurant noted for popularizing lunch counters and dairy bars.[2] The choice to produce ice cream, which may seem like an unhealthy indulgence, was motivated, in part, by nutritional concerns, as the new government sought to combat childhood malnutrition through the consumption of high-calorie foods, including the addition of dairy, to diets lacking vital nutrients.[3] Ice cream could also utilize the abundance of sugarcane on the island, stimulating another demand for refined sugar.

The flagship location of Coppelia is an enormous, shaded, circular, modern concrete pavilion supported by flying buttresses set amid a lush, park-like landscape encompassing a city block. Built on the location of a nineteenth-century children's hospital that was razed before the Revolution, this Brutalist monument to ice cream is located in the Vedado, a wealthy neighborhood in western Havana filled with new high rises, hotels, and single-family homes, a short distance from the Malecón—a five-mile esplanade along the coast of Havana. Designed by Mario Girona, Rita María Grau, and Candelario Ajuria, Coppelia opened on June 4, 1966, with the ambitious capacity to seat one thousand patrons.

Girona was familiar with the neighborhood, having previously worked on the private homes of wealthy clients in western Havana and on the Hotel Capri. After the Revolution, Girona designed differently, creating architecture that emphasized round shapes and organic forms and integrating vegetation. The focus on curves and the promotion of the circle as a revolutionary shape resonated with contemporaneous projects such as the Escuelas Nacionales de Arte (National Schools of Art; see pages 166–169). At the same time, the curving concrete structure also recalled spaces of leisure, tropicality, and pleasure built for tourists before the Revolution such as Max Borges Recio's Salon de las Arcos de Cristal ("Hall of Crystal Arches") at Cabaret Tropicana and Club Náutico.[4]

Acting as a social hub for first dates and family outings, Coppelia also became known as a cruising spot for gay men, with its own social codes. The 1993 movie *Fresa y Chocolate* (*Strawberry and Chocolate*), set in 1979 during the throes of the regime's crackdown on homosexuality, is a fictional story that

Mario Girona et al., interior view of Coppelia Ice Cream Parlor, Havana, Cuba. © Archive Eduardo Luis Rodríguez

traces an unlikely friendship between Diego, a gay artist, and David, a revolutionary university student, and comments on this phenomenon. In the film, David jokes to a friend that he was able to tell Diego was gay because he ordered strawberry ice cream when chocolate, the most popular flavor, was available.[5] Diego also makes his feelings about Castro's government known when he notes that ice cream is the only good product that they make in the country but that soon they will receive nothing but water and sugar—foreshadowing the anxiety about the scarcity of goods and materials in the 1990s.[6] After the reunification of Germany in 1990 and the collapse of the Soviet Union in 1991, Cuba could not produce enough milk domestically to provide for all its dairy needs, and eventually prioritized the production of ice cream over other staples like butter.[7] At the end of the film, David also consumes strawberry ice cream as the friends patronize Coppelia for the final time before Diego's planned flight from the island.

Despite fewer flavor choices, Coppelia continues to serve ice cream to this day, while its counterpart in America, Howard Johnson's, has closed. Mid-century furniture, such as Harry Bertoia's iconic wire chairs, proliferate around Coppelia's counters and tables, highlighting the endurance and survival of modernist design in Cuba. **ARDP**

1 Alex Mayyasi, "To Defy the United States Castro Built the World's Greatest Ice Cream Parlor," *Atlas Obscura*, November 8, 2019, published online at https://www.atlasobscura.com/articles/ice-cream-in-havana.

2 Iván L. Munuera, "Coppelia: Revolutionary Ice Creams," in *Havana Modern: Critical Readings in Cuban Architecture*, ed. Rubén Gallo (Mexico City: Arquine, 2023), 134.

3 Munuera, 134.

4 Victor Deupi and Jean-François Lejeune, *Cuban Modernism: Mid-Century Architecture 1940–1970* (Basel: Birkhauser, 2021), 216–17.

5 *Fresa y Chocolate*, directed by Tomás Gutiérrez Alea and Juan Carlos (1993, Havana), DVD.

6 *Fresa y Chocolate*, 1993.

7 Munuera, 138.

THE NATIONAL SCHOOLS OF ART

In a lush, vegetated park in western Havana, once the site of an exclusive country club, lies a complex of five sprawling brick structures, each uniquely and intricately designed. The buildings, while distinct from each other, are connected aesthetically through their organic forms and earthy materials as well as their deterioration from disuse and lack of maintenance. These buildings, known collectively as Las Escuelas Nacionales de Arte (ENA; National Schools of Art), are unlike any other mid-century architectural project built during the early years following the Cuban Revolution.

A mythologizing anecdote of the founding of the schools recounts Fidel Castro and Che Guevara deciding that the grounds of the country club should be transformed into a campus of an art school to rival the best around the world while playing a round of golf there. In 1961, the government invited architect Ricardo Porro to design buildings for five separate schools to encompass plastic arts, dramatic arts, music, ballet, and modern dance and requested that construction begin in just two months. Porro, in turn, enlisted two Italian architects living in Cuba—Vittorio Garatti from Milan and Roberto Gottardi from Venice—whom he had met while working abroad during the 1957 construction boom in Venezuela.

Ricardo Porro, School of Plastic Arts at the National Schools of Art, Havana, Cuba, detail of central courtyard with papaya fountain. © Archive Eduardo Luis Rodríguez

Vittorio Garatti, School of Ballet at the National Schools of Art, Havana, Cuba. © Archive Eduardo Luis Rodríguez

Porro, who was interested in African folkloric dance as well as sculpture, chose to design the School of Modern Dance and the School of Plastic Arts. Garatti, an amateur pianist, had previously wished to be a dancer and chose to design the schools of music and ballet. This arrangement worked well as Gottardi enjoyed the theater, making the design of the School of Dramatic Arts an appropriate assignment.

The architects chose to use brick since more modern, conventional materials such as steel and concrete were difficult to source or too expensive because of the US embargo against Cuba. To build quickly, they relied not on modern techniques, but on an ancient way of construction utilizing Catalan vaults—a method of bricklaying in which fast-setting mortar and bricks are placed over scaffolding to create a gentle curving ceiling, which needs little to no support when fully solidified.

The five schools were purposefully designed with no main entrance to the wider campus and without giving prominence to any specific building, thus rejecting architectural and disciplinary dogmatism and hierarchies.

In designing the School of Plastic Arts, Porro took inspiration from Afro-Cuban culture, in particular the Afro-Cuban painter Wifredo Lam and Oshun, a West African fertility deity prominent in the Cuban religion Santería. Evoking sensuality, the domes of the school were designed to be akin to breasts, and the center had a piazza with a statue of a papaya, representing female sexual agency. The symbolism, at large, evoked rebirth and hope for the future. Contrastingly, Porro's unfinished School of Modern Dance contains not curves, but angles of varying degrees, meant to reflect uncertainty about the future.

Porro described Garatti's design for the School of Ballet as a "uterus" when he saw the architectural drawings.[1] Purposefully built with long, dark hallways and other mysterious areas, the classrooms and performance spaces, by contrast, were well illuminated. For the music school, Garatti sought to design a building that would be completely open like the Revolution, without enclosure. Rejecting traditional temple-like architecture, there were no doors, columns, or barriers but rather long expanses of hallways, which manifested ideas of freedom instead of power.

Finally, Gottardi's School of Dramatic Arts was conceived to reflect a process of journey and arrival. The theater is not immediately apparent upon entry, and one must follow labyrinthic passageways full of circuitous turns, reminiscent of a European medieval city, to find classrooms.

Construction began smoothly, even with classes in session. Artists and students, who flocked to the site, would perform for the builders as well as volunteer their time to assist in construction. Individuals who could not previously attend art school before the Revolution due to financial circumstances were also able to study. The first years were reported to be an invigorating moment for the artistic community, with a sentiment that the mores of artistic and sexual repression had ceased. Even in terms of fashion, students felt free to explore, bucking previous conventions, as women could wear miniskirts and bikinis.

However, problems started to arise as construction dragged on. By 1965, none of the schools was fully complete, and Soviet prefabricated architecture was embraced by the government as a solution to efficiently construct buildings. Antonio Quintana Simonetti, who directed the Ministry of Construction, demanded that architects begin using prefabrication in all projects. The emphasis on uniqueness, beauty, and inspiration that Porro, Garatti, and Gottardi imbued in their work came to be framed as a bourgeois idea and a costly endeavor of what the Ministry of Construction believed were the true needs of workers and the Revolution. Potential jealousy of two foreigners tasked with such a prestigious project also fueled criticism.

Porro was also a divisive personality in Cuban architectural circles. While promoting modernist architecture, he also argued that the movement was essentially European and had various faults in its application in Cuba. He believed that architecture should reflect not just the European heritage of Cubans but also African and indigenous roots as well. His designs subverted the preponderance of rationality and easily recognizable forms, advocating for a more oneiric, or dreamlike, and sensual architectural practice. This belief caused the leading architecture critic Roberto Segre to retort, "I like sex with women, not sex with architecture," when criticizing the schools.[2]

Within this context of mounting criticism, Guevara called for changes at ENA in the article "Socialism and Man in Cuba," proposing military discipline and complaining about a lack of oversight of both the construction of the buildings and the student body at large. This turn from a "romantic revolution" to an "authoritarian revolution," as financial circumstances became more dire, led to a purge of students who were deemed ideologically deficient or exhibited queer identities—part of a larger program of oppression directed against homosexuality in Cuba. In 1965, the construction of the schools was deemed "non-productive" and ordered to a halt, with Porro's school for the visual arts being the only one close to completion. After housing a circus for a short while, the buildings were abandoned and left unmaintained, causing them to be stripped of materials and looted in times of hardship.

After the project's incompletion, Porro fled Cuba in 1966 for Paris. Garatti would work as an urban planner in Havana until he was accused of espionage and deported back to Italy in 1974. Notably, he was one of the architects of the Cuba pavilion at Expo 1967 in Montreal (see pages 170–173). Gottardi faced criticism and censorship for his perceived ideological impurity and was removed for a period of time from his university position to work at a construction site.[3]

In the 1990s, the schools became known to a wider global audience through exposure from American architect John Loomis, eventually leading the schools to become part of the World Monuments Watch list and the beginning of a rehabilitation program until the 2008 financial crisis and two hurricanes in 2009 caused all unessential construction to cease. **ARDP**

1 *Unfinished Spaces*, directed by Alysa Nahmias and Benjamin Murray (2011; Crystal City, VA: PBS, 2013), DVD.

2 *Unfinished Spaces.*

3 *Unfinished Spaces.*

EXPO 67

The 1967 International and Universal Exposition, more commonly known as Expo 67, took place in Montréal, Canada, from April 27 to October 29. It is among the most successful and well-attended of all the world's fairs of the twentieth century, hosting nearly 55 million visitors and sixty nations from around the world.[1]

Like most world's fairs, Expo 67 strove to offer visitors a glimpse of the present and a hint of the future by assembling a unique collection of national and sponsored pavilions to which they could journey. Expo 67 underscored this sense of travel by issuing visitors ersatz passports that could be stamped at their various destinations. Erected on islands specifically built for the fair in the St. Lawrence River, Expo 67's physical separation from the city of Montréal only enhanced this feeling of remote adventure.

Sergio Baroni, Huge D'Acosta, and Vittorio Garatti, Cuban pavilion at the 1967 International Universal Exposition (Expo 67), Montréal, Canada, 1967. Collection Archives de la Ville de Montréal, VM94. Photo: Armour Landry

Under the theme "Man and His World," taken from the title of a book by Antoine de Saint-Exupéry (*Terre des Hommes*, 1939), Expo 67 exuded the same kind of global humanist camaraderie that is typically associated with the Olympic Games. Despite this feeling of equanimity, this world's fair was dominated by the pavilions of three nations: Canada, the host country, which was celebrating the nation's centennial; the Soviet Union, which was recognizing the fiftieth anniversary of the Russian Revolution and had won an earlier bid to host the event but withdrew; and the United States, with a pavilion that celebrated a Pop Art-inspired "Creative America," inside a giant geodesic dome. Despite this Cold War–era superpower dominance, Expo 67 would also be an opportunity to showcase an emergent post-colonial era, such as the pavilion of a recently independent Algeria; Africa Place, a cluster of pavilions representing fifteen countries—Cameroon, Chad, Congo, Ivory Coast, Gabon, Ghana, Kenya, Madagascar, Niger, Nigeria, Uganda, Rwanda, Senegal, Tanzania, and Togo; and Cuba, which would mark its first such appearance on an international stage since the 1959 Revolution.

Expo 67 excelled in the commissioning of progressive architecture and design, which had become a mainstay expectation of world's fairs. Expo 67 proved to be one of the most compelling showcases of such experimental architecture. Perhaps the most spectacular was the US pavilion designed by Buckminster Fuller and Shoji Sadao—a 250-foot-wide and 200-foot-high geodesic dome created with a skeletal steel frame clad in transparent acrylic. Visitors could quickly pass through the structure on a monorail or ascend the seven floors of displays housed inside the bubble via a series of escalators. Habitat 67 was the thesis project of architect Moshe Safdie, who had speculated about solving housing needs through prefabricated construction techniques. The final result clusters three criss-crossed stacks of 354 prefabricated concrete boxes joined together to form 158 apartments, each with its own outdoor space. The West German pavilion designed by Frei Otto and Rolf Gutbrod would bring Otto's experiments in flexible, portable, prefabricated, and spatially efficient architecture to the international stage for the first time. Soaring to great heights in a series of graceful hyperparabolic curves, the translucent white membrane tents offered perhaps the most basic, albeit exalted, definition of architecture as shelter. The Cuban pavilion by Vittorio Garatti, Hugo D'Acosta, and Sergio Baroni offered another visually arresting design and also celebrated prefabrication techniques.[2] A series of stacked rectangular boxes crowned with triangular skylit volumes and punctured by large circular porthole-like windows, the Cuban pavilion's angular, orthogonal geometries were a clear contrast to the fluid forms of the German pavilion and the bubble-like wholeness and purity of Fuller and Sadao's dome. Although partaking of the same prefabricated ambition as the brutalist concrete Habitat 67, the Cuban pavilion displayed, instead, a physical lightness. This was achieved using aluminum panels clad in white vinyl that were easily assembled on-site and seemed to float above the ground, touching down on a series of concrete-footed pylons. While Habitat 67 exuded permanence, the Cuban pavilion implied portability and nimbleness.[3]

If Expo 67 is best remembered for the adventuresome architecture of its pavilions, another equally compelling and recurring feature of the fair was the frequent deployment of multimedia presentations. While previous world's fairs used the latest moving image technologies to engage visitors, Expo 67 doubled-down on immersive and interactive media. *Canada '67* was a film directed by Robert Barclay and produced using Circle-Vision 360 technology developed by Walt Disney Productions, which employed nine cameras mounted to a special circular rig to record in the round. Up to fifteen hundred visitors stood encircled by nine large screens that featured scenes of Canada—center ice at a Toronto Maple Leafs hockey game; a charging ring of mounted police on horseback, lances in hand; or flying in the air, circling Niagara Falls. The National Film Board of Canada produced a trilogy of films under the title *Labyrinth*, which shunted visitors through three large rooms or viewing chambers. Co-directed by Roman Kroiter and Colin Low, the multipart film was a precursor to Kroiter's later development of the IMAX movie experience. The Czech pavilion's Kino-Automat boasted the world's first interactive movie wherein visitors were given the opportunity to vote on a character's actions. The film's protagonist would appear live onstage at five different intervals in the plot's development to solicit a course of action from the audience. Like many of these media-based pavilions, the Cuban entry to Expo 67 would also indulge in the immersive nature of multimedia by incorporating still and moving images as well as texts, music, and sound into a cohesive narrative through which visitors would traverse. Although most pavilions attempted to add a kind of pan-humanist or universal sentiment to their otherwise nationalist displays, Cuba offered a more complex presentation rooted in the country's centuries-long quest for ultimate independence and its recently successful revolution against imperialism, which it saw as part of a larger global struggle.

The official guide to the Cuban pavilion asked Expo 67 visitors: "What does the name CUBA suggest to you? Sunny beaches . . . Afro-Cuban rhythms . . . the world's best rum and tobacco? Or a revolutionary people who sacrifice and struggle for a better life?" The pavilion sought to actively explicate this series of impressions. Entering on the first floor, visitors would encounter photomural displays that told "our history" of colonial and imperial exploitation and suffering, setting the stage for an uprising, before ascending stairs to the second floor, which focused on accomplishments of the Revolution in the areas of industry, healthcare, and education, and Cuba's solidarity with other liberation movements around the world.[4] The Electronic World Map lit up places where liberatory struggles had taken or were taking place since 1868, the year marking the start of Cuba's independence struggle against Spain.[5] On the top floor, visitors encountered a double-screen cinema with films by Santiago Álvarez, Pastor Vega, and others from Cuba's official film agency, the Instituto Cubano del Arte e Industria Cinematográficos (ICAIC; Cuban Institute of Cinematographic Art and Industry).[6] Throughout the pavilion visitors encountered six discrete screens, some projecting slide shows and others films, while projections were also layered onto photographs and walls, transforming the entire architecture into what Garatti described as a "projection machine."[7] The layered imagery in addition to ambient sound, music from the pavilion's canal-side bar, and a lighted, rotating, abstract sculpture added to the overall multimedia experience.

While most press accounts dismissed the Cuban pavilion as a propaganda machine, it was perhaps the most overt in its messaging. It did not shy away from the opportunity to tell its story on the world's stage, in North America, where many visitors to Expo 67 included American tourists—the very country with which Cuba was most at battle. It also did not shy away from shining a light on the independence struggles of other countries and their revolutionary heroes—places like Vietnam and Nicaragua. In this way, the Cuban pavilion at Expo 67 offered a different take on the idea of the universality of human life, arguing that resisting the kind of colonialism and imperialism that had cast its net over much of the world was indeed a shared historical struggle of global proportions. **ASB**

Sergio Baroni and Vittorio Garatti, chair from restaurant at the Cuba pavilion at Expo 67, Montréal, Canada, 1967. Collection Embassy of Italy in Cuba. Photo: Claudia Monteagudo

1 For more about the cultural and historical import of Expo 67, see: Rhonda Richman Kenneally and Johanne Sloan, eds., *Expo 67: Not Just a Souvenir* (Toronto: University of Toronto Press, 2010).

2 For more information about the pavilion, see my essay in this publication, "Becoming International: Importing Modernism, Exporting Revolution," 114–29.

3 Habitat 67 would remain one of the few permanent structures of Expo 67, becoming private residences after the fair. The Cuban pavilion was built to be disassembled and shipped back to Cuba, but this did not happen. It remains a mystery as to where its components were relocated, although several other pavilions' materials were distributed to various places in Canada.

4 For a comprehensive account of the Cuban pavilion and its design, see: Guillermo S. Arsuaga, "Exporting the Revolution: The Cuban Revolution at Expo 67, Montréal," in Rubén Gallo, ed., *Havana Modern: Critical Readings in Cuban Architecture* (Mexico City: Arquine, 2023), 146–69.

5 Arsuaga, 155.

6 Arsuaga, 158.

7 Garatti in Florian Zeyfang, Alexander Schmoeger, and Lisa Schmidt-Colinet, "Pavilion in Parts," video accessed at: https://www.florian-zeyfang.de/pavilion-in-parts/movie.

LIBERTAD PARA ANGELA DAVIS
COMITE POR LA LIBERTAD DE ANGELA DAVIS. CUBA

FÉLIX BELTRÁN

> Returning to Cuba at the end of 1962 was one of the most important opportunities, despite the blockade of Cuba, to be able to contribute to the revolution. Working in difficult, hurried conditions, with a shortage of materials, papers, inks for printing. This was one of the determining factors of a sense of synthesis in my design projects that, since New York, sought to ensure that nothing was missing or that nothing was left over in the work, and that the creative part was to facilitate persuasion in the public, in the public for whom it was intended.[1]

Félix Beltrán was born in Havana in 1938 and had studied graphic design at the School of Visual Arts in New York in the 1950s before returning to Cuba in the early 1960s. Beltrán was a child of socialist parents and a supporter of the Twenty-Sixth of July Movement, which was founded by Fidel Castro and other revolutionaries against the Batista regime and would later mount the Cuban Revolution. Beltrán would become the head graphic designer of the propaganda department of the Cuban Communist Party, where he created numerous memorable posters and graphic identities for the government, helping to solidify Cuba's international reputation in graphic design in the post-revolutionary period.

Absorbing the design lessons of mid-century modernism in America, Beltrán would be influenced in his approach to propaganda by the "big idea" or

Félix Beltrán, *Libertad para Angela Davis (Freedom for Angela Davis)*, 1971, poster for the Departamento de Orientación Revolucionaria, offset lithography on paper. The Lindsay Webster Collection of Cuban Posters, Wofford College. Courtesy Lincoln Cushing/Docs Populi

concept-driven advertising of New York City agencies such as Doyle Dane Bernbach, who achieved great acclaim with their clever, groundbreaking ads for the Volkswagen Beetle (e.g., *Think Small* of 1959 depicts the lightweight, economical car diminutively on a sea of white space in a full-page newspaper ad). An equivalently iconic design by Beltrán is his *Clik* poster (1968) for oil conservation, which depicts the phonetically spelled word set small in bright yellow at the center of a dark blue, but otherwise empty, background. Evoking the sound of a light switch within the darkness of a room, the design was initially rejected but became an iconic and successful messaging campaign in Cuba. With its minimal and modern aesthetic and its clear and direct communication, *Clik* represents the kind of grand synthesis that Beltrán most prized—nothing missing, nothing left over.

Beltrán also introduced to Cuban poster design the practice of graphic line translations in which an object or a photographic image was reduced to a kind of simplified silhouette, an outlining of the image's most essential or descriptive qualities. This method became a mainstay of how to reproduce a photographic image for screen printing by creating a high-contrast, monotonal, solarized-like image. Beltrán's masterful handling of positive and negative space can be gleaned from another famous work, *Libertad para Angela Davis* (*Freedom for Angela Davis*), a 1971 poster of the imprisoned Black American political activist, the contours of her face traced in thick, curvilinear linework and set against a striking red background (the color of her political belief in communism) with her hair, a distinctly large afro, enveloping the rest of the space and bleeding off the side of the page. The technique was referred to as *cartel marqueta* (model poster) by Cuban designer Alfredo Rostgaard, who ascribed to this reductive method an allegorical capacity in which a photograph of an object or person has been modified and selectively edited to help convey a story, impression, or message. Beltrán's other iconic portrait is of Che Guevera (*Che*, 1969), in which the famous portrait photograph of the revolutionary martyr by Alberto Korda has been rendered using only horizontal bars of red and black in varying lengths to create a linear pixel-like image of the former leader.

These techniques were born out of material constraints that had plagued Cuban society since the American embargo was initiated in the early 1960s. The designer not only embraced such limitations, but also incorporated them into his own personal design ethos, finding new creative outlets. A similar kind of asceticism can be gleaned through Beltrán's exclusive use of only Akzidenz-Grotesk, a modern, sans serif typeface, in his designs. His embrace of geometric abstraction draws upon not only elements of European modernism, but also the minimalist efficiency of Japanese culture, where he once traveled to study, as well as the influential nature of Concrete Art, which first emerged in Europe but was later exported to Latin America, where the practice flourished and was transformed.

Beyond the many posters Beltrán produced, his work in the area of logos, symbols, and graphic identities is among his most prolific. He would contribute to the graphic identity of Cuba's national pavilions at Expo 67 in Montréal and at Expo 70 in Osaka, Japan, each design based on the eccentric architectural geometries of the country's distinctively shaped buildings. Beltrán presented the first exhibition of logos to take place in a museum in Latin America at the National Museum of Fine Arts of Havana in 1971, the first of several shows dedicated to the genre that he would present.

Despite his long and productive affiliation with the major entities producing graphic design in Cuba, Beltrán would eventually elect to leave the island and emigrated to Mexico in 1980. He would continue to practice and teach graphic design there until his death in 2022. Although he left Cuba in a conflict with the National Union of Writers and Artists of Cuba (UNEAC), as he says, "without rancor,"[2] there were signs of potential disillusionment over, perhaps, the one constraint that he could no longer accept—the right to interpretation, something he always conferred upon his viewers:

> The state preferred that designers use phrases taken from the speeches of government leaders, mainly Castro. That way the messages were clear, with no risk of interpretation. As a designer in a free country, one could say no to a client, disagree, or even tell him to go to hell, but in Cuba this was not possible because the revolution and its messages were considered omnipotent and infallible.[3] **ASB**

1 Félix Beltrán, interview for Tendencias.tv, translation in Sonia Díaz and Gabriel Martínez, eds., *Félix Beltrán: Visual Intelligence: Graphic Design in a Social Sense* (Düsseldorf: Optik Books, 2022), 20.

2 Pepe Menéndez, "Interview with Félix Beltrán," *Artcrónica* 16 (2020), accessed online at: https://www.artcronica.com/revista/edicion-no-16/felix-beltran.

3 Interview with Maggy Cuesta in Sonia Díaz and Gabriel Martínez, *Félix Beltrán: Visual Intelligence*, 319.

THE MINISTRY OF LIGHT INDUSTRY AND THE TEN-MILLION-TON SUGAR HARVEST

After a disappointing sugar harvest in 1969, Fidel Castro proclaimed that Cuba would reach the ambitious goal of producing the island's annual estimated maximum capacity of ten million tons of sugar the following year.[1] Castro called half a million workers from the cities into the countryside to cut sugarcane, hoping to stimulate an economy increasingly dependent on this traditional export crop to pay spiraling debts to the Soviet Union.

The funds from the harvest were supposed to help finance the projects of government agencies such as El Ministerio de la Industria Ligera (the Ministry of Light Industry), which was created in 1967 for the purpose of exploring new technologies and innovative techniques to produce furniture, textiles, and other products for the country's growing housing sector. Focusing on the development of easily mass-produced furniture containing modular elements for multiple uses, the Ministry of Light Industry created furniture prototypes using inexpensive, readily available materials. One medium in particular, particleboard, could be made from bagasse, the dry, fibrous pulp that remains after sugarcane is extracted.

The first minister of the agency, Enrique Escalona, operated with the understanding that the development of consciously designed products could be harnessed for the purpose of industrializing the country. He entrusted Iván Espín, an architect educated at the Massachusetts Institute of Technology who wanted to create an industrial design school in Cuba, to lead a product design team. Espín was well-connected through his sister Vilma, who married Raúl Castro, brother of Fidel. The group was supported by Italian businessman Mauro Casagrandi, who supplied the Castro government with Alfa Romeo vehicles. With Casagrandi's assistance, they were able to facilitate trips to then-Czechoslovakia, Romania, Poland, Italy, and Sweden to visit furniture factories.[2]

María Teresa Muñiz Riva, *Esferas Modular Lamp* from the Ministry of Light Industry's *MueblePared (FurnitureWall)* exhibition, 1971. Courtesy Reinaldo N. Togores and María Teresa Muñiz Riva

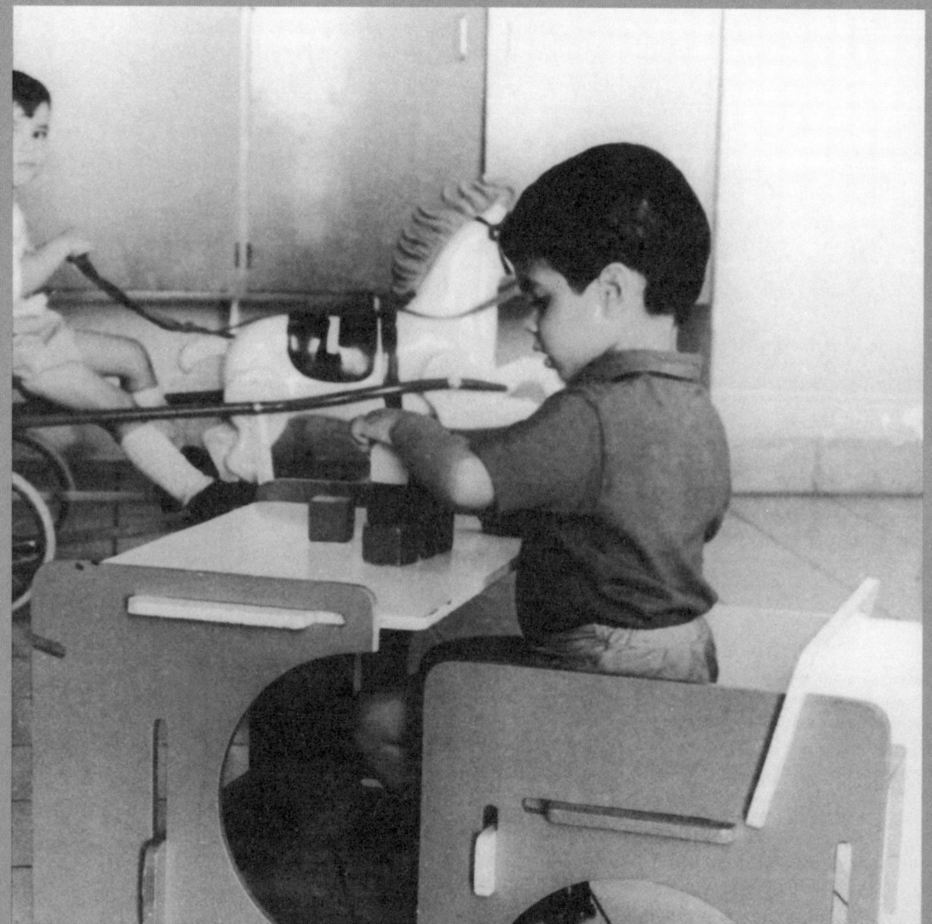

Child using chair and desk from María Teresa Muñiz Riva's line of *Jigsaw* children's furniture. Courtesy Reinaldo N. Togores and María Teresa Muñiz Riva

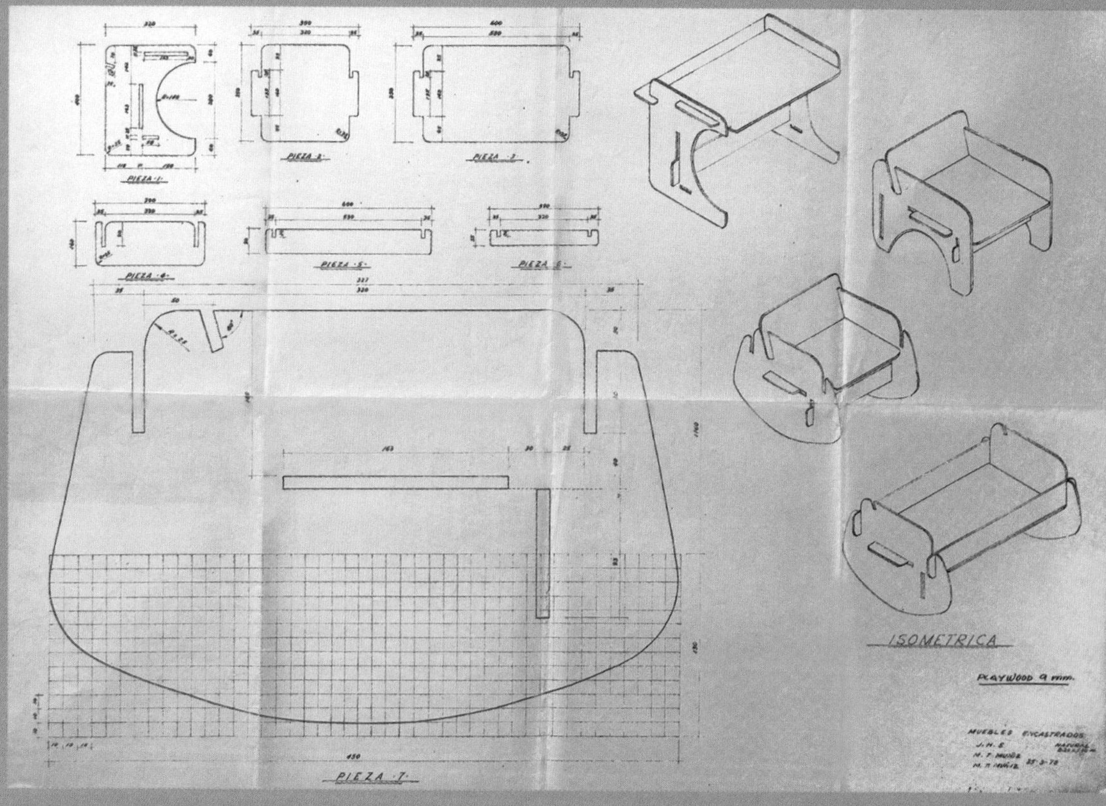

María Teresa Muñiz Riva, drawings for *Jigsaw* children's furniture. Courtesy Reinaldo N. Togores and María Teresa Muñiz Riva

Children constructing María Teresa Muñiz Riva's *Jigsaw* children's furniture. Courtesy Reinaldo N. Togores and María Teresa Muñiz Riva

Exhibition view of *MueblePared (Furniture Wall)* with *Corbu Chair* (back left), *Yab-Yum Lounge Chair* (center left), and *Esferas Modular Lamp*, 1971. Courtesy Reinaldo N. Togores and María Teresa Muñiz Riva

Heriberto Duverger, *Corbu Chairs* with the Ministry of Light Industry Group's *Mobile Table*. Courtesy Reinaldo N. Togores and María Teresa Muñiz Riva

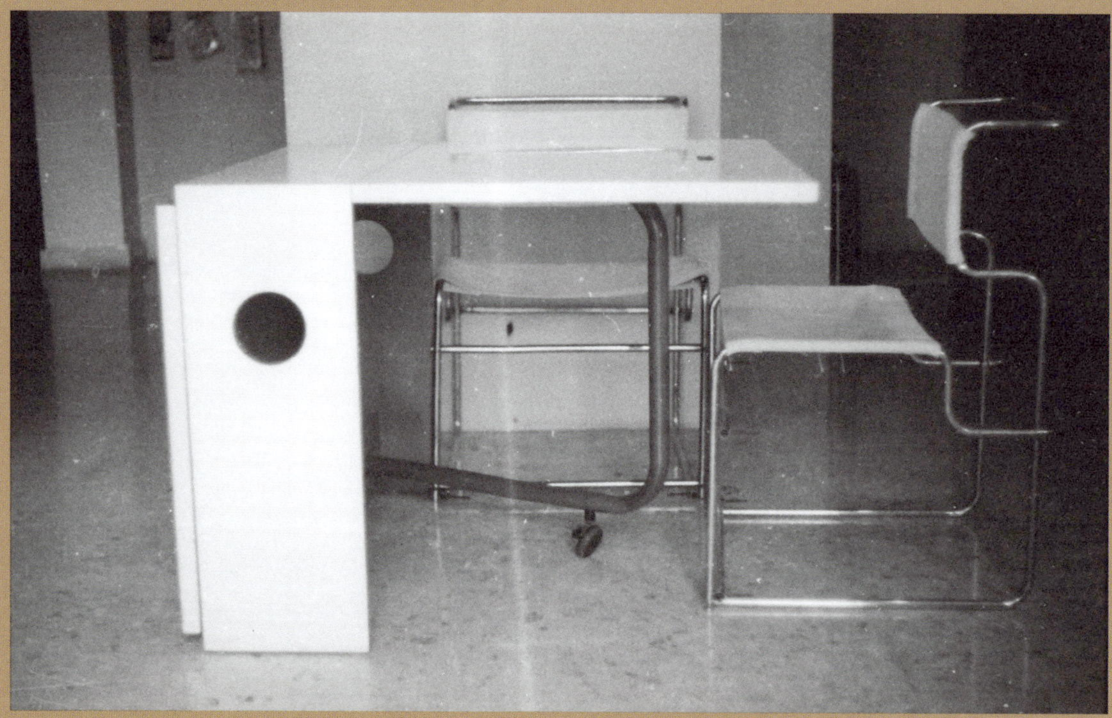

Reinaldo N. Togores, *Green Cord Chair* from the Ministry of Light Industry's *MueblePared (FurnitureWall)* exhibition, 1971. Courtesy Reinaldo N. Togores and María Teresa Muñiz Riva

The Ministry of Light Industry exhibited prototypes at a 1971 exhibition entitled *MueblePared* (*Furniture Wall*), which emphasized through its manifesto (see pages 184–185) how furniture could divide and articulate space within dwellings while still fulfilling conventional roles such as storage. The exhibition included designs by Reinaldo Togores, María Teresa Muñiz Riva, and Heriberto Duverger and focused on economical designs, including seating using plastic cordage that could be cheaply produced in Cuba; plywood furniture that could be self-assembled with slotted joints and packed flat for transport and storage; and particleboard furniture that could be manufactured from bagasse.[3] When the targets of the sugar harvest were not met in 1970, Escalona was replaced as minister, and the prototypes eventually showcased in *MueblePared* never made it to the assembly line. They were, however, used in a staging of prefabricated experimental housing designed by architect Fernando Salinas.

The only designs developed by the Ministry of Light Industry that were put into production were a type of experimental classroom furniture for schoolchildren. Muñiz Riva, a ceramicist and founding member of the Cuban Association of Craft Artists (ACAA), created a system of plywood pieces that could easily fit together without screws like a jigsaw puzzle. With this technology, children were able to build and dismantle the very chairs and tables that they used daily. Moreover, the *Jigsaw* furniture allowed for modularity, as different combinations of plywood shapes could be assembled into a variety of designs including tables, desks, rocking chairs, and doll tables, as well as for flexibility in the classroom as the chairs and tables could be packed flat for storage.

The furniture was designed at a height to help combat skeletal malformations in children, as traditional school furniture was considered inadequate;[4] tables and chairs were often too high for children, and chairs had writing surfaces only on the right armrest.

Three schools around the country utilized this furniture, including a school for the children of workers at a plastic shoe factory in Havana, a school in a fisherman's cooperative in Cienfuegos, and an elementary school in Birán where Castro was born.[5]

ARDP

1 George Volsky, "Cuba Mobilizes for Sugar," *New York Times*, Jan 26, 1970, published online at: https://www.nytimes.com/1970/01/26/archives/cuba-mobilizes-for-sugar.html.

2 Reinaldo N. Togores, "MeublePared: A Proposal (1971)," published online at: http://www.togores.net/arch-design/premisas-en/mueblepared-en.html.

3 Reinaldo N. Togores, "1969–1972: Cuba's Forgotten Late Sixties Industrial Design," published online at: http://www.togores.net/arch-design/premisas-en.html.

4 Reinaldo Togores, "An Experience in School Equipment for Children in the Lower Age Group," published online at: http://www.togores.net/arch-design/premisas-en/escuelas-en.html.

5 Togores, "An Experience in School Equipment for Children."

MINISTRY OF LIGHT INDUSTRY MANIFESTO, 1971

the built hollow is not the housing solution. the function of housing is not only to protect us from the outside environment.

THE HOUSE IS A CONTAINER FOR MAN AND HIS THINGS, BOTH USEFUL AND USELESS.

when using things, man performs different groups of activities.
each group of activities needs its space and each thing requires a place.
two problems. 1–storage 2–division of space

–OUR PROPOSAL: MUEBLEPARED–

a single solution for two problems
a single material: laminated bagasse particleboards
a single technology: squaring–grooving–edge covering–drilling–
on automated continuous lines
a single product: standardized modular panels
a multiple use: homes, schools, offices–hospitals–libraries–etc.

WITH THIS MUEBLEPARED SYSTEM, ITS ADDITIONAL COMPONENTS–TABLE, CHAIRS, ARMCHAIRS AND BEDS, ITS LAMPS, GRAPHICS AND COLOR–THIS STRUCTURE HAS BEEN COMPOSED:
THE HOUSE OF TOMORROW FOR TODAY.

Exhibition view of *MueblePared (Furniture Wall)* with the Ministry of Light Industry's manifesto. Courtesy Reinaldo N. Togores and María Teresa Muñiz Riva

THE LIGHT INDUSTRY GROUP

AN INTERVIEW WITH REINALDO TOGORES AND MARÍA TERESA MUÑIZ RIVA

THIS INTERVIEW WAS CONDUCTED ON DECEMBER 4, 2022, IN MIAMI, FLORIDA, BY ABEL GONZÁLEZ FERNÁNDEZ AND LAURA MOTT. SPANISH EXCHANGES WERE TRANSLATED BY ANDREW RUYS DE PEREZ AND BRIDGET BARTAL.

ABEL GONZÁLEZ FERNÁNDEZ (AGF) Why don't we start this interview by chronologically going through your life. Let's start with your childhood and education. Where did you go to school? How did you become an architect?

REINALDO TOGORES (RT) Okay, let's start from when I was a little child. My father was a surgeon, he had studied in the United States, and therefore spoke English. He sent me to an American school, called the Phillips School, in Havana. The director of the school, Charles E. Sargent, was a member of the Cuban Freemasonry, one its leaders. His name still appears today, among others, on a bronze plaque at the Gran Logia de Cuba building entrance in Havana. Due to these circumstances, I had the luck to learn English as a very young boy.

AGF And then you went to high school?

RT High school, yes, and it was the opposite of my primary school. I'm happy to have studied there at the Phillips School because it was a very liberal school. I then went to the opposite type of school, the Colegio de Belén, which was run by Spanish Jesuits.

AGF The same school as Fidel Castro, right?

RT Yes, the same school. In that time, I was also involved in the opposition against the [Fulgencio] Batista dictatorship. I was in a group that was led by the daughter of Aureliano Sánchez Arango.[1] So, I had a record of opposing the government of Batista, and I was very happy when Fidel Castro took power. We thought that would be the solution for the country's problems.

LAURA MOTT (LM) How old were you when the Revolution took place?

RT I was born in 1939, so I turned 19 in 1958, right before Fidel Castro took power. By the way, as I was so involved in the fight against Batista, my father worried I wouldn't be safe in Cuba. It was very dangerous to be against the Batista government. In those last months of 1958, my father sent me to Mexico. It turned out to be a great experience for me. It opened me to the whole world of Mexican culture, especially the murals of [Diego] Rivera and [David Alfaro] Siqueiros. I even thought about studying architecture in Mexico. Before that, I had started studying architecture at Villanueva in 1956 because then the University of Havana was closed.

Fig. 1 Heriberto Duverger (far left) and Reinaldo N. Togores (far right) with Mauro Casagrandi (third from left), c. 1970. Courtesy Reinaldo N. Togores and María Teresa Muñiz Riva

AGF What is Villanueva, a school?

RT It was a Catholic university that was closed in the first years after Castro took power. Surprisingly, I met people at this Catholic bourgeoisie university who were extremely left wing. Well, when Fidel Castro took power, I returned to Cuba from Mexico. I wanted to continue studying, but at the University of Havana, architecture didn't open until late into 1959. Therefore, I entered the School of Philosophy and Literature those first couple months.

AGF That's where I went.

RT Well, I joke that I went there from 1959 to 1959. When the architecture school opened, I left the School of Philosophy and Literature and changed my enrollment to the School of Architecture. I met María Teresa there. That was the beginning of our relationship.

AGF How did you get to study architecture, María Teresa?

MARÍA TERESA MUÑIZ RIVA (MTMR) [translated] I always liked architecture. I was born in Manzanillo in Oriente Province. I went to the Colegio Dominicas Francesas in Havana, a private Catholic school where in 1958 I finished my high school degree in science and letters. I had to wait until the last months of 1959 when the School of Architecture opened. There I met Reinaldo. I am younger than him.

RT [translated] Only one year.

MTMR [translated] One and a half! And more than a half!

RT She came from a wealthy family. Her father, a landowner, was the heir of an importing and exporting business established in Manzanillo since the middle of the nineteenth century. They were what were afterwards called by Castro as "Latifundistas," which were the people who had too much land, and María Teresa's family owned a lot of land. They were the victims [of the collectivization of land], even though her family had collaborated with Castro's rebels. They had a house in the foothills of the Sierra Maestra mountains in which the rebels kept a storehouse.

AGF So, María, you went to study architecture after the Revolution?

MTMR [translated] Well, then I encountered Reinaldo at the university. We were married while we were still studying in 1961. I did not finish the degree because our first child had been born, and Reinaldo was sent to work for an indefinite period of time in Santiago de Cuba in the east. I then followed him, leaving the university after completing my third year.

RT When you finished your degree, they sent you to work, God knows where. In my case, I was assigned to build houses for rural communities.

Fig. 2 María Teresa Muñiz Riva in the *MueblePared (Furniture Wall)* exhibition, 1971. Courtesy Reinaldo N. Togores and María Teresa Muñiz Riva

LM Anywhere in the country?

RT We made houses, for example, in the easternmost town of Cuba, called Gran Tierra. It was twelve kilometers from the eastern tip of the island.

AGF What did you do there?

RT We built houses for farmers.

AGF And what year was that?

RT That was from 1966 to 1968.

AGF So which year did you graduate, then?

RT It was in 1966.

AGF So then right away after graduation you started working on rural housing in Oriente? And María Teresa joined you?

RT I was originally sent to the province of Camagüey and then a few months later to Oriente. María Teresa decided she didn't want to stay alone in Havana to study, so she came with me to live in Oriente. We were given a house in Santiago de Cuba by the Ministry of Construction, so we could stay there. She was working too, making plans and projects. She wasn't an architect, but she worked like one. She also gave drafting classes to employees of the Ministry of Construction.

AGF Did you always worked together in Cuba at that time?

MTMR [translated] At that time, yes. When we came back to Havana, we started under the Ministry of Light Industry in what was called the Estudio de Productos (Product Study Department). The purpose of the ministry overall was for the development of the consumer goods industry.

RT Around 1968, I think, there was something called the "Revolutionary Offensive."[2] Fidel Castro took all the property from private businesses. He confiscated everything the private businesses owned, and this included all the small shops where furniture was made. Their excuse was that they needed all that production capacity to furnish the 100,000 new houses the government planned to build yearly from 1970 onwards. A new ministry was created, and that was the Ministry of Light Industry. They assigned someone to be minister, who curiously knew us because he was María's neighbor from Manzanillo.

AGF Enrique Escalona, no?

RT Yes, and Escalona recruited people whom he thought could be useful in this new impulse of design in Cuba. It was how he managed to get Iván Espín[3] into the ministry, and he also brought us from Oriente, so we could work for him. There was a department that María Teresa mentioned called Estudio de Productos, or Product Study. It's where Iván and Eva Björklund, who had been brought to Cuba from Sweden, worked. When we both entered, the first few months we were just exploring and proposing ideas. For example, we made some toys and jewelry designs.

AGF And when did you start working there? 1966?

RT We began there in the first months of 1968. We were both initially in the Product Study Department, but then Escalona created a development group for the furniture industry, which he assigned me to lead.

AGF But María Teresa stayed in Product Study?

RT Yes, she was in Iván's group, but María maintained her independence working for a different project. When I moved groups, an important project for a new school arose. So, she was charged with designing that school's furniture, and I went on to study how to develop the furniture industry.

MTMR [translated] Iván and his people were working on furniture for houses, and I was making furniture for schools. I worked in another studio with a separate group of designers. The furniture for the schools was also some of the first furniture that I have ever physically made. I was asked to design the furniture for a new primary school in Havana in 1969, that would occupy a building that had been the old church of Padre Sardiñas, a priest who supported Fidel fighting in Sierra Maestra. It was for children of mothers working in a new factory for plastic shoes and sandals.

RT All the furniture was innovative, with stackable chairs and tables, reversible blackboards, and other new ideas. She conceived the idea, that the younger children could play with the furniture, assembling and disassembling it.

AG A polyvalent design then?

MTMR [translated] There were eight flat individual pieces available to assemble the furniture, and with those pieces, about six combinations were possible. In reality, the children could disassemble them, but they would need help when trying to put the pieces back together. I believe it was good for them to do it.

RT There were also different sizes of furniture for different ages. Later she designed the furniture for two other experimental schools.

MTMR [translated] The other schools I designed furniture for included one in Fidel Castro's hometown and also one in a fishermen's commune in Cienfuegos. That one was an idea from Celia Sánchez[4]—a school with an open layout. That was about the only furniture from the ministry to actually be produced on a large scale.

AGF So Togores, María Teresa was in this Product Study group, designing for the schools. Iván was designing for the houses. What were you doing?

RT My department was involved in the development of the furniture industry, studying furniture production and packaging. The task was to make the entire industry more productive. Remember, there were all these small shops that made furniture before the Revolution. We were tasked to modernize this. They sent us in 1969 to Europe to visit modern furniture factories.

AGF Where do you go in Europe? Eastern Europe?

RT Eastern Europe and Western Europe. We spent some time in Romania. Then we had very brief visits to Poland, the Soviet Union, and Czechoslovakia. In western Europe, we went to Italy and finally Sweden. Eva Björklund had already returned to her home country and prepared for us a very extensive tour of the local furniture industry.

In all of those places, what we saw was how particleboard panels were cut automatically in continuous production lines, drilled at the joints, and assembled. It's what they do right now for storage furniture. Remember we were focused on increasing industrial capacity at that time. In Sweden, we saw them make storage furniture in great volume. The conclusion we arrived at after this research was basically that there should be a development of particleboard production. This coincided with a plan to harvest ten million tons of sugar in Cuba in 1970. With the great amount of money the government would have after producing these ten million tons, they could fund the modern furniture industry needed to furnish all the new houses they planned to build. We would also have so much leftover sugarcane bagasse to produce the particleboard panels. Unfortunately, all that didn't happen.

AGF You would use the sugarcane material to make particleboard?

RT Yes, a great amount of particleboard could be made from that. However, it didn't come to pass.

AGF The sugar harvest was planned after your visit to Europe?

RT The harvest took place from August 1969 to June 1970. I was in Europe in 1969. In fact, when I was there, María worked at a command center in Cuba for the harvest.

AGF My grandfather worked in one too.

RT Every minister, like our Escalona, was assigned a region of the country. On top of leading the ministry, he had to manage all of these people cutting cane and sending it to the factories. There were command centers to organize all this, and María Teresa worked in one of those

LM Can you talk a bit more about why the plan with the sugar harvest did not work out? Why were the particleboards not made from the bagasse?

RT We now know that reaching the goal of ten million tons was then considered impossible by the people in charge of planning it, but they had orders to obey. There were consequences for not reaching the ten-million-ton goal. Fidel Castro blamed certain people, and one of them was Escalona. Probably the zone he was in charge of didn't produce as much sugar as needed. So, Fidel demoted him and put someone else in charge of the ministry.

Even if the expected amount of sugar was not produced, the price of sugar was high, so they said there would be money even without the ten million tons. So, we kept making designs for all the storage furniture and also for the complementary pieces needed. That was done by exploring other inexpensive materials, like aluminum tubes and plastic cords. Initially we didn't use wood in them, but when [Salvador] Allende[5] took power in Chile, in November of 1970, we were told he would send wood to Cuba, so we could make furniture with it. We had the idea of assembling wooden parts holding them together by the tension of plastic cords. The wooden pieces and plastic cords could be made in central factories, and then small local workshops could assemble the furniture when needed. But I don't think the wood ever came from Chile.

For the particleboard, we proposed that it could be furniture that didn't need metal fasteners because there would be joints in the board, how do you say it in English—*encastrada*?

AGF Built into the board. Joints built into the board to attach to each other.

RT We went on working towards that goal. We were in contact with people who made offers for the necessary equipment for production. One of them, was Mauro Casagrandi, an Italian businessman who imported many things to Cuba, including Alfa Romeo cars. He helped us by bringing from Italy the hinges and connectors for our particleboard furniture prototypes. He also invited an Italian businessman to visit Cuba who owned furniture factories, named Alberto Zevi, who I think was a cousin of Bruno Zevi, the Italian architect and writer.

MTMR [translated] Reinaldo was then, after he came back, working on furniture design for houses.

RT Returning to Iván Espín—his work making designs was brief. What he was really was interested in was creating an industrial design school. Under Escalona, he opened a small industrial design school.

AGF You were teaching and producing furniture designs then too?

RT I was working from 1968 to 1971 on developing furniture for housing until it was evident that nothing came out of it. I started teaching at the university later, in 1972.

AGF And Heriberto Duverger was in this with you too?

MTMR [translated] Yes, it was the three of us. We two and Heriberto.

RT When we went to the Ministry of Light Industry, I had asked them to reclaim Heriberto, who was also working away from Havana. I don't remember where. During architecture school, he was part of a group of people who were very interested in cultural activities.

AGF You and Heriberto went to university together?

RT Yes. Well, this school of architecture was a bit strange because I was in a group which started the course before Heriberto's group began. It was more or less the same graduation but really there were two groups. I was in a group of people that had already started studying architecture before the Revolution. Heriberto was in another group, but later.

Fig. 3 Exhibition view of *MueblePared (Furniture Wall)* with Reinaldo N. Togores' *Red Cord Chair*, 1971. Courtesy Reinaldo N. Togores and María Teresa Muñiz Riva

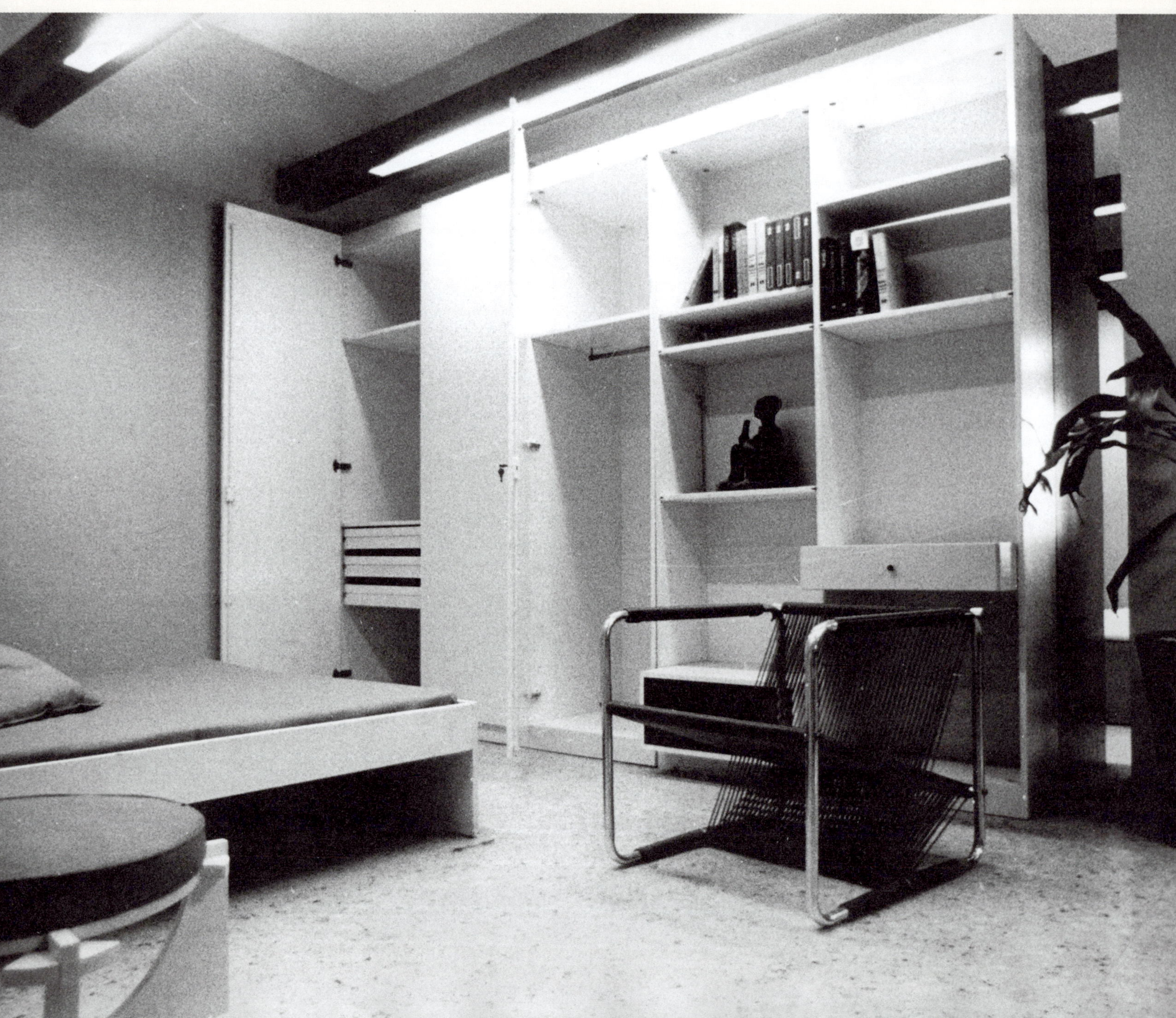

AGF And that's how you knew him and were able to call him to the Ministry of Light Industry?

RT Yes. It was through a group of people who were more interested in cultural things at that time. For example, in this group was [Antonio Fernandez] Reboiro, who was well known later as a poster designer.

AGF Between architects, designers, and painters, you have this shared experience of architecture. Was this part of the spirit of the time?

RT Painters were certainly among our mentors. Guido Llinás,[6] María Teresa's design teacher, gave us a painting before he left for Europe. We also have a Raúl Martínez (see pages 156–161) from when he was an abstract expressionist. He gave us the painting as a gift when we were married.

AGF You were all part of the same conversation then, painters, designers, and architects. When you made this furniture, what kind of spaces were you thinking of? What was your ideal layout for the furniture you designed.

RT We wanted to express our ideas and beliefs about what should be done with furniture. So, in 1971, we set up an exhibition about our proposal that we called *MueblePared: Furniture Wall*. Here we proposed a lighter solution than the Grand Panel prefabrication system that had been imported from the Soviet Union, something which was becoming more and more common at the time. We proposed an alternative construction solution, in which we could use particleboard as storage furniture but also as a division between spaces, achieving a more flexible housing layout

AGF Is this a different project from the furniture you designed for Salinas's experimental housing project?[7]

RT No, it was furniture from the same project. The thing is that we made something, if I can say so myself, so iconic of the times that everyone wanted our designs to furnish their spaces with. It was in high demand.

AGF You mean architects wanted your furniture to be included in their designs? They wanted the furniture from MueblePared? And where was that exhibition?

RT *MueblePared* was installed in a prototype workshop that the Ministry of Light Industry had by the Almendares River. The space we used for this exhibition was in the front of the ground floor, with a carpentry workshop at the back. A room a floor above had drafting tables for designers. We made chairs, lamps, and other furniture in order to fill those spaces, but what we were really promoting was *MueblePared*—a wall that also functioned as storage furniture—that defined and delineated spaces.

AGF And then when Salinas saw this exhibition, he asked for your furniture to furnish his experimental house? That's the connection?

RT Yes, Paolo Gasparini,[8] an Italian-Venezuelan photographer, took a set of photos of Salinas's project in Wajay. We collaborated with Salinas and Roberto Segre[9] in setting everything up for it. Segre even brought a photo of Che Guevara from his home to stage a picture with the *Red Cord Chair*. Our furniture was the style for the moment. The photos of the house were promoted by Iván Espín. There is an interview (see pages 212–221), where he used them.

AGF The wood for your designs didn't come from Chile? It's Cuban wood?

RT No. It's pinewood. It's actually Soviet. The wood never came from Chile. The idea was to cut lateral pieces from the wood with cylindrical connectors, and then have everything held together by the tension of plastic cords. The wooden pieces and plastic cords could be made in central factories, and then small workshops could assemble the furniture when needed.

AGF The pieces of furniture were also used for a fashion exhibition, for experimental clothing, right?

RT Yes, for Fernando Ayuso.

MTMR [translated] He was married to Ana Vega, a Cuban architect.

AGF He was a fashion designer?

RT Ayuso, yes. He had a private shop before the Revolution on La Rampa. It was named *Corinto y Oro* (Maroon and Gold). As he and his wife supported the Revolution, when Fidel Castro confiscated all the private businesses, they accepted that and changed its name to *Taller Experimental de Diseño* (Experimental Design Workshop). When this exhibition with our furniture was held, he had traveled to Spain or France, I don't remember which. He hoped to conduct business there.

AGF Can you talk about the state of furniture design in general in Cuba at the time?

RT Furniture was being made in Cuba all this time. But the furniture industry kept on making the old designs that they were used to making before the Revolution. They nationalized all the carpentry workshops, but the people who worked there were some of the same people. Some of the big owners left the country, but most of these were small workshops.

AGF Were you aware, for example, that Gonzalo Córdoba [see pages 48–59] was doing furniture? That he was doing projects like Fidel Castro's office? Can you tell us the difference between that group and your own group?

Fig. 4 Reinaldo N. Togores, *Red Cord Chair* in Fernando Salinas's *Modular Multiflex Housing System*, Wajay, Cuba, 1971. Courtesy Reinaldo N. Togores and María Teresa Muñiz Riva. Photo: Paolo Gasparini

RT The difference was that Córdoba was making luxury furniture. We were using plastic cord and particleboard and he had materials like leather, hair-on hide, and other luxury material.

AGF Like mahogany.

RT Yes, and for wood, we were hoping that Chile would send pinewood. We didn't want to do that type of luxury furniture design. We liked those designs, but for us, it was the same thing that was always going on before the Revolution. There was nothing new.

AGF And why do you think they didn't produce your furniture at a large scale? Why was it kept in prototypes? It is designed to be easy to produce. Was it because they imported Soviet furniture?

RT No, it wasn't because of importing Soviet furniture. There was already an entrenched system in place that continued on. We had meetings with Celia Sánchez, and of course with Salinas when we put our prototypes in his experimental housing. Here we tried to explain our ideas, but with no success.

LM I'm trying to understand. You would present these projects—for example, you would put your furniture in the Salinas house—and then nothing would happen? Nothing would come of it? I'm asking if they ever told you something official like we're going to be able to put your prototypes into production.

RT No, we know there were several offers related to facilities for producing the furniture.

Mauro Casagrandi, the Italian businessman we were connected with, had made a proposal for a particleboard furniture factory, and all the other things, like the connectors and all that, needed for the furniture. But the government said no, it was too expensive. It seems they had other priorities. In fact, Salinas's innovative houses also remained as prototypes. They were never built on a large scale.

LM Where was Iván Espín in all of this? We talked to Eva Björklund a few months ago. We went to Sweden to see her. She was saying that he had this idea for a design revolution, and that was the narrative he was driving. Then because of his closeness to the Castro family, there was this potential engine to move this forward. Can you talk a little more about that?

RT We met Iván in university through Olga, his wife. In 1959, when I came to the University of Havana, I met Olga, and she was the girlfriend of a fellow who was from my primary school. Afterwards this fellow left Cuba in 1959 or 1960. We still had a friendly relation with Olga in the university when she met Iván. Then we went to Oriente after graduation and lost contact, but when we returned, we had a close friendship with Iván and Eva. Really, Iván was not so much a designer himself, but he had these great ideas and what he really wanted was to start an industrial design school. He managed to open the school in 1969–1970, under the Ministry of Light Industry. After the sugar harvest failed, and Escalona was thrown out of the ministry, this school was closed.

LM What year did it close, the school?

RT 1970 or 1971. The school had a very brief existence. But as Iván had so many relations, later he managed to create another school: the Higher Institute for Design (ISDI).[10]

AGF Yes, he created the current design institute. So, were you a professor in 1970 then? I'm interested to know what kind of people went to that school. Artisans, craftspeople, architects?

RT I began teaching at ISDI when it was created in 1984. Young people with an artistic vocation, some of them already with their own small workshops, came there. I still know people who were my students during that time. For example, the last time I was in Havana, I went to the offices of UNEAC [National Union of Writers and Artists of Cuba][11] to pay my dues. When I was leaving, I met a fellow that incredibly recognized me. He shouted "Togores!" and told me that he had been my student. And he told me about his life, he designs furniture and has a small private workshop.

AGF This leads to an important question about the Revolution and your views on it. This is important to us because you are an interesting figure. You went to a private American school. You were part of the Cuban bourgeois before the Revolution. But you are still part of UNEAC now.

There is intense separation between the history of the Republic and the history of the Revolution. In Miami, they claimed to be the repository of the memory of the Republic, and they don't see it connected with the Revolution (dictatorship today). When they study modernism, they don't want to include what was made after the Revolution. I'm really curious if you could talk about how your ideas and designs came from the Republic and the connection before and after the Revolution. How do you feel that your work related with people like [Mario] Romañach?[12] We know that the work of bourgeois architecture of the 1950s was made for the rich people. Did you have some ideas about a social project that was coming or hoped for change in the country, or is it something that's just happening?

RT Well, we admired Romañach and other architects that were changing the way our city looked. I grew up in a city that was growing, especially in Miramar, where my parents lived. There was, in the last ten or fifteen years before the Revolution, a huge amount of housing being built. In fact, one of the most iconic Romañach buildings was built just one block away from our home. My father had friends who were architects. One of them took me with him on several occasions to see the things he was building.

Fig. 5 *Taller de Experimental Diseños* fashion show with Reinaldo N. Togores's *Green Cord Chair* (left), *Red Cord Chair* (center), and unnamed prototype (right), Havana, Cuba, 1970. Courtesy Reinaldo N. Togores and María Teresa Muñiz Riva. Photo: Jesús García Saavedra (Kuko)

Fig. 6 *Taller de Experimental Diseños* fashion show with María Teresa Muñiz Riva's *Esferas Modular Lamp* (left) and Heriberto Duverger's *Yab-Yum Lounge Chair* (right), Havana, Cuba, 1970. Courtesy Reinaldo N. Togores and María Teresa Muñiz Riva. Photo: Jesús García Saavedra (Kuko)

About architecture I knew little, I was more inclined initially towards painting, and especially cinematography. In my adolescence I was a cinema enthusiast. I attended regularly the International Catholic Film Office [cinema], one of whose heads was Father Tomás Macho, who was my high school teacher at the Colegio de Belén.

On the other hand, I was also a member of the leftist Sociedad Cultural Nuestro Tiempo[13] and a regular attendant to their cinema club sessions and other activities. So, my ideological experience spanned both extremes. Not to miss a thing of what happened in this milieu, I even attended the opening session of the first short-lived Cinematheque of Cuba, promoted among others by my Colegio de Belén schoolmate Adrian García-Hernández.

At *Nuestro Tiempo* I met Ricardo Porro, during a presentation in which he explained his vision of architecture. What architecture would be for me was clear when he defined it as "a poetic framework for the activity of man."

I don't think there was much of a difference between the understanding of architecture and design of our generation and that of those working before 1959. The revolutionary government is known for its prefabricated school buildings, but the first prefabricated school building in Cuba was designed and built before the Revolution by architect Manuel Gutierrez for the Villanueva University's Mechanical Engineering school.[14]

LM I'm interested in the notion of "design for all." I'm curious about the ideology of "design for all" in your practice and where these ideas came from. Did it come from this group of left-wing thinking, or was it also thinking of design ideologies you found in other places? Other designers outside Cuba?

RT Well, of course we read all the magazines we could about design. We knew about the work of people working in architecture and furniture design like the Eameses.[15] All of this was part of our formation and training. María Teresa and I spent much of our time when students in the National Library. There we read architecture journals like *Domus* and *Casabella*. Those years they also had a lot of American magazines. I remember that I found the name by which Heriberto's slotted panel chair is known—*Yab-Yum*—in an article I read in *Evergreen*. I also read a lot of books dealing with art and philosophy. One text

Fig. 7 Eva Björklund, *Little Monster Chairs*, 1968–1972. Courtesy Reinaldo N. Togores and María Teresa Muñiz Riva

that had a great influence in my way of thinking about design was Walter Benjamin's essay "The Work of Art in the Age of Mechanical Reproduction." I read it in an English translation that appeared in the *Studies on the Left* magazine about 1961.

AGF I also find very interesting how these products you designed were an effort to industrialize. Iván Espín was concerned with taking design beyond craft and trying to produce an automation of the work to expand for massive consumers.

LM What you were proposing was very ambitious. The aesthetic is very modern, of its time, and it seemed that there was an incompatibility between that vision and the ideology of the government and the reality of the supply chains.

RT The problem is that, for example, we were proposing to create big factories with automatic production lines. What really existed as the infrastructure for manufacturing furniture were only small workshops. Anyway, all that furniture would have been necessary if Castro's housing plans—100,000 units a year—would have become a reality. But this goal was never reached. Aesthetics, modern or not, was never the government's concern.

AGF And how did you leave the Ministry of Light Industry, Togores? At some point, when you realized that what you were doing wasn't going to happen?

RT Around 1970 a new plan related to schools was proposed. When we saw nothing would come out of our efforts related to furniture and that there was an opportunity to design and build real schools, we left the Ministry of Light Industry and went to the Ministry of Construction's group for school construction.

At that time, we took a liking to artisanal ceramics. And we set up a small ceramics workshop in our house. As our second child had then been born, María Teresa started dedicating most of her time to ceramics. In those years, the Cuban Association of Artisan Artists (ACAA) was created. We are founding members of its ceramics section.

In summary, there were three stages of our professional lives in Cuba. First stage was related to experimental furniture. The second stage was devoted to designing schools in a different ministry. I designed a school in Camagüey that according to Fidel Castro was the best-designed school in Cuba. To me, that was like building a new utopia, but this plan lost importance in the 1980s.

Finally, the third phase was when I was invited to be a part of a design group that was created within the Secretariat for Nuclear Energy. This secretariat was led by Fidel Castro's oldest son. I thought that working with the leader's son would be the best way to create the architecture that we wished. But then, suddenly, Fidel Castro's son was removed from his position.

LM What was the design aspect of the department of nuclear energy?

RT Architecture.

LM For facilities?

RT Yes, for example, I worked on plans for an office building that included an underground bunker designed to resist atomic bombs. I also designed a nuclear radiation laboratory that was built in Wajay. We had counseling by the International Atomic Energy Agency. Officials from Europe came to advise.

AGF And then at a certain point, you left Cuba. What year did you leave?

RT Early 1992.

AG And you went to Spain?

MTMR [translated] Due to my family. My parents were Spanish, but they had already passed away in Cuba by then. I had Spanish citizenship by descent.

RT Yes, María also had family in Spain. During my work in Cuba, especially in that last stage I told you about, I got involved in computer-aided design. My first computer was given to me when I worked at Secretariat for Nuclear Energy. Due to this specific background, I had useful skills, so after a while I was invited to work in a Spanish university teaching computer-aided design. I've written a couple books now—two or three—about this very topic, but that's another story.

1 Aureliano Sánchez Arango was a member of President Carlos Prío Socarrás's government as the Education and Foreign Minister before Fulgencio Batista's coup in 1952. In exile, he went on to finance Fidel Castro's revolution against Batista.

2 The so-called *Ofensiva Revolucionaria* (Revolutionary Offensive) was the confiscation of medium and small businesses by the Castro government in 1968. Its goal was to remove the remnants of the pre-revolutionary capitalist economy and it led to the closing of nearly 58,000 businesses and economic decline.

3 Iván Espín was a Cuban architect educated at the Massachusetts Institute of Technology. His sister Vilma Espín was the wife of Raúl Castro.

4 Celia Sánchez was a Cuban revolutionary who was a close friend and colleague of Fidel Castro.

5 Salvador Allende was a socialist politician who led Chile from 1970 to 1973. He committed suicide during a military coup supported by the Central Intelligence Agency of the United States of America.

6 Guido Llinás was a Cuban painter who lived and worked in Paris after the Cuban Revolution.

7 Fernando Salinas was a Cuban architect known for the use of prefabricated concrete slabs in years after the Revolution. Furniture designed by the Ministry of Light Industry was staged and photographed in his Modular Multiflex Housing System (see pages 212–221).

8 Paolo Gasparini has published numerous books, including *La ciudad de las columnas* (Havana, 1970), with a text by his friend Alejo Carpentier.

9 Born in Milan in 1934, Roberto Segre was one of the most renowned historians and critics of Latin American architecture. He lived in Cuba from 1963 to 1994.

10 Iván Espín later founded the Institute Superior de Diseño (Higher Institute of Design) in 1984.

11 UNEAC: Unión Nacional de Escritores y Artistas de Cuba (The National Union of Writers and Artists of Cuba).

12 Mario Romañach was a Cuban architect, best known for his single-family modernist homes built in the 1940s and 1950s. He lived in the United States after the Cuban Revolution.

13 Sociedad Cultural Nuestro Tiempo was a leftist intellectual interdisciplinary group with a leading role in Cuban culture during the 1950s. Ideologically, the group leaned towards communism, and its interests spanned experimental art, music, literature, and cinema in dialogue with the European vanguard.

14 This building received an award from the American Institute of Architects (AIA) in consideration of its advanced design concepts.

15 The couple Charles Eames and Ray Kaiser Eames were American industrial designers noted for their contributions to mid-century furniture design and architecture.

Heriberto Duverger, *Corbu Chair*, 1968–1972, for the Ministry of Light Industry, metal and canvas. Collection Cuban Modern. Photo: Claudia Monteagudo

Reinaldo N. Togores, *Red Cord Chair*, 1970, for the Ministry of Light Industry, metal and plastic cord. Collection Luis Ramirez. Photo: Claudia Monteagudo

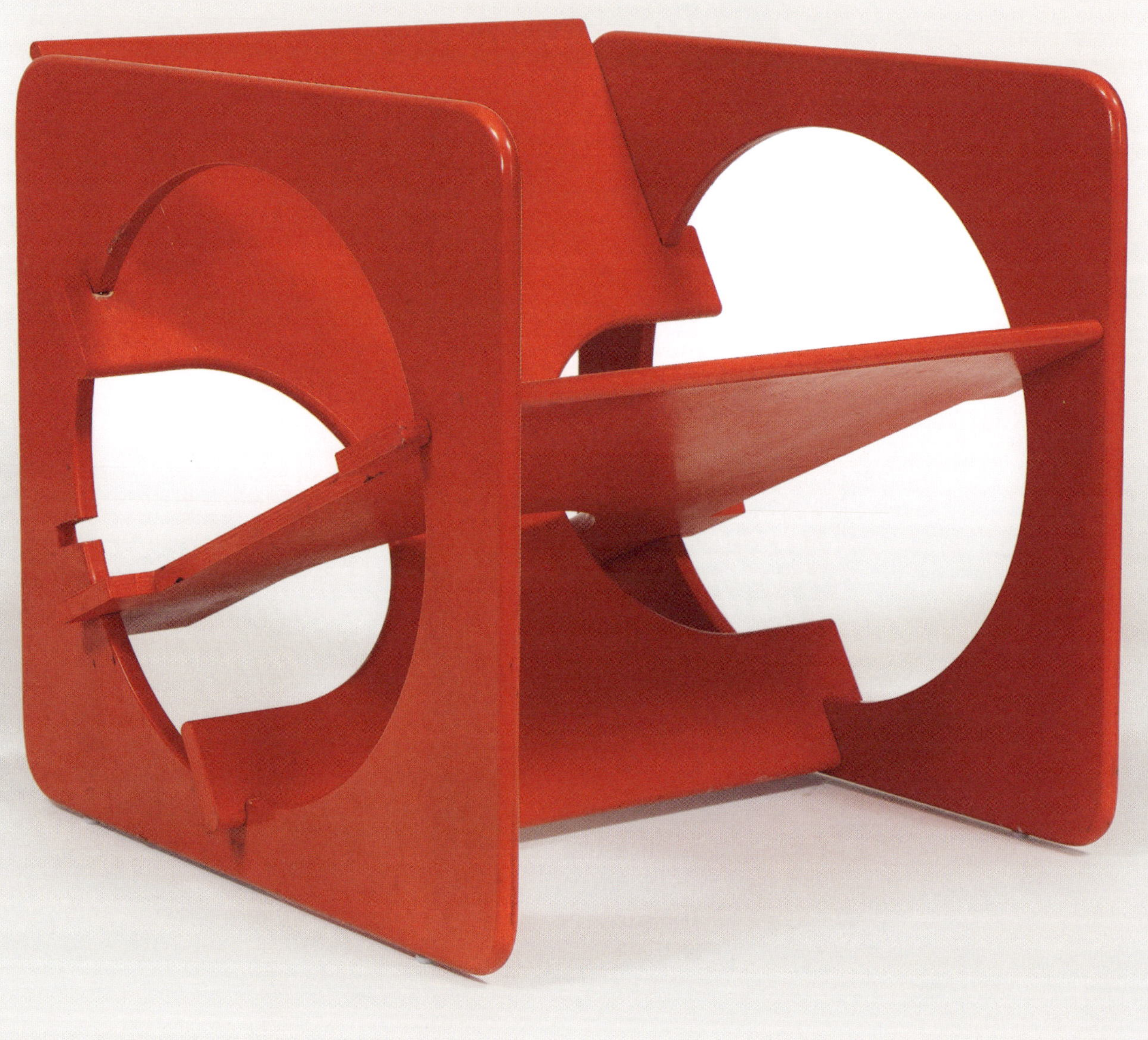

Heriberto Duverger, *Yab-Yum Lounge Chair*, 1968–1972, for the Ministry of Light Industry, lacquered plywood. Collection Cuban Modern. Photo: David Avilés

Heriberto Duverger, *Yab-Yum Lounge Chair*, 1968–1972, for the Ministry of Light Industry, lacquered plywood. Collection Cuban Modern. Photo: David Avilés

Reinaldo N. Togores, Reproduction of *Green Cord Chair*, 1971, for the Ministry of Light Industry, lacquered wood and plastic cord. Collection Cuban Modern. Photo: Claudia Monteagudo

Reinaldo Togores, *Balance Rocking Chair*, 1968–1972, for the Ministry of Light Industry, lacquered wood and canvas. Collection Cuban Modern. Photo: Claudia Monteagudo

Eva Björklund, *Little Monster Chair*, 1968–1972, for the Ministry of Light Industry, painted plywood, foam, and fabric. Collection Cuban Modern. Photo: Claudia Monteagudo

María Teresa Muñiz Riva, *Esferas Modular Lamp*, painted wood, metal, electrical components, 1968–1972. Collection Reinaldo N. Togores and María Teresa Muñiz Riva. Eva Björklund, *Little Monster Table* for the Ministry of Light Industry, 1968–1972, painted plywood. Collection Cuba Modern. Photo: Claudia Monteagudo

TOWARDS A CUBAN INDUSTRIAL DESIGN, 1971

THE MINISTRY OF LIGHT INDUSTRY

FIRST PUBLISHED AS "PREMISAS PARA UN DISEÑO INDUSTRIAL CUBANO," ("PREMISES FOR A CUBAN INDUSTRIAL DESIGN"). TRANSLATED INTO ENGLISH AND ABRIDGED BY REINALDO TOGORES.

Our life is largely conditioned by designed objects. So close is the relationship between our activities and objects which concur in them, that we can reconstruct the life of a culture that disappeared long ago based only on the remains of its utensils. Clothing, furniture, utensils, and other items that a civilization uses have always been its most faithful image. Always, but in our time. Today, useful objects—-and increasingly aesthetic ones—are reproduced in growing quantities by industry. But the bulk of industrial production is concentrated in a small number of countries. Those who lack adequate facilities shall be limited to acquire, in exchange for raw materials and at increasingly high prices, objects characteristic of an alien culture.

Now, laying the foundations of our own industry, we create the conditions for the recovery of an appearance which is truly ours. One by one, each new product from our industry that reaches the people will contribute to the realization of this renewed environment to which we aspire. The choice of the shape for the objects that our industry will produce involves decisions of great importance. For the industrial designer responsible for this task no object lacks significance. If its design is correct, every object encloses a lesson of order; it is just a special case within this comprehensive program for the design of the society to which we aspire.

We are not satisfied with its characterization of the formal residues of a more or less distant past. The incorporation of cultural values from the past does not justify the imitation of a formal language that responds to social and technological conditions that disappeared long ago. We must seek sound principles for action through the rigorous analysis of our reality and its fundamental development trends.

Thus, although the persistence of a certain typology—as in the case of the rocking chair—can be inferred from ecological and cultural constants, the final shape will be affected by the choice of technologies and materials as well as factors related to the scale of our current dwellings.

From these factors, the necessity is also derived for folding, collapsible, transformable furniture that will ensure a more efficient use of built space. Moreover, a number of different lamps emerge from a study of the role that artificial lighting plays in the dwelling: from diffuse ambient light, up to that which can be controlled, precisely directed to where it is needed.

For these objects tradition does not provide many precedents. Some are already a reality in our industrial designers' prototypes. In them, we have a glimpse of the features of that environmental countenance to which we aspire. First, the search for a synthetic expression where the superfluous, the merely decorative, is rejected for the sake of structural clarity and a more rigorous functionality.

A close correspondence between aesthetics and intentions is evident in the choice of forms—the circle, the triangle, the square—always the most elementary, the repeated use of primary colors and the clear articulation of the various components, where the design of the joints is often loaded with a strong expressive content.

This does not imply an impoverishment of the object's formal qualities; in suppressing the ambiguous and confusing, the essentially structural is raised onto a plane of aesthetic significance, and further achieves a higher synthesis in which the object is no longer appreciated in isolation, but in terms of its role in the characterization of an environment in which this restricted formal vocabulary makes its insertion possible.

For example, a lamp and an armchair—distinct themes and materials—are solved on the basis of circles and squares, these forms also preserving one

Taller de Experimental Diseños fashion show with Reinaldo N. Togores's *Balance Rocking Chair*, Havana, Cuba, 1970. Courtesy Reinaldo N. Togores and María Teresa Muñiz Riva. Photo: Jesús García Saavedra (Kuko)

and the same structural sense: The circle as a support and articulation allowing movement both for the seat and for the lampshade. These objects are formally coherent even without having been designed as part of a "set."

The possibility of achieving this integration of disparate pieces is imposed by a conception that abandoning old conventionalisms supports the plurality of functions that use superimposes within the same space. The idea of living room, dining room, bedroom "sets," holds for us increasingly less validity. And the type and quantity of items that concur in an ambiance should depend only on their specific functions. Instead of the sofa, a bed allows the living room to also be used as a bedroom. Meanwhile, bedrooms will no longer be exclusively so, transforming themselves into areas of study, work, or living.

In that certain totalizing intention at an ambiance scale, and in the reiteration of formal themes, a persistence of that tempered baroque that has characterized the highlights of our cultural past is discovered. But this recovery of the essence in tradition is not imposed as a precondition to the designer's action; it arises from a deep identification with our environmental culture's constants. These premises, on which today we base our work as industrial designers, have—besides a profound cultural meaning—a great importance in the field of the economy, since it is precisely this simplicity and this economy of means that modern industry requires from designed objects in order to achieve their mass reproduction.

TO DESIGN THE FUTURE

CONVERSATIONS ABOUT HAVANA'S NEW INDUSTRIAL DESIGN SCHOOL, 1971

AN INTERVIEW WITH IVÁN ESPÍN AND CARLOS RUIZ DE LA TEJERA WITH ADDITIONAL COMMENTARY BY OLGA ASTORQUIZA AND EDMUNDO DESNOES ABOUT THE MINISTRY OF LIGHT INDUSTRY'S SCHOOL OF INDUSTRIAL DESIGN, WHICH WAS FOUNDED IN 1969. CONDUCTED BY NILS CASTRO. EDITED FOR CLARITY AND TRANSLATED INTO ENGLISH BY REINALDO TOGORES.

Originally published in *Cuadernos de Arquitectura y Urbanismo*, 82 (May–June 1971): 62–68. This issue of the magazine was devoted to activities and events associated with the 1971 ICSID (International Council of Societies of Industrial Design) Congress held in Ibiza.

NILS CASTRO (NC) The fashion of revaluing the Bauhaus is widespread; this makes me fear that the School of Industrial Design, is a Creole version of such a fashion. Is it really something that responds to a specifically Cuban need?

IVÁN ESPÍN (IE) The last alternative is the correct one; this does not correspond in a straightforward manner to a continuity with the Bauhaus, there is however, an organic connection with our reality. The school arises from a very strong need within the Ministry of Light Industry. We wanted to develop a branch of industry; for example, toy manufacturing, to replace imports that cost little to manufacture, but a lot in transportation, because of its volume. . . . We started to organize an industrial design team and we found a very concrete problem: it was impossible to find enough people prepared in this field, which is something of such cultural significance. People here had never been prepared at a "higher" level in this area. The closest are architects, who have another kind of preparation and are taken over by tasks in the field of construction. It was evident that the problem would be solved only with highly trained designers, constantly focused on the field of industrial design, unmixed with artisanal design. This, for example, was not well defined in the Bauhaus: much of its production processes involved handicraft and were therefore costly and insufficient. The school, however, is designed from the beginning to target mass production and with the most efficient technology. Oscar, do you want to say something about this?

OSCAR RUIZ DE LA TEJERA (ORT) In contrast to the Bauhaus, we start from a very concrete analysis of our own reality. From the need for a special kind of creator, linked to our future industrial development. The concept of the designer, from the beginning, must therefore be different from that of the Bauhaus. They did not define their criteria from social pressure, as is our case, that is, to consider meeting the needs of large populations at the best quality level our manufacturing facilities can allow in the coming years (for which the handicraft conception is not valid). There is, therefore, at school, an awareness of social responsibility, that of the designer as an individual immersed within a social group, which forms him and to which he must provide his services. At school it arises even in its composition, that is, its structure and organic composition that correspond to our country's social structure.

NC How do these differences manifest themselves from the point of view of the skills taught at school? So, what does this mean regarding the training students must be given?

IE The answer lies in the ideological distinction that Oscar spoke about. It follows that, because by us being directly connected with the resolution of social problems, it colors all our teaching. The problem of the designer is posed as a problem of transforming reality, not just as the production of beautiful and useful objects. . . . The only way to effectively contribute to this transformation of society is with a series of instruments, largely coming from Marxism as the concrete analysis of a concrete reality. That is, this type of continuous confrontation, of continuous analysis of a reality to act effectively on it, permeates the whole school's pedagogical approach, it is the spirit that we want to instill. This implies that the designer's school training must be of a much higher level than is generally conceived. First, it should not be that of an individual who is a bit isolated, who faces a drawing table, and who given a few indications about an object devotes himself to prepare its drawing.

NC We must clarify, then, what you mean by a designer, unlike the established idea. Then we'll see how you manage it.

IE The concept of the designer should be precisely the opposite of that image of a man bent over the drawing table. We define the design process in two major sections: that part about making the drawing, which is the least important, since it results from work previously done, and what is central, the analytical part of information processing, which leads to defining precisely, first, the design problem; second, what the parameters and limits of that problem are; and, third, seeing the limits of the possible solution. And here, then, is when it can be drawn, but already most of the work has been done, the part of greater intellectual level.

NC What is this preliminary stage, what steps does it comprise? Therefore, what training will the future designer need to undertake it?

IE Well, we are temporarily using terminology borrowed from cybernetics, because it is useful to us. This first part we call software, that is, information processing, and the "design" itself, the drawing, we call hardware. We are emphasizing the first. The designer needs some instruments of analysis to capture the whole reality, since the problem is transforming it, in their sector, of course. Anyway, it's a career of synthesis, he is a professional who works with the data prepared by specialists in many branches—economists, engineers, psychologists, educators, sociologists, physicians—and he is the one who must synthesize, in an object, all those parameters, giving them its final shape. He is forced to analyze the whole situation to communicate and evaluate the results with different specialists. The designer is not a specialist in the sense that other professionals are, limited within a narrow range of knowledge, reaching deeper; the designer belongs to a new type of professional that "specializes" precisely in methods of analysis and synthesis. In this sense, he has many things in common with those professionals engaged in information theory, semiotics, or cybernetics, which also have certain generalizing principles that apply to different sectors of reality. This makes the designer a very peculiar specialist, dealing with methods rather than specific knowledge of a certain phenomenon or area.

ORT More specifically, this is made clear in the teaching method we are using to form that designer. Students do not make the first contact with the design based on an isolated individual learning to draw, but what comes first is to do what we call questioning the object. That is, before you start designing a particular object, you must begin by discovering what need that object responds to, that is, what problems are hidden behind the object, what does that object satisfy, in which environment does it work, what is needed to produce it. From here, design analysis begins.

NC And from here the research method and the interdisciplinary nature of research on the object springs, right?

ORT Suppose we had a matchbox. What is the functional problem a matchbox represents? What purpose is it needed for? To produce a flame through physical means, by friction. What scratching surface is needed for a given quantity of matches from a given type? Is it possible to use a better economical method than that of scratching? It is also a means of transportation with a capacity, volume, weight, strength. Are they the most appropriate? A flatter and larger box, for what kind of pocket, or briefcase, or for the kitchen shelf? Wooden, cardboard, plastic? The box may carry information, through color, drawing, texts. How much information and which contents? The box can serve other purposes—educating, saving coins, filing nails—which can be addressed by modifying its design. It is in this first analysis that different images shall be created starting from that image we have before us, that is—or was—a box of matches. Well, knowing how many ways flames can be produced, by what means, with what resources, based on what actions, carried out under what conditions. . . . I mean, there are a number of problems that lie behind the image of an object, and one must learn to describe them.

NC So, the designer as his first step examines an everyday object, in a way that problematizes it. He shall not accept its usual way of presenting itself—being so usual may lead us to believe that Havana's Industrial Design School is not natural or necessary—but will investigate looking for ways to maximize its performance, its functionality. Is it like that?

IE Well, you see, from the moment you approach the designer's work as a task of transforming society, rather than designing specific objects, of which the actual connection with social needs is ignored, examining the real needs of society, and proposing answers in the field of design is mandatory. So, we arrive at a conception which is central to this school, and to our work as designers, which is systems design. That is, when you identify all these needs, you find that they can be met by different sets of objects. You realize the absurdity of thinking about objects in isolation since the problem is to meet a set of requirements in an optimal way, and not to satisfy atomically this or that need. Immediately it becomes obvious that the designer cannot do so without sufficient knowledge of the economic, political, and moral issues involved in the problems of consumption

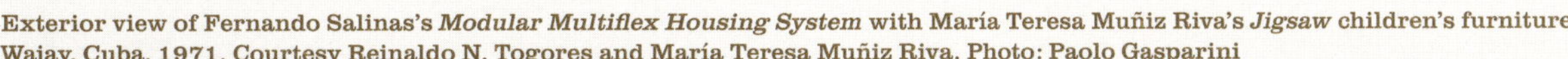

Exterior view of Fernando Salinas's *Modular Multiflex Housing System* with María Teresa Muñiz Riva's *Jigsaw* children's furniture, Wajay, Cuba, 1971. Courtesy Reinaldo N. Togores and María Teresa Muñiz Riva. Photo: Paolo Gasparini

and the resulting needs, and the economic and technological problems of the country to pose it in terms of optimization.

NC So, the conclusion is structural: there is a system of needs, on the one hand, and a system of objects, on the other. It is about getting the most rational, satisfactory formula to link both systems, to establish their homology.

IE Yes, but the existing technological system also remains, and more importantly, that which is possible for the country because this is a country that has to increase its production of industrial objects to more than the double in less than ten years. Thus, the means of production, which are crucial in meeting the needs, are our major concern as industrial designers.

NC This introduces another concern. The designer is suggested to be working slightly as a technologist, a bit as an economist, in the sense of obtaining more efficient solutions at a lower cost which can be achieved in a certain technological state. But it is not only these factors, we need to consider that these objects are part of the world that surrounds man, which requires regarding their design as an ethical-psychological problem, as a pedagogical, aesthetic problem, etc.

IE Yes, of course. That is the area in between these two poles, that of the needs and that of the intrinsic rationality of existing technologies. When I speak of needs, I understand them as a whole, not just as utilitarian needs, but in the sense that the object meets the needs of the human being as a whole. However, technology has a kind of rationality of production, an internal logic that doesn't match a priori with human needs. Then, one of the main functions of the designer is to establish a balance between these two poles, based always on the integral human being. Because if you focus on meeting the needs from a broader, ethical, aesthetic, point of view, and ignore the technological part, you're not actually being very effective in the transformation of human beings. You would be working on an ideological level without a real base; the object as design can be exquisite, but if you fail to produce it in series, and at an acceptable cost, because it does not conform to technology, it will not have a wide distribution, and your effectiveness will be reduced. We must precisely find the point of optimum efficiency, but this has to include the consideration of technology and its laws.

NC But only technology?

IE No, not at all. The ideological and cultural factors are key to the designer, as they are the designer's goal, while technology is the means. The designer's task begins with ideological and cultural work. In Cuba, for example, you have the problem of furniture: obviously there is a great need for furniture and a large consumer sector reclaims a type of furniture that, from a technological point of view, is very irrational. Furniture that is a truly degenerate version of "style" furniture, upholstered, with carvings, etc., each time in cheaper versions that are truly monstrous. Why? Because we lived in a society in which that model had a meaning.

NC A prestige . . .

IE Exactly. We are well aware that when it comes to a system of objects there is a double meaning: system as objects to fulfill needs, to be used according to their particular purposes, and at the same time, system in the sense that they are a kind of "vocabulary" of "language," because these objects are not neutral in people's psychology but have meaning. The furniture is so full of class meaning—among others—a situation we have inherited from a class

Interior view of Fernando Salinas's *Modular Multiflex Housing System* with María Teresa Muñiz Riva's *Esferas Modular Lamp* (back, middle), Wajay, Cuba, 1971. Courtesy Reinaldo N. Togores and María Teresa Muñiz Riva. Photo: Paolo Gasparini

society. This acts unconsciously, but in fact they still insist on such a kind of furniture—exorbitant, hot, heavy, scarcely functional. There lies the responsibility of the designer, who must deal with this situation and transform it. He cannot be passive; he cannot adapt to a flawed situation. Here we have, too, the deep connection of design with mass media, which plays a key role in educating the consumer; consumption is one of the major areas of cultural education and cultural transformation, perhaps its key area.

In the concrete analysis of concrete reality and the axis of our method, we consider that this situation is transformed through the play of the analysis of the situation of consumption or, it may be said, the in-depth psychology of the reasons why the consumer asks for that, the knowledge of the mass media, the available technology, and the educational work. Then making a design that is culturally and technically valid, that does not represent a class situation, and that meets the aesthetic and ethical aspirations to a higher average level than that of the older furniture, while studying how to educate consumers at the same time on the use of this new furniture.

So, you find yourself with the basic fact that the designer's main task is in the field of changing mindsets. Of course, design in the modern world cannot act alone, but forms a system, say, with mass communication, with sociological analysis, with the technological apparatus. . . . These things cannot be conceived separately, and together their essential purpose must be this modification, this permanent renewal of mental structures.

NC The large and abrupt changes that have taken place in our society give rise to another type of problem, that they may not always be in harmony. The Revolution hits first and strongest on the most urgent points, and other points lag behind. Different social sectors develop at different rates, as do different ideological and psychological levels in each individual. Many delays are not perceived until they become, in turn, problematic. There are cases in which men who are radically revolutionary in some fields don't know how to be the same in other fields. For example, the teacher who is radical in politics but remains traditionalist and normativist in the teaching of Spanish grammar, or a man advanced in economic tasks who is a conservative in his family relationships. Sometimes the structures of theoretical thinking and of emotional life are mismatched, for example, the old coherence is lost with the rapid transformation of the environment, and a more rational and fairer one must be developed. At the same time, the designers themselves are involved in this problem and suffer the disharmonies and contradictions.

IE Well, of course, it is clear from the responsibility and role that we attribute to the designer that he must have a very strong ideological soundness. It is no longer about the designer "being clear" politically as a citizen, but he must also be politically sound, even as a professional need, to be able to design well. Moreover, as people improve their development in knowledge structures, they are more likely to properly develop emotional structures. There is a great relationship between these two aspects: one helps the other, or forms it or deforms it, as appropriate. This we have in mind regarding the pedagogical approach we have in the school. Perhaps Edmundo would like to elaborate on this topic.

EDMUNDO DESNOES (ED) Well, I come from another city of culture, from literature and art criticism, and I am not a designer. In the early years of the Revolution, I was an arts critic of traditional forms but today I think that's ridiculous because a popular revolution must also have a popular art form, mass reproduced, and I think that includes the whole problem of industrial design. Even painting itself is in crisis in Cuba, even though it is one of our most developed cultural forms, and in the Revolution's early years it was given a big boost. But a work uniquely reproduced, a picture, say, can go to a museum, to an office, or can be purchased as a present for a head of state abroad, etc. Mass reproduction is the solution to the creator's problem, including to the problem of alienation of the artist, who almost always felt excluded from society, who did not participate. I think that through design, which includes the poster and even the design of a pot, a useful solution can be attained. Another question that I had was the critical aspect. Through painting and literature, you may have greater independence to be critical, but that independence is actually useless because in capitalist countries this independence is in direct relation to its inefficiency. A writer or a painter can say all they want because nothing of what they say is effective. However, a journalist, who works in the media, or a movie star, or a designer of an object, is subject to a number of laws because it does have a real function within society. The designer is not free in that sense but depends on a whole series of pressures from needs, including from moral concerns.

On the other hand, what interests us most, instead of transmitting knowledge, is to develop an analysis system, so that students are endowed with a capacity to question and understand things for themselves. The development of information, of technology, is dizzying, and the knowledge we can give students is limited. Therefore, what we can convey to them is a working and analysis method. In this case we have seen how students feel that a revolution has taken place in them, a new way to see the objects around them, a new way of thinking. They expect rules, categorical statements, laws, and, indeed, we have always rejected that. Consider a specific case, because always when we analyze cases theoretically, we are somewhat up in the air. Say, the film *Antonio das Mortes* was discussed; what matters is not the conclusion, whether it be good or bad, but the ability to analyze the film, with a range of views, both aesthetic, political, and social, about design. The conclusion depends on each individual student, but the key is a method of analysis, namely placing the work in context—social, historical, cultural, artistic. Generally traditional methods were the other way around, right? What you get is the conclusion.

IE I believe that teaching is in crisis, not only because of ideological reasons, but because of practical ones. It is impossible to deliver to the student in five years the knowledge produced in a year. If design is not conceived as information processing, i.e., as the ability to sift information through methods of analysis and synthesis, and process it, and do this in a consistent way, the problem cannot be resolved. Reality already rejects that old conception of education.

NC Teaching can be the unlimited accumulation of tiny details; knowledge not as training, investigating, and doing, but as the ability to recite. . . . A very interesting thing in our school is the teaching method, which is the presentation of problems to solve and not the memorization of rules and data. From the analysis of the results come theorizable suggestions. Would you elaborate on this?

IE At school, we have totally abandoned the traditional classroom in which a teacher stood at one end of the classroom and dictated or spoke from there, and then went away. The connection it had with that audience, passive and patient, was unknown. For us, it is essential to start from the students' actual knowledge, because it is the only way to connect knowledge with them. We start from a practical problem in the area in question, which necessarily implies a response from them. This gives them a level of awareness of their own knowledge, and their limitations and failures, and to us a concrete and objective view about what their level is. Incidentally, we are not using the old terminology of "subject" or "discipline," precisely because we want to emphasize that difference in character, rejecting traditional connotations. We are talking about "minimum codes," a name designating the essential knowledge system on which to base the operations of a given area, the effective minimum for a subsequent design, the bare minimum to start with. Then, the minimum "presentation of information" code was presented at the first "class" one of those Italian coffee makers, the domestic type, so that they could see and manipulate it, and they were presented the following problem, without any prior explanation: they were given pencil and paper and asked to communicate as designers with the people that were in charge of its production. They had to communicate everything necessary so the coffee maker could be reproduced exactly, communicating it in the most efficient way. The issue of drawing was not even raised, the word "drawing" was not even mentioned, it was a practical problem of communicating the information (which is the problem behind all technical drawing). The results were extraordinary, as almost all produced exploded perspectives. This was amazing for most of us, who come from schools of architecture of the traditional type, in which it is very difficult for students to do those kinds of drawings even in the last years of their training. They just concluded that this was the most effective way to do it, quite spontaneously, without ever learning that it was supposedly difficult. The criterion they had was to communicate or not to communicate the information.

OLGA ASTORQUIZA (OA) Indeed, its success was due to its having been raised as a problem of communication with factory workers and not as a drawing exercise, forcing them to think in terms of a totality. Therefore, they did not feel the drawing as a constraint—although there is drawing anyway—but simply as an instrument they spontaneously used to achieve a certain goal. That is, changing the problem leads them to an intellectual effort, which if stated otherwise, they would have resisted, as if they had never received a drawing "class." In traditional schools, the student starts by drawing in the abstract—parallels, circles, squares, letters—draws without having a purpose. Well, you can achieve manual training, but it is still very frustrating to be drawing with no purpose; in this case the goal was set without even saying they had to draw.

ORT Manual training is implicit in achieving the stated problem's goal, which is to effectively address that communication.

NC Well, often when one wants to explain how to get to a certain place, one makes little sketches of streets and blocks, with arrows and crosses, bad as drawings, but allowing one to tell so-and-so exactly how to get to what's-his-name's home. Iván said at the beginning that the designer's problem was being able to analyze the problem and not so much knowing how to draw. Now the need for transmitting the resulting design efficiently is added, and drawing is not essential; it remains a subsequent medium.

OA Yes, a psychomotor technique that comes through practice.

ORT But mastery of this medium is what gives you the efficiency—clearness and accuracy—in that communication.

NC When you list your minimum codes, I see that you mention "value analysis." Do you mean by this, the cost of production within a given technological level, or do you refer to the semantic value, or otherwise, which the object possesses? Aesthetic, psychological? Which "value" do you mean?

IE We are not referring to the cost of production but to the social value derived from practical usefulness and, on the other hand, to semantic value.

ORT If we reversed the terms, it is also the value of the analysis. That is, how we can enhance our own analysis, our research, our final product, regarding which standards, which scale of values, and that scale corresponds to a specific society, which is ours. There you have an ethical evaluation, an aesthetic evaluation, an evaluation of work, of the effectiveness of our own work.

NC What are the other minimum codes?

ORT There is ergonomics, the relationship between man and object, the minimum energy used by man within that relationship. Anthropometry, physiology, and psychology are all involved. To make it clear: if I design a water jug, I must consider the weight that it may have when full so it can be manipulated; I consider the handle's shape to achieve the minimal effort solution; its shape and color so we don't have a psychological rejection, etc. On the other hand, there is the study of culture as a context in which the object should be acceptable, so it responds precisely to its ideological environment. In presenting the information, of which we have spoken, apart from communication, perception is also involved—to be aware of the laws of perception, to develop on them and achieve an enhanced performance from the experience of perceiving the universe. Then, of course, we have design itself ranging from the problems of analysis to the drawing. Each of these minimum codes resulting from this analysis is an area in which you must have training to reach a decision; therefore, they cannot be considered in isolation, as separate disciplines, but as units of knowledge that are synthesized in the task of designing an object, items of one and only one thing.

NC Now when we talk about presenting information, I noticed something that I do not know whether it is covered in other minimum codes, or in other aspects of your work. You spoke about the designer's communication with the object's manufacturer. But the designer also communicates with the housewife who uses the example's coffee maker, with guests who see the coffee maker on the table, etc. Besides communicating with manufacturers, communicating with consumers should also be considered. Is this also studied within these minimum codes? Is it considered as a different theory or is it also presenting the information? Communication with the worker is a technological problem, it's a matter of specialties within the factory. It is in the other aspect where great problems arise—aesthetic, psychological, ethical, etc. I wanted to allude to them when asking about the object's semantic value.

OA Through new practical tasks, students move from communicating with the workers to other forms of individual communication, then to group communication, and later, to mass communication. Always, of course, based on a specific analysis of tasks until the structure of each code is assimilated.

IE We've been talking all the time about objects. In fact, although the school is about industrial design, this also involves designing information objects, such as posters, films, TV programs, which are designed with the primary purpose of transmitting information. This is an essential axis in the conception we have, which is mainly information design.

NC It is not only about semantic objects specifically intended as such. Should we also consider a spoon as a means of communication, albeit this is not its primary purpose?

Interior of Fernando Salinas's *Modular Multiflex Housing System* with Heriberto Duverger's *Corbu Chairs* (back) and *Yab-Yum Lounge Chair* (front), Wajay, Cuba, 1971. Courtesy Reinaldo N. Togores and María Teresa Muñiz Riva. Photo: Paolo Gasparini

IE As we conceive it, the spoon is part of a system, and this confers on it a semantic value. If you look at the value that people confer on objects, you'll see a huge part of that value are factors of meaning, although this is unconscious, and consumers have only presented the immediate usefulness of the object. We talked about that with respect to furniture as a "language" that speaks about the social status of the venue or of its owner. Communication with the consumer is the designer's catalytic role, the truly important one, while the other, yes, is a technical function. Within the school this aspect is studied in the general design workshop, where all the minimum codes are synthesized.

ORT That is, communication is from a man, as a designer to others as consumers, by means of objects. For the object being produced, there is an intermediate communication with the manufacturers.

NC Now, as to the systematicity of that semantic value, I think it would be worthwhile to clearly observe something else: You can be, or should be, extremely aware of something that others manipulate without noting it. So often an archaeologist goes in search of certain artifacts, without much interest in finding the type of object that could be displayed in a museum; he rather seeks for remains of broken pots, coal, fish bones, pieces of shells, etc. He specially looks for the garbage dumps from communities that left few traces. This happens for example with Martinez Arango's research at our university. Then, from a series of fragments, he begins reconstructing an entire culture, step by step. He finds a piece of a pot: it is painted or not, the clay is fired or not, it is shaped this way or the other, it has a certain thickness, it appears associated with other remains at a certain depth, in a certain kind of place, from which he infers the technological level of community that produced the pot, their livelihoods, etc. From that dump we know if they were gatherers or hunters, whether they fished or knew about agriculture, and so on. There comes a time when the archaeologist is already establishing hypotheses about their likely family organization, daily life habits, beliefs, etc.

That is, the archaeologist reconstructs the system from some loose fragments, because these elements are coherent, consistent within a totality endowed with a certain order. However, he is not involved in the system and can make a reading of this system from the outside, from another system. It often happens that one does not perceive this, but as you have seen things all your life, occupying a certain place, one believes it to be the only normal way of being, accepting it without questioning its rationale, without comparing it with other real or possible ways of being. But one also lives within a system, one an archaeologist of the future could read from outside it; we are occupying the place where Martinez Arango places the aborigines. Can we study ourselves through the eyes of an archaeologist, the system in which we are immersed, becoming aware of the systematicities we practice without knowing it? This is implicit in the question posed by the matchbox example by Oscar earlier. Say, a chair: its form, materials, its association with other furniture and of a certain place, involving a sitting position, different functions, events, habits, living arrangements, technology, beliefs . . . a way of living that can be inferred from the way and occasion of sitting. A divan, a rocking chair, a high-back chair, a throne, a desk (with or without a chair) don't imply the same things. An archaeologist discovers how a culture existed in a certain way; the designer is inserted into contemporary culture's conditioning and shape.

IE Historically, the designer has overlooked or ignored that the system of objects is a culture-shaping code, that shapes a way of being, not an unquestionable system given beforehand.

NC The act of communication is achieved by all with apparent ease, but when linguistics inquires into this act, an extraordinary mechanical complexity for its implementation is made evident. Now, behind the universe of more or less necessary objects—that habit or propaganda made necessary and commonplace—there is also a no less complex language, and perhaps, more so but we do not realize it—we don't figure out its "grammar." The designer is, in this case, somewhat of a grammarian of civilization's objects.

IE For a society that has set as its goal forming the new man, approaching design from this point of view is mandatory, inescapable.

NC All right, back to the point about the school's origin, to the inclusion of this theory in Cuba, with the problem of underdevelopment and accelerated development. How does it figure within all this?

IE Throughout the interview that question has been partly answered. We want to transform society. Now we are interested in how we must do it. To create the new man for that new society, design has to face two interrelated aspects: the imbalance between the many aspects of necessity, and the economic and technological possibilities. If we manage to establish that balance, we'll be able to not only serve the new man but also speak to the depths of his mind through the language of the objects of his civilization. These are new terms, but they are not free; they are instruments of thought applied to a very specific situation, our need to transform man by transforming his environment. That communication, that language, must be established through the objects themselves.

NC It is a disturbing thought, but a very agreeable one, that a cup and even a bottle's cork shall be considered as mass media. Not as obvious as a television set, perhaps. However, the aesthetic value lies mainly in the object's semantic charge, in the object's capacity to transmit large, broad, and complex information in a single stroke, by simply showing the object. Why, then, don't you talk about aesthetics?

IE I think there has always been a project of being implicit in art, right? That is, the artist always raises the possibility of a different way of existence for the social being, so the work of art has a strong content in the sense that it offers a solution. However, that solution is given only within that aesthetic level. I understand that this is a most important aspect of art: giving a vision, a higher possibility, a solution to the improvement of being. That is art's great strength. Thus, today's truly vital artist is closely linked to these general problems of mass communication and the production of industrial objects. Design is replacing the "classical" artist because our times transform the approach for a new kind of action, from the hope that was before, to a possibility subject to the artist's will.

NC In Cuba, a pictorial revolution is taking place, not in painting in general, but in poster art. You cannot always distinguish, right now, a poster from a painting, and more and more artists are looking to express themselves by means of the poster.

IE However, I think many of those artists have acted more by instinct than by awareness, or, in any case, have assumed a political and social consciousness, but not an aesthetic one. I think the important thing is that we are in the midst of a mutation in art: artists such as Picasso or Le Corbusier are almost the last of a breed, because the basis of their work has been taken from them, i.e., one can no longer paint a picture in the same way that Picasso painted and still be a vital artist. Picasso could do so because in his time he had no alternative, and he had to accomplish the function of art that way. Today, the artist does not simply present the image of a better world, rather, he can connect his art in a concrete way with the effective transformation of reality. So much so that this society has proposed for itself a new man.

1 The School of Industrial Design was one initiative of Enrique Escalona, the inaugural head of the Ministry of Light Industry. Promoted by Escalona, the school would cease to exist along with other initiatives when he was replaced as head of the ministry in 1971.

Exterior of Fernando Salinas's *Modular Multiflex Housing System* with María Teresa Muñiz Riva's *Jigsaw* children's furniture (front) and Reinaldo N. Togores's *Balance Rocking Chair* (back), Wajay, Cuba, 1971. Courtesy Reinaldo N. Togores and María Teresa Muñiz Riva. Photo: Paolo Gasparini

LA CASA ORUGA (THE CATERPILLAR HOUSE)

Mercedes Álvarez and Hugo D'Acosta, *Módulo Experimental de Vivienda de Asbesto-Cemento (Experimental Asbestos Cement Housing Module)*, Havana, Cuba, 1964–1968. Photo: Rigoberto Diaz

In 1967, while inaugurating a new group of buildings in Gran Tierra, a remote town in eastern Cuba, Fidel Castro announced a plan to drastically increase the supply of residential housing in the country over the next decade, utilizing incoming technology from the Soviet Union: "As of next year, we will be able to increase housing construction greatly and by 1970 we shall be able to construct some 100,000 living quarters a year. Therefore, between 1970 and 1980, 1 million houses must be built."[1]

In the decade following the Revolution, the consideration of housing as a social right rather than a commodity necessitated new technology to be imple-mented to fulfill construction needs. Although Castro eventually chose to mechanize construction on the island by building large high-rises made from prefabricated panels similar to Khrushchyovkas in Eastern Europe, named for their promotion by Nikita Khrushchev, Cuban architects also experimented with prefabrication in order to innovate.[2] The Soviet panel system, in particular, brought worries about cost and unsuitability for the tropical climate, as the high-rises were designed with heavy, rigid panels to accommodate the heavy snow loads of the Russian winter.[3]

One alternative solution, called Módulo Experimental de Vivienda de Asbesto-Cemento (Experimental Asbestos Cement Housing Module), more colloquially known as "La Casa Oruga" or "The Caterpillar House," was designed by the husband-and-wife team Mercedes Álvarez and Hugo D'Acosta. The pair developed their solution between 1964 and 1968, proposing that houses could be built out of six-millimeter-thick asbestos cement sheets formed by single molds, making them available for mass production. Easily transportable because of their light weight and assembled using mechanical joints, the sheets could comprise a highly configurable system of cells to fit specific needs through individualized floor plans.

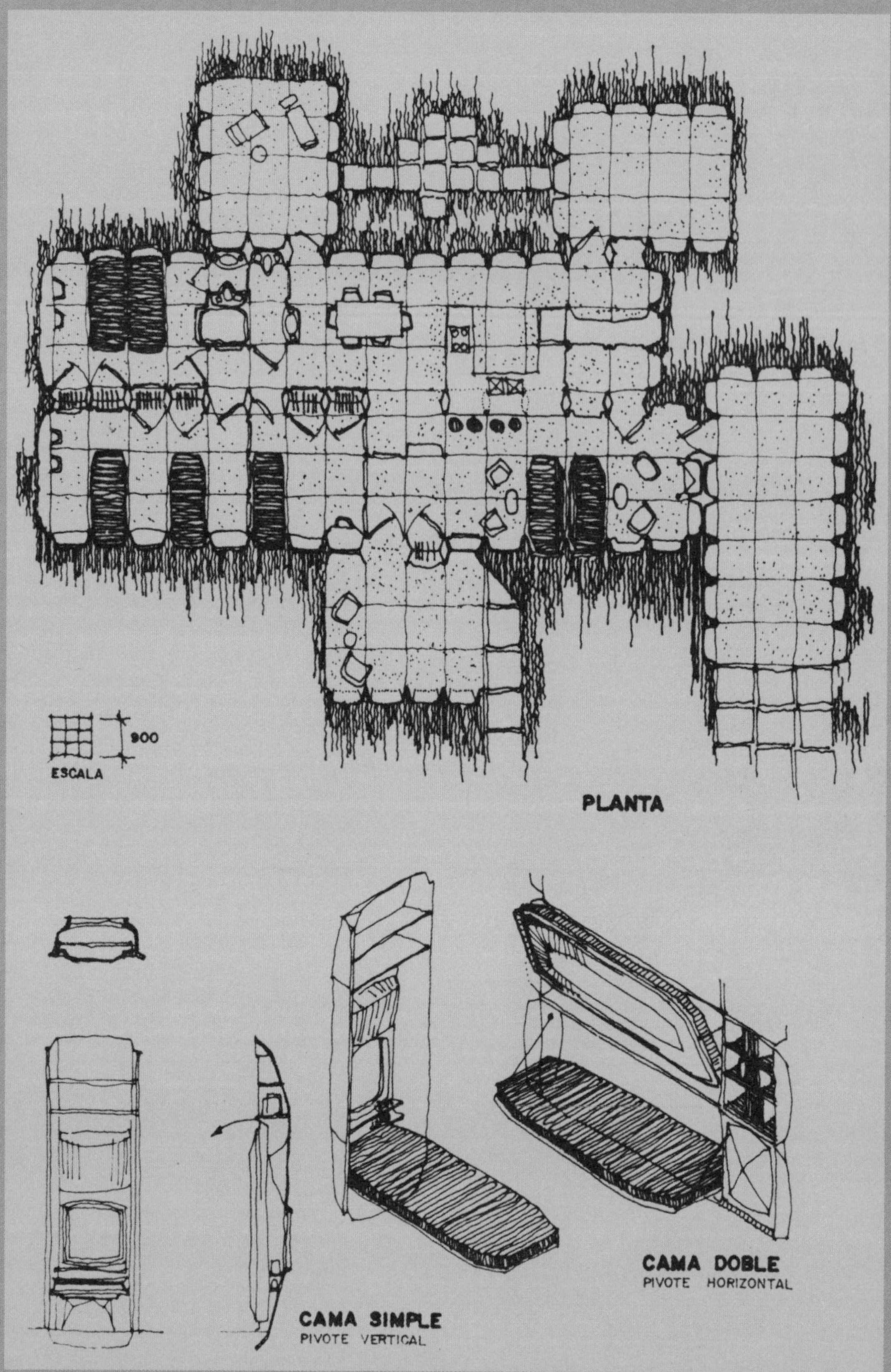

Mercedes Álvarez and Hugo D'Acosta, Sketch showing large-scale configuration and built-in beds for the *Asbestos Cement Experimental Housing Unit*, Havana, Cuba, 1964–1968. © Archive Eduardo Luis Rodríguez

Mercedes Álvarez and Hugo D'Acosta, exterior view of the *Asbestos Cement Experimental Housing Unit*, Havana, Cuba, 1964–1968.
© Archive Eduardo Luis Rodríguez

Designed for both urban and rural settings, the housing units could be stacked to create multistory dwellings. This consideration of multiple climates and contexts was important, as the concentration of housing construction was initially nonurban and focused in rural areas due to the Revolution's beginning and sustained presence in the countryside.[4]

While the exterior of the Caterpillar House appears spacecraft-like with repeating rounded, voluminous protrusions punctuated with grate-like windows, the smooth interior walls contained molded cavities meant for built-in furniture and other storage to be similarly mass-produced alongside the asbestos-cement sheets. The curvilinear walls, undulating spaces, and even the furniture resonate with architect Ricardo Porro's criticism of the boxy, rectilinear facades and the repeating quadrilaterals found in modernist single-family homes before the Revolution; he believed that more organic designs, with softer, rounded corners better represented Cuba architecturally than the pre-revolution emphasis on European orthogonal rationalism.[5]

D'Acosta and Álvarez, as part of a young generation of Cuban architects committed to the revolutionary ideal of the expansion of housing for all, had previously worked together on the first social housing project of Castro's government, Vecinal Unidad No. 1 (Neighborhood Unit No. 1), in Havana del Este, the most deprived area of the capital. Built immediately after the Revolution, from 1959 to 1961, the

Mercedes Álvarez and Hugo D'Acosta, interior view of the *Asbestos Cement Experimental Housing Unit*, Havana, Cuba, 1964–1968. © Archive Eduardo Luis Rodríguez

project was a superblock of one thousand apartments, divided into four sectors of walkable cul-de-sac neighborhoods. Nonetheless, a more efficient solution to address the country's housing shortage needed to be developed. Unofficial sources estimated that half of the housing units for the poorest half of the population were deemed uninhabitable.[6]

Cuba faced a particular challenge since constructing houses was considered the responsibility primarily of the private sector before the Revolution and, therefore, few large social housing projects, such as those completed elsewhere in Latin America by the likes of Mario Pani in Mexico City, Affonso Reidy in Rio de Janeiro, and Carlos Raúl Villanueva in Caracas, were undertaken in Cuba.[7] Pedro Martínez Inclán, an architect and city planner, identified a lack of housing in Havana as a problem as early as 1925, when he calculated that 35,000 new housing units needed to be built to house an incoming population moving to the city.[8] He eventually led one of only three pre-revolutionary social housing projects in Havana between 1944 and 1948, the Barrio Obrero de Luyanó, which accounted for only fifteen hundred modest single-family homes.[9]

Ten iterations of the Caterpillar House were constructed, but only one remains and was brought to international attention when it was rediscovered by architectural historian Eduardo Luis Rodríguez in 2004. While the production of units was never realized, the Caterpillar House is an example of cutting-edge architectural experimentation in Cuba, particularly within a wider global context of developing modular living spaces in the 1960s and 1970s. For example, the avant-garde British architectural group Archigram designed its Plug-In City concept in the 1960s, which transformed architecture into a form of scaffolding with dwelling units to be considered as portable and interchangeable vessels. This kind of configuration was imagined to be helpful for humans as life became more nomadic through the introduction of new technologies.[10] The Japanese Metabolist movement also focused on the creation of "megastructures" by inserting prefabricated units into larger building structures.[11] Ettore Sottsass Jr.'s Mobile and Flexible Environment Module (1972) also envisioned an adaptable way of living in which containers could house different functions for living.[12] The gray, curvilinear modular units bear striking aesthetic resemblance to the Caterpillar House, a project that also conceived architecture to be an adaptable tool for people's constantly changing needs rather than a constant that forced humans to adapt their own lives to the living space available for them. **ARDP**

Mercedes Álvarez and Hugo D'Acosta, chair for the *Asbestos Cement Experimental Housing Unit*, 1964–1968. Collection Concha Fontenla. Photo: Claudia Monteagudo

1 Reinaldo Togores, "MueblePared: A Proposal (1971)," http://www.togores.net/arch-design/premisas-en/mueblepared-en.html.

2 Barry Bergdoll and Peter Christensen, *Home Delivery: Fabricating the Modern Dwelling* (New York: The Museum of Modern Art, 2008), 100.

3 Reinaldo Togores, "MueblePared."

4 Victor Deupi and Jean-François Lejeune, *Cuban Modernism: Mid-Century Architecture 1940–1970* (Basel: Birkhauser, 2021), 129.

5 Deupi and Lejeune, 86.

6 Gary Fields, "Economic Development and Housing Policy in Cuba," *Berkeley Planning Journal 2* (2012): 56, citing Sergio Roca, "Housing in Socialist Cuba," in *Housing: Planning, Financing, Construction*, ed. Oktay Ural (New York: Pergamon Press, 1980), 63.

7 Deupi and Lejeune, 170.

8 Deupi and Lejeune, 168.

9 Deupi and Lejeune, 170.

10 Bergdoll and Christensen, 123.

11 Bergdoll and Christensen, 144.

12 Ettore Sottsass Jr., "Design as Postulation," in *Italy: The New Domestic Landscape* (New York: The Museum of Modern Art, 1972), 163.

A CONTEMPORARY LENS ON CUBAN MID-CENTURY DESIGN

LAURA J. MOTT

AHORA O NUNCA

In early 2020 at the entrance of Cuba's national fine art museum, the Museo Nacional de Bellas Artes de La Habana (National Museum of Fine Arts of Havana), sat a light sculpture, *Untitled (Ahora o nunca . . .)* by artist Raúl Cordero (fig. 1).[1] The color LED lights sear the words *ahora o nunca* ("now or never") into the retina, and it takes awhile to blink away the imprint of the phrase. The artwork conveys an existential contradiction—a message of fleeting urgency in the form of a large static object. As a text-based artwork, its interpretation is especially contingent on its placement, like a conceptual chameleon that changes meaning based on its surroundings.

In Havana, the sculpture was auspiciously installed directly across the street and in the sight line of Fidel Castro's yacht *Granma*, which sits entombed in protective glass as a commemorative monument. In 1956, the boat took Castro and eighty-one other exiled revolutionaries from Mexico to Cuba on a perilous journey to overthrow the authoritarian government of Fulgencio Batista (fig. 2). The eventual success of the Revolution in 1959 and the establishment of Castro's communist regime can be traced back to the *Granma* expedition.[2]

Isolated, the message and the monument together tell a succinct hero's journey. However, if one widens the frame to the streets of Havana and the country of Cuba as a whole, the boat and the phrase could be interpreted as relics of a broken utopian promise—a now that never truly came to be. The social evolution that was to result from Castro's Revolution dissolved into a strict dictatorship that continues today even after his death in 2016. The works included in *A Modernist Regime: Cuban Mid-Century Design* are conduits for understanding the realities of Cuban politics and social life from the period of the Revolution to the present. The impetus for their creation was to communicate post-revolutionary achievement and spread the communist agenda of the new Cuba.

Fig. 1 Raúl Cordero, *Untitled (Ahora o nunca . . .)*, 2019, LED bulbs and electric installation on wall. Courtesy the artist

Fig. 2 Fighters disembarking from the yacht *Granma* onto the Cuban coast, 1956

In the context of today, they tell stories of neglected histories and social hierarchies of privilege that contradict an ethos rooted in communism. As a counter-tactical act, the mid-century aesthetic in design and graphic design has ultimately been co-opted and appropriated by a current generation of Cuban artists and designers to broadcast a ground-up narrative of oppression under authoritarianism.

The Parable of Dujo

The story of the Dujo furniture brand serves as an allegory for the evolving interests of Fidel Castro and the economic challenges in Cuba since the Revolution. The Dujo furniture brand was formed as a government entity in 1959 for the design practice of Gonzolo Córdoba, an Argentinian-born designer who had been successfully working in Cuba designing restaurants and hotels before the Revolution (see pages 48–59). He was able to gain the confidence of Castro through Celia Sánchez, the guerrilla fighter who organized the landing of *Granma* and one of Castro's most trusted advisors. Sánchez, alongside Iván Espín, the brother of Raúl Castro's wife Vilma Espín, led the initiatives in Cuban design during the 1960s and early 1970s for a new Cuban aesthetic identity, helping to legitimize the fledgling government on an international stage was a priority. Their ambitions included the design of new furniture and interiors for the architecture that had been seized during the transfer of power, including offices and residences of high-ranking government officials, tourist hotels, and the Palace of the Revolution. In Cuba, the Dujo brand populated these spaces with furniture made with high-end materials primarily sourced from the country, including local woods such as mahogany and cedar, woven rattan, and Bayamo marble. Essential to the cultural identity of the Revolution was the notion of authentic *Cubanía* (Cubanness), which the designers embedded in the brand, in part, through their choice of materials.

The Dujo furniture brand takes its name from the *dujo* chair used by pre-Columbian peoples referred to as Taínos, who were located throughout the Caribbean, including Cuba. Using the Dujo name was a way to link the newly founded company to an older and thus more authentic Cuban past. This strategy worked both for domestic audiences in support of the state's new utopian project and to justify its relevance as a commercial enterprise under the Revolution's umbrella. It also served as an effective marketing tool to help differentiate an otherwise aspiring international brand by accentuating its Cubanness. Contradictory to its socially egalitarian domestic agenda, this meant presentations of Dujo at high-end furniture salons, expos, and exhibitions primarily throughout Europe, including a partnership and ongoing commercial presence at Steph Simon Gallery in Paris. Córdoba's partner in Dujo was María Victoria Caignet, who created textiles and functional objects, and collaborated on exhibition design, while he took the lead on designing furniture and overseeing a team of designers and carpentry shops to execute the brand. Between 1967 and 1971, Córdoba and Caignet created dynamic international presentations of the Dujo brand in Paris and Milan, and had an exhibition at the Liljab Museum in Stockholm and the headquarters of the United Nation's Food and Agriculture Organization (FAO) in Rome.[3] As seen in the *Salon de Meubles* in Paris in 1967, they often adopted aesthetics from Cuba's tropical setting, including living plants, wood-paneled walls, straw rugs, and carved trellises (see pages 86–87). With this stage set, they were capitalizing on an imagination of Cuba by the public, who had only grown more curious since the Revolution.

This type of design display typically has a specific type of person in mind. For instance, American mid-century design was advertised in places such as *Playboy* magazine to appeal to the "modern executive man" through objects that communicated success, wealth, and capitalism at its finest. When one looks at the presentation of Dujo design in these international contexts, one questions: Whom is this for? Who is the person that inhabits this room? A room staged with high-end furniture seems to target the antithesis of Che Guevara's vision of the "new man" who would embody the communitarian values of the Revolution. Guevara preached the superiority of moral over material incentives, which would be eliminated in this new society in which the "new man" would work to produce for the whole society instead of himself. In a speech to an association of small farmers Castro explained his dream: "there will arrive the day when money will have no value. Money is a vile intermediary between man and the products man creates."[4]

By the early 1970s, the international Dujo initiative was abandoned due to a lack of capital, the absence of a sustainable market, and the stigmatization that it was "bourgeois taste"—too closely connected to pre-revolutionary Cuba. Ultimately, it was this existential conflict that would halt high-end production and exportation of the Dujo furniture brand. The framing around the design was parallel to Castro's mindset at the time. Marco Castillo, an artist and collector of Cuban modernism, explains: "[Castro] got radicalized, he got very into Soviet politics, and he militarized the country. And so, artists became the enemy because they were the creative people. By the seventies,

Castro also began his censorship of artists and writers. The government destroyed the movement, the design, and the taste."[5] In 1974, Córdoba and Caignet were shifted to a new furniture line called EMPROVA, conceived by Sánchez, that was solely focused on economic design production for Cubans and prioritized Cuban public spaces, such as hospitals and schools. The high-end Dujo furniture could also be found in government administrative offices, where it was used until it was worn down, and then passed down to rank-and-file workers. These workers, who rarely understand its origins and thus its value, are a primary source for collecting Dujo furniture in Cuba today, where what is found is often in poor condition, with broken parts, missing leather, abraded fiber seats, etc. Paradoxically, the Dujo furniture in the best condition can be found in Europe, where it was originally purchased from salons and galleries. These objects have been treated as high design and cared for over the decades.

Although the lead designers moved on and Dujo ceased producing higher-end luxury furniture, the Dujo furniture business persists even today, but in a completely altered form. The current state of Dujo speaks to the realities of contemporary Cuban life, its economy, and the government's stringent control over material goods for its citizens. There are two factions of the current business: a public store of basic furniture and a private sector that services the production of furniture for primarily new hotels and the tourism industry. The public store has what are called "liberated" objects for sale, which means that Cuban officials have approved them to be sold to the people.[6] A typical experience at the store would start with a long queue to get in when it opens at 12:30 p.m. Such long lines are a common experience when purchasing food, clothes, or any other material goods of limited access in the country due to the US embargo and a general lack of local industries. The public store that sells furnishings looks like a warehouse of inexpensive and unrelated objects without any distinctive design or cohesion. One of the more popular items is a rocking chair made of aluminum tubes and plastic cords, often found on patios, which in fact resembles the materials and aesthetic of Reinaldo Togores's version of this common chair designed for the Ministry of Light Industry in 1970 (see page 201).

The furniture production of Dujo today remains dedicated to government enterprises. All the production is done in Cuba in purportedly eleven factories located throughout the country, including one in Las Tunas that specializes in more advanced carpentry. The Dujo designers today focus exclusively on executing designs referred to as "the line of desire," which are dictated to them by a French company called Bouygues Bâtiment International. The European company was hired by the Ministry of Construction to design interiors for Cuban hotels owned by the government. According to one Dujo designer, the government has a policy of making all the furniture in Cuba, however, all materials are imported, so no Cuban wood or local materials are used anymore. As of today, there is no autonomous Cuban design produced by Dujo. "We have been fighting this battle, those hotels should have furniture of Cuban design, but nothing in those hotels resembles Cuba once you close the windows," an anonymous designer stated; "but we aren't our own bosses."[7] Ironically, at the headquarters of Dujo, there is a large replica of a Clara Porset chair and the original Dujo sign with the indigenous *dujo* chair as its emblem (fig. 3). Today, Dujo is rumored to be owned or run by Mariela Castro Espín, who is the paternal niece of Fidel Castro and maternal niece of Iván Espín. Even though the "Cubanness" of the design and materials has dissipated, the intimate relationship between power and access to objects remains present. The storefront of Dujo today is a mid-century remnant—a facade that does not match what is transpiring inside—a metaphor of the contradictions and lack of transparency of the authoritarian government.

Fig. 3 Dujo Muebles headquarters, Havana, Cuba 2023.

A Contemporary Lens

Cuban mid-century design and its aesthetic history is used as a tool by contemporary artists and graphic designers to represent the ideological shift from the Revolution's utopian intentions to the resulting dictatorship. On July 11, 2021, thousands of Cubans spontaneously took to the streets in dozens of cities to protest—the first nationwide demonstrations against the Cuban government in decades. The protests took place as an act of collective desperation due to poor living conditions throughout the country, including shortages of food and medicine, constant electrical blackouts, Covid-19 restrictions, and oppressive policies, including the repression of artistic freedom. In 2018, President Miguel Díaz-Canel signed into law

Fig. 4 Marco Castillo, *Córdoba*, 2019, mahogany and cane. Courtesy the artist and Nara Roesler Gallery

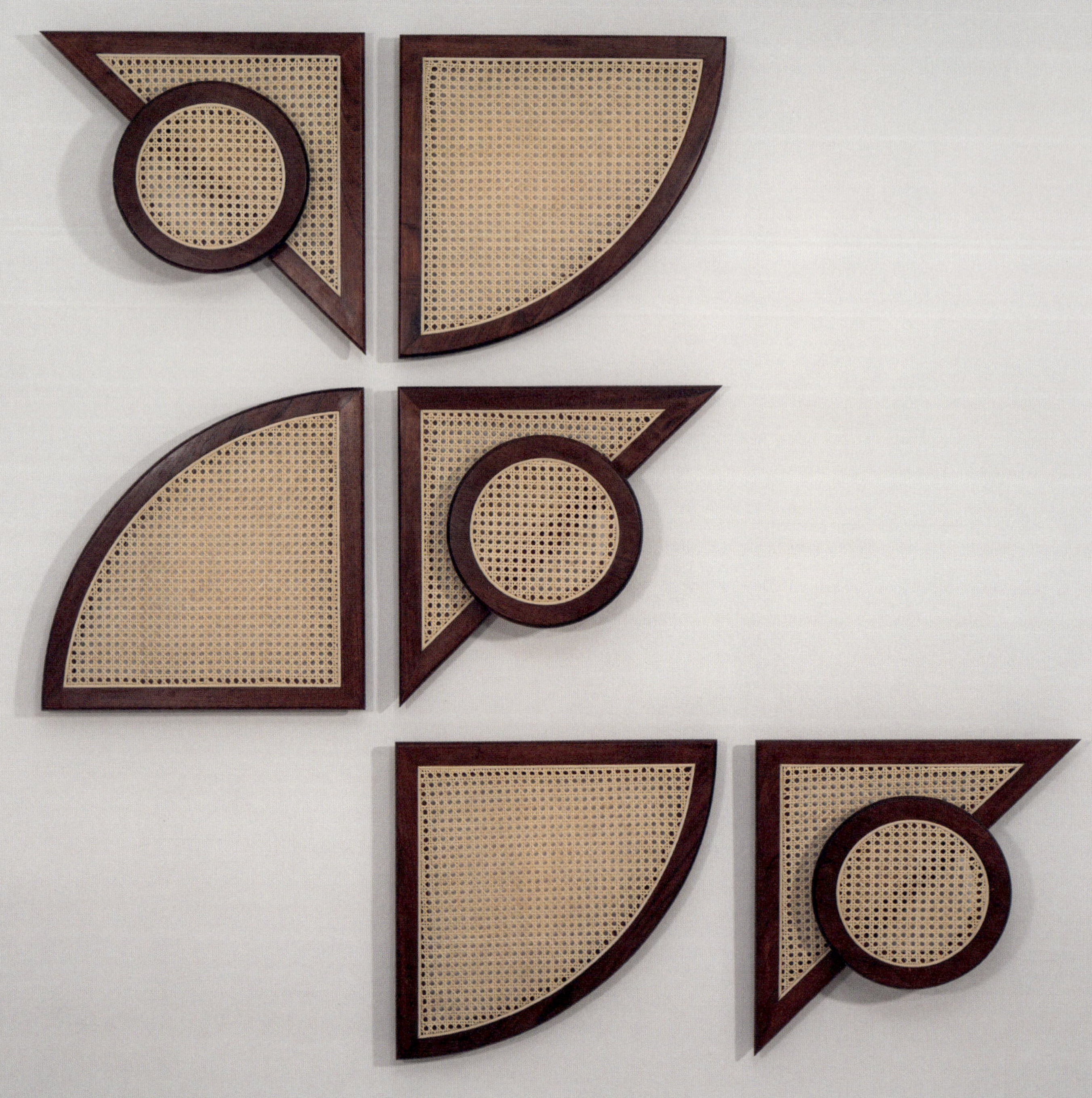

Fig. 5 Marco Castillo, *Beltrán*, 2019, mahogany and cane. Courtesy the artist and Nara Roesler Gallery

Decree 349, stating that all artists, including collectives, musicians, and performers, are prohibited from operating in public or private spaces without prior approval by the Ministry of Culture.[8] It launched a campaign by the Cuban government to suppress the artistic community and control creative production through official legislation in an attempt to quell the outpouring of anti-government artwork and music. The backlash led to the formation of organized protest groups by artists and intellectuals, such as the San Isidro Movement. Three weeks before the historic protest, artist Hamlet Lavastida was arrested and imprisoned for more than three months because he shared an idea for an anti-government art project through a private messaging app that was being secretly monitored. He was later forcibly exiled to Poland. His experience inside the police interrogation room informs his artwork and speaks to how the legacy of mid-century materiality is experienced today: "They took me to a very small room. It seems that was the way they could soundproof in the 1960s with an aesthetic that was used a lot in communism. In the interiors, they covered cement in wood. It reminds me of the provincial scenery that Fidel Castro liked so much: having everything in wood, making everything *wood*. It seems that this comes from the world of the cedar of Holguín; this is a rather rustic imagery that I find interesting."[9] Lavastida's recollection is reminiscent of the stylized sets of the Dujo brand that foregrounded the authentically Cuban woods (see pages 86–87). The aesthetic carries with it a nostalgia for the seeding days of the Revolution when Castro created his guerrilla camp in the Sierra Maestra mountains. Nostalgia is a powerful political tool that materiality reinforces.

Marco Castillo, in addition to being a prolific collector and researcher on Cuban mid-century design, is an artist and was one of the founding members of the artist collective Los Carpinteros (1992–2018). There is a divided Cuban art scene; a minority of which supports the communist government and a robust critical contingent, including Castillo and his work, that began to exhibit internationally in earnest starting in the 1990s and to voice the artists' dissent to a global audience. Castillo incorporates the aesthetics derived from Cuban modernism in his practice both to resurrect this neglected history and to critique the political oppression of creative life in Cuba. In his series titled *The Decorator's Home* (2018–present), the artworks are named after modernist Cuban architects and designers in homage to this forgotten generation of creators, including Gonzalo Córdoba, María Victoria Caignet, Iván Espín, Reinaldo Togores, Heriberto Duverger, Clara Porset, and Félix Beltrán—all of whom are featured in *A Modernist Regime*. The series uses traditional materials and techniques associated with Cuban mid-century design, like mahogany wood and rattan caning. In the sculpture titled *Córdoba* (fig. 4), a round chair seat evolves in shape to ultimately form a five-pointed star, a symbol of communism. The modular *Beltrán* (fig. 5), created in 2019, refers to Félix Beltrán, one of the most important figures in Latin American graphic design, and mimics the domestic wall hangings found in many mid-century homes. The shapes are inspired by the logo Beltrán designed for the Cuban pavilion at Expo 67 in Montréal (see pages 170–173). In this series, Castillo is also referencing the aerial view of the kind of plans that interior designers use to lay out a room, but here the objects are in turbulence. The work is a like a freeze-frame of deconstruction, which conceptually links to the demise of autonomy of Cuban artists and the loss of creative life in a dictatorship.

Visual communication to both local and global audiences has had a rich history in Cuba even before the Revolution, with iconic tourist posters promising an exotic paradise of music, dance, and sunshine. The poster campaigns to aestheticize the communist agenda were crucial to the Castro propaganda machine following the Revolution, as seen through initiatives such as the Organization of Solidarity with the People of Asia, Africa, and Latin America, or OSPAAAL (see pages 130–133). However, the current generation of graphic artists have co-opted this modernist aesthetic as a counter-tactical act; they use the aesthetics of OSPAAAL and other mid-century propaganda against the government—a strategic mirror to show what the regime has become. Today, they utilize twenty-first-century technological platforms including social media to reach their audiences. This is reminiscent of how the director of OSPAAAL's poster program, Alfredo Rostgaard, applied a by-any-means-necessary approach to distributing its agenda and sought out forms of communication that were immediate and would make their posters "more effective and modern."[10] For OSPAAAL, it was about forming a solidarity amongst communist and socialist liberation movements in Asia, Latin America, and Africa based on shared subjugation under colonialism; today, the Cuban community of artists and designers, most of whom now live in exile, use it as a communication platform to inform a global audience of subjugation under dictatorship.

Social media and messaging apps like Telegram and WhatsApp are the primary platforms of exchange for Cuban graphic designers. A common hashtag is #27N, which is the handle for independent Cuban artists, writers, thinkers, and civil society members who bonded together in the wake of the unjust arrest of rapper Denis Solís González and other aggressions against artists, which resulted in a sit-in protest in front of the Ministry of Culture in Havana on November 27, 2020. Since then, artists have faced continuous surveillance, harassment, and arrests, to the effect that almost all of the artists mentioned in this text have been in prison or exile, primarily in Mexico, Spain, and the United States, since 2021. These acts against participants in #27N are part of a broader crackdown on artistic expression in Cuba through laws like Decree 349 that gives the government discretionary power to criminally prosecute artists who create works of protest. Around the same time as Lavastita's arrest, artist Luis Manuel Otero Alcántara and musician Maykel "Osorbo" Castillo were imprisoned for the vague crime of "insulting national symbols" and were subsequently sentenced to five years in prison.[11] A leader of the San Isidro Movement, Alcántara is a sculptor and performance artist who challenges societal hierarchies with works like *Welcome to Yumas—Miss Bienal de La Habana* (2015), in which he dressed in drag, traversing the streets of Havana as an iconic Tropicana dancer. Castillo co-authored the protest song "Patria y Vida" ("Homeland and Life"), which was released in February 2021 and gained an international following as the anthem for resistance against the Cuban government.[12]

In the last few years, Alcántara has become a prominent figure as a political prisoner. Graphic designer

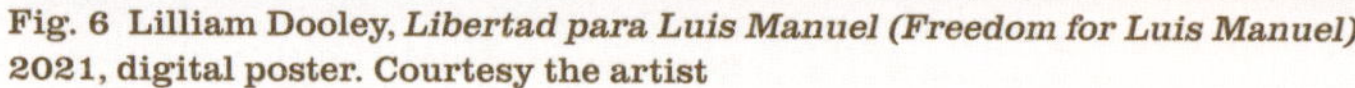

Fig. 6 Lilliam Dooley, *Libertad para Luis Manuel (Freedom for Luis Manuel)*, 2021, digital poster. Courtesy the artist

Fig. 7 Anet Melo Glaria, *Despierta, Cuba (Wake Up, Cuba)*, 2020, digital poster. Courtesy the artist

Liliam Dooley adapted Beltrán's famous 1971 poster of activist Angela Davis, who was wrongfully imprisoned, and added Alcántara's face to the image to equate the two injustices (fig. 6). While ideologically the two have supposedly opposing views about communism, the arc of time has altered perception of this simplified duel, owing to how the ideology ultimately manifested itself as authoritarianism. The mid-century graphic design legacy is pervasive and fraught with a combination of admiration and internal conflict for this generation, as graphic designer Anet Melo Glaria (fig. 7) writes: "As a child I used to lie on my back for hours and hours to look at the wall of my uncle's room, covered from side to side by a sea of posters that stimulated my curiosity, my fantasy, my aesthetic sense and, without suspecting it, my vocation itself. Many times, I imagined what it would be like to have lived two decades ago, in that fertile time for creation with a cause, which gave rise to one of the most beautiful periods of Cuban graphic art. A time when they 'believed' in the possibility of building a country of just aspirations and noble promises. Then everything changed in Cuba. From one day to the next the light went out, and with it the inspiration of all those artists from my childhood."[13]

Conceptual artist and graphic designer Julio Llópiz-Casal has created a social media series of iconic portraits of Cuban political prisoners with a single vertical bar representing a tear running down their faces: the red bars are for political prisoners (fig. 8); the black bar is for deceased individuals who died by hunger strike or police brutality (fig. 9); and the colors of the transgender and queer flag are for injustices to those communities (fig. 10). His portrait of Alcántara has been widely shared and is the primary image of his political prisoner campaign. Human rights organizations and the United States government have called for Alcántara's release since he was detained on July 11, 2021, after he posted a video to social media saying he planned to join the historic protests. Later that same year he was named a "prisoner of consciousness" by Amnesty International and, along with the San Isidro Movement, was recognized in *Time* magazine's Top 100 list of important figures of 2021. Also that year, Castillo's "Patria y Vida" won the Latin Grammy Award for Song of the Year and racked up more than 13 million views on YouTube as of 2023. Llópiz-Casal's social media images are accompanied by political commentary and reference "Castrism," the condition of continued oppression in Cuba and a reference to the metaphorical castration of the growing population

Fig. 8 Julio Llopiz-Casal, *Luis Manuel Otero Alcántara*, 2021, digital poster. Courtesy the artist

Fig. 9 Julio Llopiz-Casal, *Diubis Laurencio Tejeda*, 2021, digital poster. Courtesy the artist

Fig. 10 Julio Llopiz-Casal, *Brenda Díaz*, 2021, digital poster. Courtesy the artist

of artists and intellectuals forced into exile. "Castrism cannot be reformed. And not only can't it be, but in its continued evolution it will only increase its anti-democratic character. What was allowed in the 1960s is not allowed today. That's why we see in the '60s considerable worship to Fidel Castro and in the middle of 2023 millions of people now hate his political legacy. . . . There is no logic in creating laws on the backs of human beings if it is not precisely to prevail over him or her. #ElCastrismoNoPuedereformarse (#Castrismcannotbereformed.)"[14]

The goal in this creative production is to create a fever pitch that ultimately leads to reform in the country. The call of urgency—now or never—is a daily practice for many of these artists who work strategically to communicate amongst each other, to the people in Cuba, and to the global community. In reflecting on the current state of Cuba, one asks: what can be gained by resurrecting this design history with the current trajectory of Cuba and its artist and intellectual community primarily in exile? Curator Abel González Fernández offers, "For us, the importance of memory is its liberatory potential. We come back to modernist movements because it is the time when all the political possibilities of democracy and progress were grounded in our national tradition. Through the unveiling of this knowledge, it offers optimism to Cuban people both on the island and in exile. It is a place of our collective dreams to be recovered in the future, and we recover the past now to inform the present. When looking at Cuba, we must recognize what we need to keep from the fascinating, tragic, elegant, and complex Cuban history. What are we going to keep? We may not have a land for all Cubans to be reunited now, but we have a shared memory that will unite us."[15]

1 The artwork was on view as part of Raúl Cordero's solo exhibition "Arte Para la Mente Distraída / Art for the Distracted Mind" on view from November 2019 to March 2020, when the Covid-19 pandemic closed down the museum.

2 "Granma" is an affectionate term for a grandmother; the yacht is said to have been named for the previous owner's grandmother.

3 Abel González Fernández, unpublished interview with Córdoba, 2017.

4 Jamie Suchlicki, "The Making of the 'New Socialist Men' in Cuba," Cuban Studies Institute, January 8, 2020, published online at: https://cubanstudiesinstitute.us/principal/the-making-of-the-new-socialist-men-in-cuba.

5 Oliver Kupper, "The Decorator's Home: An interview with Marco Castillo on Cuba's Incomplete Aesthetic Revolution," *Autre*, July 2, 2019, published online at: https://autre.love/interviewsmain/2019/7/2/9ay8opsu61u03ywmderyrw99m550pw.

6 José Manuel Mesías, Interview with the author, June 6, 2023.

7 The source of this quote is anonymous to protect the designer's employment.

8 Amnesty International, "Cuba: New administration's Degree 349 is a dystopian prospect for Cuban artists," August 24, 2018, published online at: https://www.amnesty.org/en/latest/news/2018/08/cuba-new-administrations-decree-349-is-a-dystopian-prospect-for-cubas-artists.

9 Carlos Manuel Álvarez, *El Estornudo*, "El prisionero 2239 de Villa Marista. Una conversación con Hamlet Lavastida," October 11, 2021, published online at: https://revistaelestornudo.com/hamlet-lavastida-entrevista-artista-cubano-preso/

10 Richard Frick quoting Rostgaard in Luigino Bardellotto, ed., *¡Mira Cuba!: manifesti cinematografici, politici e sociali = carteles de cine, políticos y sociales* (Milan: SilvanaEditoriale, 2013), 181.

11 Daniel Cassady, "Cuban government sentences dissent artist Luis Manuel Otero Alcantara to five years in prison," *The Art Newspaper*, June 27, 2022, published online at https://www.theartnewspaper.com/2022/06/27/luis-manuel-otero-alcantara-sentenced.

12 "Patria y Vida" was released in February 2021 as a collaboration between exiled Cuban musicians Alexander Delgado and Randy Malcom of the duo Gente De Zona; Yotuel Romero, founding member of the pioneering Cuban hip-hop band Orishas; and singer-songwriter Descemer Bueno. Contributors Maykel Osboro (Castillo) and Eliécer "el Funky" Márquez both remain in Cuba.

13 Anet Melo Glaria, *El Estornudo*, "Inspiración con causa," December 8, 2020, published online at: https://revistaelestornudo.com/carteles-cubanos-libertad-movimiento-san-isidro-expresion/.

14 Julio Llópiz-Casal, Boris González Arenas: "El castrismo no puede reformarse," *Hypermedia*, March 15, 2023, published online at: https://hypermediamagazine.com/columnistas/con-c-minuscula-julio-llopiz-casal/boris-gonzalez-arenas-el-castrismo-no-puede-reformarse.

15 Abel González Fernández, communication with the author, July 21, 2023.

Contributors

Curatorial Team

Abel González Fernández is, since 2023, Assistant Curator at the Museum of Contemporary Art Detroit and a graduate of the Center for Curatorial Studies at Bard College. He has curated projects in Havana, Berlin, New York, and Tokyo, including *Sin Autorización: Contemporary Cuban Art* (2022) at the Wallach Gallery of Columbia University.

Laura J. Mott is Chief Curator at Cranbrook Art Museum, where she since 2014 has organized numerous exhibitions and publications, including: *Sonya Clark: We Are Each Other* (2023); *Olga de Amaral: To Weave a Rock* (2021); *Landlord Colors: On Art, Economy, and Materiality* (2019); and *Nick Cave: Here Hear* (2015).

Andrew Satake Blauvelt is Director of Cranbrook Art Museum and was previously at the Walker Art Center, Minneapolis, where he served in a variety of roles, including as Senior Curator of Architecture and Design. He has organized numerous exhibitions and publications on a variety of subjects, including: *With Eyes Opened: Cranbrook Academy of Art Since 1932* (2021); *Too Fast to Live, Too Young to Die: Punk Graphics, 1976–1986* (2018); and *Hippie Modernism: The Struggle for Utopia* (2015).

Andrew Ruys de Perez is the Jeanne and Ralph Graham Curatorial Fellow at Cranbrook Art Museum. A graduate of the Courtauld Institute of Art of the University of London and Yale University, he is the curator of the exhibition *Ash Arder: Flesh Tones* (2023) for Cranbrook Art Museum.

Museum Staff

Administration
Andrew Satake Blauvelt, Director
Sarah Doty, Associate Director, Museum Operations and Visitor Experience
Kelsey Cumbow, Senior Administrative Assistant

Curatorial and Collections
Laura Mott, Chief Curator
Kat Goffnett, Assistant Curator of Collections
Andrew Ruys de Perez, Jeanne and Ralph Graham Curatorial Fellow
Bridget Bartal, MillerKnoll Curatorial Fellow
Brian McLean, Head Preparator and Exhibition Coordinator
Madlyn Moskowitz, Registrar
Jordan Stohl, Associate Preparator

Education and Public Programs
Lyla Catellier, Curator of Public Programs
Meghan Morrow, Coordinator, School and Family Programs

Marketing and Communications
Julie Fracker, Director of Communications
Amanda Coe, Digital Marketing Manager
Danielle (deo) Owensby, Digital Marketing and Social Media Coordinator

Membership and Development
Autumn Parrott, Director of Development
Caryn Brooke Emmer, Donor and Volunteer Relations Manager
Katie Jaede, Membership Coordinator
Kelly Lewis-Gump, Director of Annual Giving and Membership, CEC
Michael Stachowiak, Director of Grant Development and Administration, CEC
Alexis Weisbrod, Principal and Major Gifts Officer, CEC

Visitor Services
Nickie Gunning, Lead Visitor Services Supervisor
Suzanne Maxwell, Visitor Services Supervisor
Samantha Hohmann, Visitor Services Supervisor
Gabrielle Centurione, Visitor Services Supervisor

Museum Committee

2023–2024
Denise Anton David (ex-officio)
Rebecca Applebaum-Wyett
Karen Bacon
Ebi Baralaye
Nia Batts
Jim Berline (ex-officio)
Christine Colman
J.J. Curis
Gretchen Davidson
Dirk Denison
Frank M. Edwards
Elyse Foltyn
Jennifer Gilbert (ex-officio)
Jennifer L. Hermelin
Samara (Johnson) Furlong
Phillip Morici
Jo Obasuyi
Senghor Reid
Pamela Rodgers
Catherine S. Rosenthal
Catherine J. Schwartz
Marc Schwartz (Chair)
Sandra Seligman
Nate Wallace
Alison Wong
Carol S. Ziecik

Published on the occasion of the exhibition

A MODERNIST REGIME

organized by Cranbrook Art Museum, Bloomfield Hills, Michigan, and curated by Abel González Fernández and Laura J. Mott with Andrew Satake Blauvelt and Andrew Ruys de Perez

CUBAN MID-CENTURY DESIGN

Exhibition Itinerary
Cranbrook Art Museum, Bloomfield Hills, Michigan: June 15–September 22, 2024

This publication and the Cranbrook Art Museum presentation of the exhibition *A Modernist Regime: Cuban Mid-Century Design* has been generously funded, in part, by the Andy Warhol Foundation for the Visual Arts, the National Endowment for the Arts, the Gilbert Family Foundation, and the George Francoeur Art Museum Exhibition Fund.

Front cover Illustrations by David Karwan of (left to right) a child's rocking chair from the *Jigsaw* series by María Teresa Muñiz Riva and the *Torquino Chair* by L. Rosado.

Page 2 Heriberto Duverger, *Yab-Yum Lounge Chair*, 1968–1972, for the Ministry of Light Industry, lacquered plywood. Collection Cuban Modern. Photo: David Avilés

Back cover Illustration by David Karwan of an unnamed EMPROVA armchair by Gonzalo Córdoba; "eye" design element derived from a poster by Anet Melo Glaria, *Despierta, Cuba (Wake Up, Cuba)*, 2020 (see page 236). Used by permission.

This page Illustration by David Karwan.

First published in the United States of America in 2024 by

Rizzoli Electa
A Division of Rizzoli International Publications, Inc.
300 Park Avenue South
New York, NY 10010
www.rizzoliusa.com

in association with

Cranbrook Art Museum
A program unit of Cranbrook Educational Community
39221 Woodward Avenue
Bloomfield Hills, MI 48303
www.cranbrookartmuseum.org

For Cranbrook Art Museum
Publication management and editing: Andrew Satake Blauvelt
Proofreaders: Andrew Satake Blauvelt, Laura J. Mott, Andrew Ruys de Perez, and Abel González Fernández
Photographic acquisition: Andrew Ruys de Perez
Photographic preparation: Danielle (deo) Owenshy and Andrew Satake Blauvelt
Illustrations: David Karwan

For Rizzoli Electa
Publisher: Charles Miers
Associate Publisher: Margaret Rennolds Chace
Acquisitions Editor: Isabel Venero
Editor: Sarah Scheffel
Production Manager: Colin Hough-Trapp
Managing Editor: Lynn Scrabis

Design: Lorraine Wild and Xiaoqing Wang with Naveen Hattis and Tommy Huang, Green Dragon Office, Los Angeles

This book has been typeset in Clarendon URW and Alternate Gothic Condensed ATF and printed in China on 140 gsm uncoated Luckybird.

Library of Congress Control Number: 2023951162
ISBN: 978-0-8478-3140-1

2024 2025 2026 2027 / 10 9 8 7 6 5 4 3 2 1

Printed in China

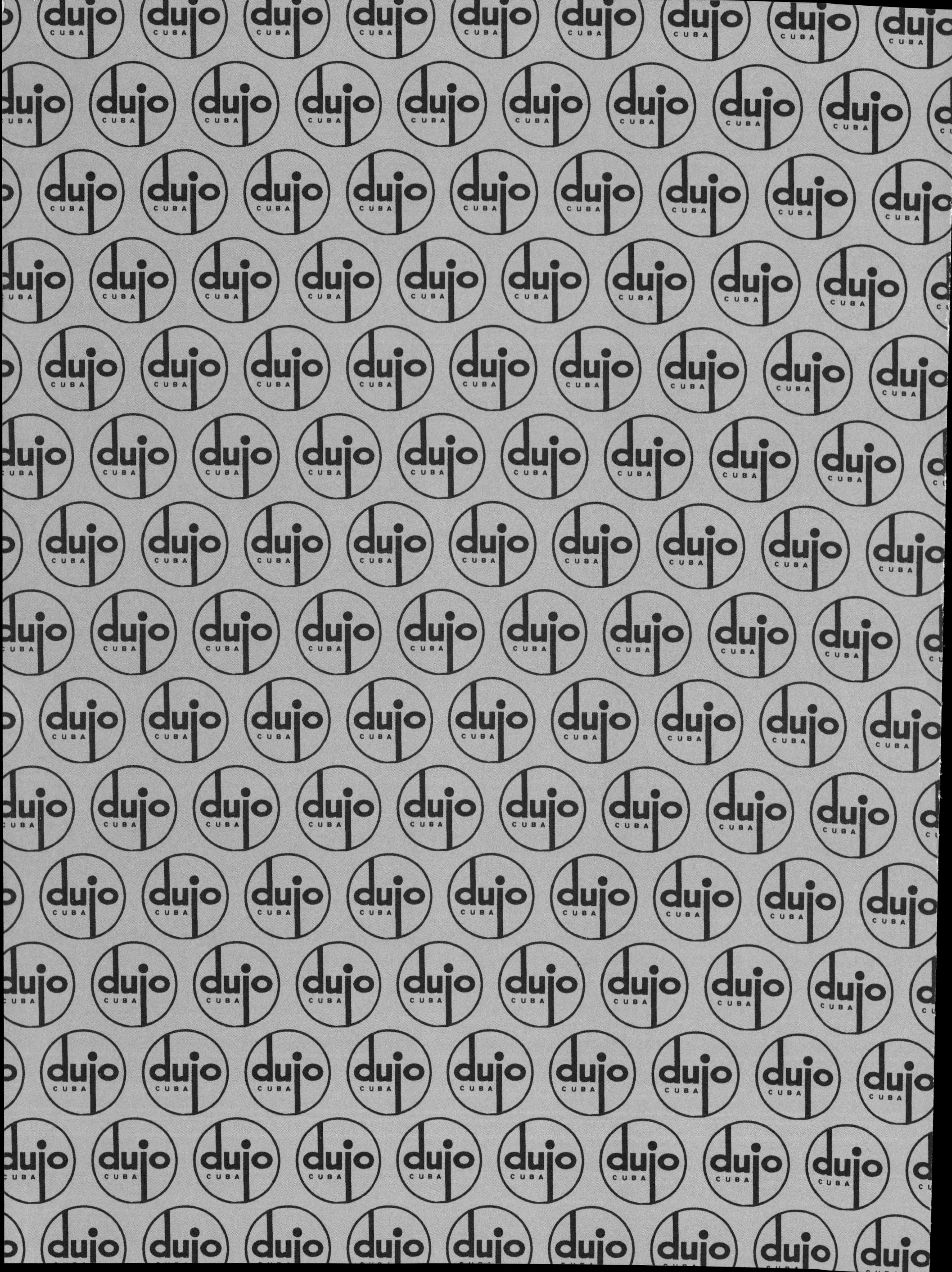
dujo
CUBA